"Illuminating, informative, and deeply personal, *It's Not What You Think* is a refreshing and complex antidote to the harmful and outdated stereotypes of Muslim women and the Middle East that still dominate America's media and political landscape. Sabeeha Rehman weaves a complex and empowering narrative of Muslim women reclaiming their identity, gender, and religion from men who seek to hijack all to ensure control and power."
—Wajahat Ali, author of *Go Back to Where You Came From* and contributing *New York Times* op-ed writer

"Easy to read, engaging, and informative, *It's Not What You Think* will be a great help to all who aspire to visit/work in Middle East in general and Saudi Arabia in particular. For folks navigating different cultures/traditions/faiths, it provides a great introduction from an author who successfully navigated these challenges. I was privileged to consult for the ailing King Fahd in June 2005 and attest to the high standards of health care and the great medical institution at KFSH&RC where the author held a very senior administrative position."
—Prof. Faroque Ahmad Khan, MB MACP. Chairman, Interfaith Institute of Long Island

"In this charming book, Sabeeha shows how even a devout Muslim who had previously visited Saudi Arabia for pilgrimage can have her stereotypical views of the Kingdom continually shattered for the better. She reveals how Saudi women both exercise their power and irreversibly expand the boundaries of their power within the confines of a patriarchal society subject to the unavoidable winds of societal change."
—Imam Feisal Abdul Rauf, founder of Cordoba House, author of *Defining Islamic Statehood* and *What's Right with Islam*

"Sabeeha Rehman's travelogue memoir invites as well as entertains, inspiring the reader with personal adventures and insight into Saudi Arabia—a modest masterpiece."
—Sidney Offit, former president of the Authors Guild Foundation and Authors League Fund and author of *Memoirs of a Bookie's Son*

It's Not What You Think

Also by Sabeeha Rehman

Threading My Prayer Rug

With Walter Ruby:

We Refuse to Be Enemies

It's Not What You Think

AN AMERICAN WOMAN IN SAUDI ARABIA

SABEEHA REHMAN

Arcade Publishing • New York

First Edition

Arcade Publishing books may be purchased in bulk at special discounts for sales promotion, corporate gifts, fund-raising, or educational purposes. Special editions can also be created to specifications. For details, contact the Special Sales Department, Arcade Publishing, 307 West 36th Street, 11th Floor, New York, NY 10018 or arcade@skyhorsepublishing.com.

Arcade Publishing® is a registered trademark of Skyhorse Publishing, Inc.®, a Delaware corporation.

Visit our website at www.arcadepub.com.
Visit the author's site at sabeeharehman.com.

10 9 8 7 6 5 4 3 2 1

Library of Congress Cataloging-in-Publication Data is available on file.
Library of Congress Control Number: 2022937475

Cover design by Erin Seaward-Hiatt
Cover illustration: Treeline © A-Digit / Getty Images; background © Okta Libriansyah Putra / Getty Images; cityscape © Mohammed Assem / EyeEm / Getty Images

ISBN: 978-1-956763-02-7
Ebook ISBN: 978-1-956763-23-2

Printed in the United States of America

To my Saudi colleagues at King Faisal Specialist
Hospital and Research Center, Riyadh,
who welcomed me, offered me professional
opportunities to achieve my potential,
and made my stay in Saudi Arabia a
memorable one

CONTENTS

AUTHOR'S NOTE

I had my trepidation about relocating to Saudi Arabia, even though it was for only two years. My friends shared my apprehension. A week before my departure, I attended my last book club meeting. As we transitioned from discussing the book to talking about my move to Saudi Arabia and wondering what it would be like, one of my friends said to me, "Write to us every day about your experiences. Start writing the day you get off the plane. First impressions need to be captured immediately." It struck a note with me, and I did just that.

The morning after my husband and I arrived in Riyadh, I wrote a long email describing my Day 1 experience: what I discovered and how it made me feel. And believe me, there was a lot in those first few hours after landing. And it took off from there—the daily reports, that is. I beamed these emails to family, friends, and colleagues in the US and to my family in Pakistan. Their responses energized me, and I found myself looking for stories to write home about. The chapter "First Impressions" is devoted to a chronological day-by-day account of my first month in Riyadh. From there on, you will read about my life on the job and life after work, a compilation of observations made in real time and my reminiscences.

As you read my stories, you are likely to wonder if any of this cultural phenomenon has changed. In fact, I am sure you will. Since most of these episodes were narrated in real time, look for updates in the epilogue, and in some cases in the footnotes.

You will come across Arabic terms that may sound unfamiliar. Check the glossary at the back of the book. It's as good as Google, if I may say so humbly.

To protect the privacy of my colleagues and friends, I have changed most of the names of the people in this book. These are people who had a remarkable impact on my life in Saudi Arabia and who made this book possible.

And now dear reader, turn to the prologue. I hope it entices you to continue reading. Sit back and relax and enjoy the journey. Thank you for flying with me.

PROLOGUE

"Don't leave home without it," my neighbor across the hall had cautioned me. Not my American Express card but the abaya. I reached for the black cloak hanging on the coat rack just before stepping out of my apartment, buttoned it up from neck to ankle, draped the black scarf over my hair, wrapped it around my neck, and turned around to face my husband.

"Am I covered enough?"

He smiled.

We were in Riyadh, the capital city of Saudi Arabia, where my husband, Khalid, and I had come to work in the country's premier hospital.

As we made our way through the courtyard, I waved to my Canadian friend Melanie lounging by the pool, sunbathing in her bright yellow bikini, with her husband, Larry, and their children.

"Going shopping?" she said.

"Yes. Need anything?"

"No thanks."

"Stay cool," Larry said, and waved as we walked past, stepping out of the compound.

"Why are you shaking your head?" Khalid asked.

"I still can't get over it. Every time I step out, I must cloak myself in the abaya, yet in the compound, it's acceptable for women to be lounging in a bikini."

"I know."

Saudi Arabia is a land of contradictions, a country that struggles to balance tradition with practicality. Saudi and Western expat cultures coexist in a "don't ask, don't tell" policy. There is room for everyone, with boundaries.

Saudi culture, I learned during the six years I lived there, is as varied as its geography. In the early 2000s, urban women were forbidden from getting behind the wheel, yet Bedouin women drove freely in the desert. In the conservative city of Riyadh, women did not work in public places frequented by men; they were conspicuously absent at the cashier and sales counters in stores and restaurants. In the mountains of Abha, women-owned and -operated businesses flourished. I was struck by the commanding voice of a woman issuing orders to her assistant, a Saudi man, to hurry and get the lady—me—a straw hat. Hers was just one in the rows of women-owned shops in a choice location: the touristy souk of Abha. While men and women were pushing cultural boundaries on the coasts in Jeddah and Dammam, Harvard grads in Riyadh were bound by traditional rules.

In the West, where our knowledge of Muslim countries is sometimes reduced to sound bites and headlines, we're prone to a mistaken idea of homogeneity. The truth is, if you have seen one Saudi, you have seen one Saudi. And for that matter, if you have seen one Muslim country, you have seen one Muslim country. There is the Middle East where women cover their hair, and Turkey, where until 2013 head scarves were banned; West African nations of Senegal and Sierra Leone where religious freedom is protected by law, and Saudi Arabia where churches, temples, or other non-Muslim houses of worship are forbidden. Iran is a theocracy, and Albania is a secular state. In Pakistan and Indonesia, women have been heads of state, and in Afghanistan, a woman's right to an education and a seat at the table is being curtailed—a consequence of culture, tradition, and politics—a fact erroneously attributed to shari'a.

Coming back to Saudi Arabia, while there was a time when this was the only country on the planet where women were not allowed to drive in cities and could not travel without their male guardian, those restrictions have been repealed by Royal decree. But, and there is a but: whereas the laws have changed, the traditions and culture that define the identity of that nation remain intact. Beliefs and traditional ways observed by families prevail.

Those traditional ways, I learned, are grounded in a culture that is tribal, patriarchal, family-oriented, hospitable, private, insular, and nationalistic; a culture that dates to the pre-Islamic era. These are values they hold dear. Tribal loyalty can be counted upon. Patriarchy is in its DNA. Family is primary, and Saudi culture, both social and corporate, is structured around family values. A closed society, Saudis welcome expatriates (like myself) into the Kingdom but keep them at a safe distance. Permanent residency and citizenship laws are restrictive. All that has not changed.

Saudi Arabia is a benevolent and absolute monarchy where freedom of religion, freedom to assemble, and freedom of expression are limited. That has not changed.

Beyond the walls of the hospital where I worked exists a rigid bureaucracy, exploitation of expat laborers, mismanagement, and waste. This contrasts with the striking efficiency with which the royal family's activities and the pilgrimage of hajj are managed. That has not changed.

Today, as I read about Saudi Arabia relaxing its restrictions on women, I can't help reminiscing about my experiences living there. I recall my confusion as I tried to distinguish the legal from the cultural, as in "am I *required* to cover my hair?" and "what is the *culturally appropriate* thing to do?" I feared the morality police, who had the power to have you arrested if your conduct defied undefined expectations. In struggling to find my footing, I lived the contradictions, adopting one persona in public and another in the conference rooms of the hospital. I was charmed by the respect my Saudi colleagues accorded an American—a woman, no less—seduced by the luxury of not being in the driver's seat, and believe it or not, surprised at the sense of freedom afforded by being cloaked in the abaya. When compelled to wear the veil, I was struck by its power. What astounded me was the influence Saudi women wielded in the workplace. It was embarrassing to confront my ignorance: how precisely I had stereotyped the Saudis, erased the gray areas, and viewed them through the lens of black and white, women in black, men in white. I would live and learn that Saudis, while not "just like us," are every bit as complex and various as we are.

This is the place my husband and I planned to live for two years. We ended up choosing to stay for six.

It's Not What You Think

CHAPTER 1

Why Saudi Arabia

Why would anyone give up her lifestyle in the United States, leave her children behind, and relocate to Saudi Arabia—albeit temporarily? Made no sense to me, yet that is precisely what I did—my husband and I, that is. Let me qualify: our children were in their twenties. Still!

It wasn't my idea. My husband, whose parents named him Khalid, which means "forever"—as in my belief that I would live forever in my beautiful house overlooking the valley dotted with trees and homes on the slope of Lighthouse Hill—looked up from his medical journal and said, "A hospital in Saudi Arabia has an opening for an oncologist."

So?

But I didn't say that. Why would a position in a hospital in Saudi Arabia get him excited? A thriving private practice for twenty-five years, a settled life in Staten Island, good marriage—I believe—two wonderful adult sons coming into their own, active in organized medicine, Muslim community building, Pakistani cultural affairs, politics: the all-you-ever-wanted kind of life.

From nowhere, in comes midlife itch. Khalid was restless. The practice of medicine had lost its luster. HMOs, Managed Care, and PPOs all brought in more regulations, more constraints, and less independence, until doctors found themselves being second-guessed by paraprofessionals. Looking for a change, Khalid had started pursuing options: Cleveland Clinic and a hospice in Connecticut, a fulltime job freer of the constraints. I went along with it, visiting these out-of-state options. I didn't want to give up my beautiful home, but I would do that for him. He had always supported me in my endeavors, and if this is what he wanted, I'd stand by him.

But Saudi Arabia! *He can't be serious. He knows we can't just move all the way to the other end of the world and leave our children behind.*

"I will email the hospital," he said.

He *was* serious.

"I don't want to go to Saudi Arabia," I said, and put forth all the arguments that you have already been thinking of:

Women can't drive. (I like being in the driver's seat.)

I will miss my children.

Our younger son isn't married yet. We can't just leave him alone.

I won't be able to work. (I had a career as a hospital executive.)

I don't speak Arabic. (I could read Arabic but didn't understand a word.)

I don't want to go through another identity crisis. Khalid and I were raised in traditional Pakistani homes as devout Muslims before coming to the US, where we set down Muslim roots while also expanding our circle to people of all faiths. We made the journey from Pakistani Muslims to American Muslims. How would my American Muslim identity fit in the Saudi culture?

Et cetera, et cetera.

If you can think of more reasons, those too.

"Let me write to them and see what they say."

They said: come for a one-month locum tenens and see if you like it here.

Good idea. Let him go, and he will see for himself that this is not for him; not for us.

And so it came to pass that Khalid took time off, asked a colleague to cover him, and flew alone to Riyadh. By the way, Riyadh is the most conservative city in Saudi Arabia.

My mother was aghast at the idea that we might move. "You can't just leave your home and take off. Your children are here."

I know.

Our sons, twenty-nine-year-old Saqib, married and doing his residency in orthopedics, and our twenty-six-year-old, Asim, who was starting a career in law, both in New York, weren't happy about it either. From their perspective, we were adults and should be trusted to know what we are doing. So American.

No sooner had Khalid landed than I started getting emails from him. It didn't look good: he liked the place.

"They want you to come for a week," he emailed. "They will pay for your airfare. Bring your CV."

Uh-oh!

I'll go and make the case that this isn't for us, I thought. *I will have hard facts and evidence on the ground.*

Walking out of Immigration at Riyadh airport and seeing the look on Khalid's face, I felt my resolve crumble. He looked happy. On our way from the airport, he filled me in.

"Bia, practicing medicine is so much less stressful." He calls me by my nickname. "No preauthorizations, no billing, no insurance issues, patients are very appreciative and accepting, no language barrier, nurses are bilingual and serve as translators, I have the freedom to treat patients as I see fit without a third party second-guessing my decision. . . ."

I was getting the picture.

The hospital had organized a packed schedule for me. A tour, meet-and-greet, plus a couple of—are you ready for this?—job interviews. I hadn't thought that was possible. Everyone in the workplace spoke English. Most of the people working at the hospital were expats. Pakistani doctors invited us for dinner and introduced us to the thriving expat Pakistani community. The ladies were telling me: "This is the most peaceful place on earth," and "We get so much vacation time that as soon as we come back from one trip, we start making plans for the next." Khalid's prospective boss's wife, a Christian American from North Carolina, also a hospital executive, took me out for lunch along with another American employee and spent the hour wooing me. I listened to her tell me how much she valued working here, the various job opportunities I would have, the connections she would make for me, the social life of an expat, and all the delightful travel opportunities.

"But you can't drive!"

Her response was: "It's a luxury to be driven."

"I will miss my children," to which she said: "You will. But you get so much vacation time that you can visit them twice a year with travel expenses paid for."

"What is it like getting by without knowing Arabic?"

"It is not a problem. The stores are manned by and large by Filipinos, and they all speak English. Cab drivers and gas stations attendants are Pakistanis, Indians, and Bangladeshis and speak English."

Then some advice: "You should ask for accommodations in the Diplomatic Quarter. Those villas are the best, and the expat lifestyle there will agree with you. Go check them out."

If she, a born-and-bred American from the South, was loving it here, I suppose . . . By the time I was done with the mouth-watering Um-Ali desert—rice pudding with almonds—I was sold. Not on the dessert—though that too—but on Saudi Arabia.

Within hours she had me scheduled for two job interviews. I wasn't impressed with the salary but was taken by the level of scrutiny one interviewer gave my portfolio. By late afternoon, she had made an appointment for me to visit a doctor's wife in the Diplomatic Quarter (DQ) and check out the accommodations. The doctor arranged for the hospital's limo service to drive me. Modern kitchen with bar-height counter seating, lots of natural light, tastefully furnished, all the closet space I would need, sliding glass doors opening out to a brick patio and garden with red bougainvillea draping the boundary walls, it had an open yet cozy feeling and just the right size for the two of us. I loved it.

A two-year stint didn't seem like such a bad idea. The hospital setting felt like an American hospital, the staff was mostly North American and European, the environment where I would feel at home. They promised to find me a job. Every expat I met told me how happy they were. So maybe a temporary change of place would be almost like an adventure kind of thing. *Hmmm!*

Breaking the news to our sons was hard on me and hard on them, not to mention my mom. The fact that I would be closer to Pakistan— where she lived—was inconsequential. Dislodging ourselves from our current setup was another story. Khalid signed a two-year contract with the hospital, handed over his practice to a colleague, and sold his office building—a house converted into an office. I resigned from my job, leaving all my colleagues in shock, and accepted an informal job offer at the hospital in Riyadh. Our children were bewildered, and I was oh so sad at leaving Asim behind alone, even though he was moving into an apartment in Manhattan with two friends and starting his first job clerking for a federal judge. But he was not yet married, and to me that meant: alone. By the time we left, Saqib's wife was pregnant, and now I carried the added emotion of missing the birth of our first grandchild.

Our entire extended family descended at JFK to bid us goodbye, and when boarding was announced, I broke into tears.

CHAPTER 2

First Impressions

Emails sent from Saudi Arabia to family and friends in the US and Pakistan

April 14, 2001
Subject: Day 1. Just Arrived

Dear family and friends,

It is 7:00 p.m. Saudi time and 12 noon New York time. We are almost settled in our temporary apartment in Riyadh.

An eleven-hour flight in business class (paid for by the hospital) is far more restful than a seven-hour transatlantic flight in economy. They don't wake you up just as you have fallen asleep, and you get to stretch on those comfy reclining seats. Thank you, hospital, for the treat.

"Dr. Rehman?" Two Saudi men in white robes and red-and-white-checkered headscarves approached Khalid as soon as we got through Immigration at Riyadh airport.

"Yes," Khalid said.

"Welcome to King Faisal Hospital. We will be taking you to your accommodation. This way, please." They guided us to Customs. We watched as the Customs officers in Saudi garb opened our suitcases. That was fine until they started opening the cartons we had so carefully taped, flipped through every medical book, and read the title and back side of each CD.

The fun was just beginning. Contrary to our understanding, the staff had not come prepared to transport our luggage—all thirteen pieces. Their instructions were to welcome us and take us to our lodging. To arrange for baggage transport for a family relocating for two years was somehow not in the equation. So, after we got through Customs and stepped out to a glorious cool breeze, they hailed a pickup truck and, between their minivan and the pickup, got everything loaded.

Driving in from the airport, I was struck by the highway infrastructure. By and large, the drivers drive by the rules and traffic is orderly. The city looks modern, well laid out, and very clean.

When we got to our apartment building, they deposited our cartons curbside and waved us goodbye.

There we were, standing by the roadside with thirteen bulky and heavy cartons. Khalid went in to speak to the doorman, who told him to take the elevator down to the basement and get the trolley.

O-kay.

Khalid came back laughing, pushing a wobbly shopping cart. The doorman stepped out, glanced at our thirteen boxes, and laughed, saying that the shopping cart wouldn't cut it, it wouldn't even fit one box.

You are not kidding.

"Call Housing," he said.

Khalid called Housing. I stood guard outside.

"It will take them twenty minutes to get here with the trolley," Khalid said. "Let me get started."

Getting started meant loading one box on the wobbly shopping cart, balancing it kitty-cornered and wheeling it all the way down the maze of hallways to the other end of the building to Apartment #120, and then wheeling the shopping cart back and reloading another carton while I stood guard. Just then an American gentleman came jogging. He and Khalid recognized each other, as he was the first person that Khalid had run into at the same spot when he had first come to Saudi Arabia for a locum last November.

"Need assistance?" he asked.

In minutes he retrieved another shopping cart from who knows where (I guess he knew his way around) and was carting the cartons to our apartment. I waited outside watching our luggage. Not that you need to guard your belongings in Saudi Arabia, but old habits are hard to break, especially when you are fresh off the Boeing. Exactly twenty minutes later the housing person pulled up in a pickup van. He thought we wanted a pickup van. No, we needed someone to pick up *our bags* and haul them to the apartment.

"No problem." He found another cart and now there were three.

Nice apartment—spacious two-bedroom with the kitchen stocked with a two-day supply of food, plus pots and pans, flatware, dishes, linen in the bed and bath—you get the picture. As soon as I had toured the apartment, I went across the hall to say hello to Sangeeta and her husband, Dr. Pai.* Of Indian descent, this was a couple who we befriended on our last visit. They had shown us around town and kept us company. It was a welcome coincidence that our apartment was right across from theirs. Tired as we were, it felt more important to beat the feeling of loneliness.

"Oh, you are here! Come in, come in. Please join us for dinner. Biryani. Come, come." Dr. Pai opened the door and stepped aside. Sangeeta, dressed in a shalwar kameez, her dark brown hair framing her face in shoulder-length waves, gestured, "Please come in."

"No thank you. We are stuffed, and very tired. But come, take a look at our apartment." I showed them around, and after inspecting the apartment one more time, we turned in.

Next morning, I woke up missing my children and sobbing like a lost child. This E.T. couldn't phone home; we are not yet hooked up for long distance. Must be telepathy—Saqib and Asim called. *Bless them. I guess we get long distance but not outgoing calls.* Just listening to their

---

* It's cultural. South Asians are formal in addressing members of the opposite sex, hence Sangeeta and Dr. Pai; likewise Sangeeta would call us Sabeeha and Dr. Rehman.

voices, I was cured. It reminded me of the scene at JFK when we were boarding. A flight attendant was saying goodbye to her baby and the baby was crying uncontrollably. As soon as she picked up the baby, he stopped crying. My boys had reached out and touched me, and I was consoled for now.

Khalid left for his first day of work, excited at the prospect of a new beginning. I unpacked. We are in temporary accommodations until a villa becomes available in the Diplomatic Quarter, so it was difficult to decide how much to unpack, not knowing how long we will be here. The hospital is right across the street, so Khalid can come by each time he has a small break. We have gotten our internet access, are reading our mail, and writing to you all. It is nice to have mail as soon as you arrive.

The weather is glorious. I sat for a while in the backyard reading a book, and it felt like utter luxury. I wanted to go out and explore, but you cannot go out without an abaya (black cloak), and I don't have one. When Sangeeta stopped by to invite us for dinner, she asked if I needed anything.

"Yes, I need to borrow your abaya, and I need you to take me out shopping to get me my own, so I can go out."

So, that is our plan for tonight.

More to come.
Sabeeha

Cloaked in the Abaya

Sunday, April 15
Subject: Day 2

Dear all,

Today I wore my own abaya for the first time. It was rather exciting to be donning a new outfit of sorts. If you haven't seen one, it's a black ankle-length long-sleeved cloak worn over the clothing, plain—although they come fancy too—with black-on-black embroidery and a scarf to drape over your hair. Inside the walled compound of apartments where expatriate employees of the hospital live, you don't need to wear the abaya. The compound's two-level structure forms a square around a courtyard with a swimming pool right in the middle. From my apartment windows, I have a view of bikini-clad women lounging in the glorious morning sun.

Last night, Sangeeta had us over for dinner and then she and Dr. Pai (also an oncologist) took us shopping. I had to borrow one of her abayas to go abaya shopping. They took us to the Pakistani grocery market—like we have Chinatown and Little Italy in New York. Well, here they have a Pakistan-Town. I got all my spices including the same Shan Chicken Tikka Masala. Small world!

Everything revolves around prayer times. When Sangeeta stopped by to ask us to come for dinner, she said, "Since *Maghrib* (evening prayer) is at 6:15 (no daylight-saving time in Saudi), and *Isha* (night prayer) is at 7:45, come at 7 p.m. for dinner. We will go out shopping after *Isha*." Got it. Speaking of prayers, here in Riyadh, I turn in a different direction. Unlike New York, where we turned east to face the Kaaba in Mecca, or in Pakistan where I prayed facing west, here the *qibla*—direction of the Kaaba—is southwest. I don't have a compass, so when I asked the receptionist in the lobby, he smiled and told me that in the living room of my apartment, one of the walls has an arrow painted indicating the direction of the *qibla*. Cool!

This morning, after Khalid went to work—Sunday is a working day—Sangeeta and I took the Ladies Shuttle Bus to the supermarket, courtesy of the hospital. There is a supermarket in walking distance, but it is expensive as they sell only American products. I went local. Of course, the passengers were all wearing the abaya, all black. I did see one woman wearing a dusty rose abaya. I suppose going colored is kosher. Covering the head seems to be optional. Some women had the scarf draped loosely over their hair, some had it pinned hijab style, and some just wore it around their neck, leaving their hair exposed. I decided to let my scarf slip off my head, wondering if the women would cover their hair once we entered a public place. Well, they didn't, so neither did I. Two women in the bus were veiled in the niqab, their faces concealed, and all you could see was their eyes. They were talking to each other in Arabic, so I presumed they were Saudi. Watching the passengers was like being at the United Nations. Pakistanis chatting in Urdu, Americans in American English, British in their clipped English accent (love the sound), Filipinos in a language foreign to me; all skin colors, all accents, all a friendly bunch of women.

"And how long have you been here?" one with an American accent asked me.

"One day!"

She had no hesitation asking for my phone number, saying, "I'll call you." And I had no hesitation giving it to her. I was yearning for friends.

I went crazy buying what you wouldn't find in a supermarket in the States: halal deli meat. "Give me a kilo of this, a kilo of that. . . ." Here is the other thing: besides having to convert riyals into dollars each time I check the price ($1=3.75 riyals), here they have the metric system. American products such as Rice Krispies (small world) are marked both ways, but local products are strictly metric. Now what was the conversion for grams and ounces, for kilograms and pounds? I can never remember, so I will just have to learn the metric system. The supermarket has groceries on one side and a Kmart-type outfit on the other. Prices of American products are comparable. Saudi teenage boys in their white robes and red-and-white-checkered *ghutras* draped over their heads work the checkout counter. Their robes are so clean—sparkling white and neatly pressed. From cab drivers to cashiers to everyone else: clean, pure, gleaming white. Men in white, women in black, black and white, all so uniform.

The director of the Quality Resource Management (QRM) department at the hospital called me. He wants me to start work as soon as I am settled. "How about tomorrow?" I said. I have no jetlag, I am unpacked, I am ready to start work. So, I am going tomorrow and see what they have to offer.

Two days in a row, Khalid has come home twice during the day for extended breaks. So far, his workload is light. And speaking of light, our apartment is very well-lit, lots of windows and glass doors. A linear layout, with every room opening out to the courtyard. But it's an old building and looks old. We will see how long this temporary arrangement lasts. We are on the waiting list for accommodations in the Diplomatic Quarter.

This evening we decided to experience "hanging out" in a Saudi mall. We are not big shoppers or mall frequenters. Nevertheless, I was curious to see what kind of clothes were being sold, how people shopped, etc. So, after *Isha* prayers, we called a Pakistani colleague of Khalid's and asked for a list of malls and how to get a cab. The hospital has contracted with a limo company and has negotiated the rates for its employees. So we called Haala Cab and, after pulling the name out of a scarf, asked to be taken to the Sahara mall. The cabbie was Bangladeshi and entertained us with his experiences in Saudi. Dropping us off at 8:30 p.m., he offered to come pick us up at 10:00 p.m. Due to prayer timings, the malls stay open late after *Isha* prayers. What a mall! New, spacious, vast, with high ceilings, not too ostentatious but modern. I headed straight to the clothing store—the abaya whets your curiosity, as in: what do women wear underneath it?

Well, it's American all the way. Nine out of ten stores had western clothing: jeans, pants, blouses, and a rather nice selection, I must say. I saw Saudi women buying all this apparel. Beneath the black abaya is a very stylish lady. And men's clothing was entirely western too. Yet, all the men in the mall were wearing traditional attire, as in white robes. Not sure when they wear jeans and tee shirts. Most of the clothing stores were for ladies' apparel—why should Saudi women be any different! Then there were the evening-wear stores. One store displayed long A-line gowns of organza material with glittering embroidery. The gowns were three-piece: a long sleeve gown, a front opening sleeveless cape, and a full-length scarf worn around the neck and hanging at the backside. I could use one of those! By the way, the mannequins wore nail-polish. And after all that, no fitting rooms. I suppose it is considered unseemly to undress, even in a women's fitting room.

Another store carried made-to-order evening gowns of western designs. The mannequins wore tightly fitted gowns, strapless or halter—Hollywood style. Inside the store were rolls and rolls of heavily beaded and sequined fabrics, and women cloaked in abayas were ordering custom-tailored gowns. Men manned all these stores; I didn't see any female staff, not in sales, not at the cashiers, no women period. I spotted Victoria's Secret.

"Khalid, I want to take a peek. You wait outside." I presumed that men were not allowed in *that* store.

A round table in the center had lingerie on display. As I picked up a piece, I heard a voice from behind.

"Can I help you?"

A man's voice!

The sales*man* walked up to me. "These are on sale," he said, making eye contact and handling one of the pieces on the table.

I dropped the thing like a hot potato and dashed out.

"Khalid, a man is selling ladies underwear. To women!"

Khalid chuckled. "Did you buy any?"

I cannot rationalize this contradiction. Can you?

Most of the shoppers were women, some with children, some with friends, and very few with their husbands. I noticed couples holding hands, discreetly. They were all arriving in cabs and cars, mostly women in groups of two or with children. Children wore jeans and shirts, but there were no bare legs; not girls, not boys. Taking a look around, all I saw was black and white, women in black abayas, men in white robes. I wonder at what age the girls must wear the abaya. At puberty perhaps?

Now listen to this: I was wandering in one of the apparel stores by myself when I heard Khalid's laughter. Spotting him at the other end of the store, I rushed up to him.

"Why are you laughing?"

"I couldn't find you. Normally when you wander off, all I have to do is look above the racks and spot your tuft of curly hair. This time when I looked around, all I could see was black scarves."

How delightful! Until now, I hadn't experienced the freedom the veil offers. Had my face been veiled, he would never have found me, but

I would have spotted *him*. See the advantage women have! They can disappear in the crowd of black-cloaked and veiled women. It suddenly dawned on me: the power of the veil, the security it offers, and complete privacy and anonymity. No one knows your identity or your business. It is all safely tucked behind the veil and beneath the abaya. Maybe I will start wearing the veil. Just kidding! Think of the women who go to work wearing the abaya. No fussing over what to wear, the right color lipstick. Bad hair day? No problem. Just throw the abaya over yourself and you are set to go. Get dolled up when you come home. Keeps life simple. I guess if you can get past the idea that it is being forced on you, it can be pretty liberating.

There was a sign in the mall that pointed to the food court on the left, mosque on the right. How about that: a mosque in the mall! So, when it is prayer time, the stores close, and shoppers walk to the mosque. I wondered how it works for women. I will have to go to the mall during prayer time to find out. Anyhow, getting back to the food court—it has all the same eateries as in the US and more: for example, Baskin-Robbins, Pizza Hut, KFC. Each stall has two checkout lines with two large signs: Men's Line and Women's Line. I like that. I get served sooner and have my privileged line. The seating area has a men's-only space and a family space. Women and men with families sit in the family space, where each seating is screened off, offering privacy. Nice! I wondered how the women with the niqab eat. The screens got in the way of my prying eyes.

The arcade? Massive. I peeked and saw children having a ball! But, and it's a huge but: no movie theater at the mall. There are no public movie theaters in Saudi Arabia, period. But they have video stores. True to his word, our cabbie came at 10 p.m. By then, there were more shoppers coming than leaving. The round-trip cost the equivalent of $10 for a thirty-minute drive. Not bad. I don't think we will need a car here. Cabs are cheap and shuttle buses are free.

Goodnight for now.
Sabeeha

♦ ♦ ♦

Monday, April 16
Subject: Day 3: Job Offer

Dear All,

I called Sangeeta this morning and invited the family over for dinner tonight.

"No, no," she protested. "You are too new to be entertaining."

"Yes, yes," I insisted. "Now that I have groceries in the pantry, I am ready." Did I mention that she had invited me to lunch yesterday and served fried fish—sizzling, crisp, and spicy Pomfrey fish from the Arabian Sea.

I got the cooking done early in the morning and then went off for my job interview.

The director, a Saudi whom I will call Samir, had interviewed me back in November. This time Khalid accompanied me—just to say hello to my prospective boss. He greeted Khalid with a warm smile, holding him by the hand and bringing him into his spacious office. When Khalid left, we got down to business. Samir offered me a position doing utilization management. He explained that this was a new position, created to address over-utilization of clinical services and patients overstaying; with my prior experience and American credentials, I could be effective in molding physician practices.

He suggested I look into other job possibilities within the institution before accepting his offer and escorted me to the Personnel Office. I appreciated his gracious gesture. He advised me to inquire into my benefits and notify Personnel that I was being hired as my husband's dependent. Got that? This is what it means: my visa is in my capacity as the dependent of Khalid. *He* was hired on a two-year contract, not me; therefore I, being his wife, am allowed entry into the Kingdom by virtue of being his dependent. That being my status, my job with the same employer would be in the category of an employee's dependent. Translated, it means that I don't get any duplicate benefits such as a second apartment. Makes sense from a practical standpoint. It did not ruffle my feminist instincts.

The Personnel office is located in the administration building. I continue to be amazed by the sparkling cleanliness of the hospital. Sarah, a light-skinned young lady of Arab descent and bilingual, wearing a white lab coat and a black hijab, briefed me: I was entitled to all my husband's benefits and no more. Sounds fair. All vacant positions were listed on the website, and she gave me the specifications of the position being offered to me, the hospital's table of organization, other available positions and contact persons. A rather pleasant and helpful person.

When I got back to the apartment, the doorbell rang. A young lady in a shalwar kameez greeted me.

"I am Nasreen, your neighbor next door. Sangeeta told me that a couple from Pakistan had arrived, so I stopped by to welcome you."

I invited her in.

"No, no, you must be busy."

"No, I am not busy. Come in, please."

I first straightened out my demographic history. Yes, I am originally from Pakistan, but I am really from the United States, as in the last thirty years.

That makes me a Pakistani-American-living-in-Saudi-Arabia, for now. Talk about super hyphenation. She was sweet and offered all her help. We exchanged phone numbers. Here the telephone numbers coincide with one's apartment number, like a hotel room.

Today the hospital hooked us up with cable TV. The choices of TV channels include: CNN, BBC, CNBC, MTV, America Plus, ESPN, Hollywood, Disney, Discovery, Zee TV, Pakistan TV, Saudi, Kuwait, Bahrain, Syria, Egypt, Dubai, Jordan, Filipino, etc. etc. To get cable TV, I had to join the employee Social Club. I now have a club card and all the promotional material.

Every time Khalid logs on to the internet, he calls out, "You have fifteen emails," or however many. That is music to my ears, and I go running to check. Yesterday when I sent my email to you all, I got an error message: "Unable to send. Can send only fifty emails at a time. You have sixty-one!"

"You sent sixty-one emails!" Khalid gasped.

I had to resend in batches of two. I am also hooked up on Dialpad with the US and call my children every day.

Sangeeta, Dr. Pai, and her children showed up at 7:30 for dinner. I made *matar pulao* and *koftas*. She brought her favorite music cassette of Indian Bollywood songs, and I played the Pakistani mystical music of Abida Parveen and Pathana Khan's melancholic ghazals for them.

Let's see what tomorrow brings. Goodnight for now.

Human Resource Encounter

Tuesday, April 17
Subject: Day 4 & 5

Dear All,

Day 4

Working hours are 8 a.m. to 6 p.m. But then, there is no commute.

Today I called Lorraine, the secretary in the chairman's office (Oncology) and asked for names of the secretaries in offices where I planned to inquire for job opportunities. I had paid Lorraine a visit two days ago, so she knew me. Then I called them, and they asked that I bring in my CV. That afternoon I timed my "drop-in" before their lunch hour and got all of them in their offices. The secretary in the CEO's office looked like an American model. Tall, slim, green-eyed, and elegant. I closed the loop with Samir, filling him in. His sense was that Personnel did not give me the correct information regarding my benefits, specifically that Khalid gets six days business leave, which I will not be entitled to. They had *not* told me that. He asked that I go back and get them to spell it out. So, I went back to Sarah.

"OK. What is the difference between my benefits and my husband's?"

"No difference," Sarah said.

"But I am told that I don't get business leave, which my husband gets."

"Oh yes. That is correct."

Am I glad I asked!

"OK. Let's go over my leave benefits," I said.

"You get thirty days annual leave, five days for Ramadan, five days for hajj, and seven days post leave."

"That adds up to forty-seven days. I understand that it should be fifty-four days." *Don't bother asking whatever post leave is. Focus on the number fifty-four.*

"No, no."

Yes, yes, I pressed on.

"Are you Muslim?" she said.

"Yes."

"OK, then you get seven days for Ramadan."

A Muslim perk. Am I glad I asked!

I did the math: 30 annual +7 Ramadan +5 hajj +7 post leave=49

"It still doesn't add up to fifty-four."

"Why don't you talk to the Benefits staff."

So I went to the Benefits office. A sour-faced man in a Saudi garb who looked like he didn't want to be disturbed sat by his window desk.

"Sir, I am being hired as my husband's dependent and I want to know if and how my benefits are different from his."

He gave me that don't-bother-me look.

"Like what?" he asked.

"Like time-off."

"You get what he gets."

"No. I don't get business leave, or do I?"

"No, you don't, but you can."

Aha!

"How is that?"

"Ask your supervisor to approve it."

Am I glad I asked!

"OK. Now, let's go down the list of all my entitled leave."

"Like what?"

Young man, probably with all his teeth intact. I started pulling.

"Like annual leave, like post leave, like Ramadan leave . . ."

"You get thirty annual, seven post leave, five Ramadan, seven for hajj."

"I was told I got seven for Ramadan."

"Are you Muslim?"

I guess I don't look Muslim. No hijab. Could pass for a Lebanese Christian.

"Yes," I said.

Hello world, I am a Muslim.

"You get seven days for Ramadan and ten days for hajj."

Bingo! The magic number fifty-four.

First tooth out.

"Do you have a package that spells this out?"

"Yes."

"Can I have it?" I don't think I said *please.*

He reached out and handed me the package.

Am I glad I asked!

Second tooth out.

All the time the package was right under his nose. I felt completely at home. There are helpful people with good customer service skills, and then there are the "I can't be bothered" people, and that is the way it is no matter where you are in this whole wide world. No culture shock here.

What *is* culture shock for us Americans is the religious perks in the workplace. Whether I fast or not, perform hajj or not, I get five extra holidays. Is that religious discrimination? *Hmmm!*

Back in the apartment, the phone rang again.

"Assalam Alaikum, this is Razia. Welcome back." Actually, she spoke in Urdu.

I had met Razia during my November visit. Her husband is also an oncologist and they had invited us to their home along with other Pakistani families to introduce us to the group. I was so happy to hear from her.

"I am placing the order for meat with the butcher. Can I place an order for you? My husband will pick up the meat and deliver it to your apartment."

"Thank you so much but I am fully stocked for now."

That was very nice of her. She proceeded to give me all kinds of orientation tips that newcomers crave. Everyone is so welcoming.

I now hear the *adhan* for *Maghrib* prayer. I am going to get really spoiled. I no longer have to keep a salat timetable to keep track of prayer time. No one here should have any excuse for missing prayer. You cannot forget—the call for prayer reminds you and beckons you. You cannot let work get in the way—all business stops when the *adhan* is called. Even if you *wanted* to conduct business, you couldn't. You would have to wait for people to come back from prayer to attend to you. This culture of prayer clears the way, makes it easy, makes it possible—for Muslims, that is. Living in the US, whereas I was able to say my prayers at work, I had to work at it, and sometimes, I did miss my prayers if a meeting ran long. In this respect, Muslims living here are fortunate.

In the evening Khalid suggested that we go for a walk. With me in my abaya, we headed out. It's exciting to be in this new attire. There is a strip mall at the end of a long block. We decided to check it out. There is the Al-Azizia supermarket to anchor it, a bank, the Body Shop, McDonalds, Domino's Pizza, KFC, Mothercare, the Learning Center, Internet Café, Telephone Exchange, Milano Shoes, etc., and believe it or not, Cheesecake Factory. We decided to try the ATM machine at the bank and see if it worked. It looked like a Citibank with a different name. We put our Citi card in the door, and it opened. We poked around with the ATM machine, which was in English and Arabic. It swallowed our card and gave us our checking balance. It works! Isn't the world a small place? You put in your NY bank card in Saudi Arabia, and it beams it off the satellite and, in an instant, you know that your last paycheck was deposited. The thrill of connectivity can only be appreciated when you are far from home.

We needed milk and checked out the supermarket. It was flooded with people from the hospital—mostly the female staff. They work here, they live here, and they shop here. In the produce section, I ran into the model from the CEO's office. What I had really wanted to experience was Arabian food. But you just don't see it. This supermarket was Shoprite USA all the way. The closest I came to local food was tahini in cans. But I'll find it—it can't be too far behind.

Day 5
It is Wednesday, April 18. The work week ends today. Weekends are on Thursday and Friday, and on Saturday, the new week starts. How is that for getting disoriented!

Today the doorbell rang. A young man handed me a flyer. Aerobic classes starting May 1 right here in my apartment building. Just what I need.

"You have to come in person to the recreation building to register."

"Where is that?"

"It's on hospital grounds across from the bus stop. And bring your Social Club card with you."

During lunch break Khalid walked in with another flyer. The Social Club was arranging an overnight trip to the city of Medina. Just what I wanted. Medina is the city Prophet Muhammad migrated to and where he established an Islamic State. He is buried there. So I called them and got the same answer: come in person to sign up.

Khalid and I went to the recreation building. It looks like a resort. Terraced gardens, covered conical walkways, tennis courts, and playgrounds with large toy turtles. First, I had to have my ID badge made. The waiting area had a designer's touch: plush sofas, modern-looking coffee table and lamps, neat artwork on the walls. . . . I'd wait here anytime.

When I had called to sign up for the Medina trip, I was told to bring in our *iqama*. It's a residence permit. Every expat living in Saudi Arabia is required to carry it on their person at all times or one can be put in jail—no questions asked—unless you have your passport on you. That is the law. Since we are new and our *iqama* isn't ready, we are allowed to use the passport with our visa stating we are here on employment. Once the *iqama* is issued, the employer holds your passport until you need it for travel. The Social Club accepted our passport, and we were told to get travel papers from the hospital within the next few days. All this was explained to us when we had come in November, and Americans living here had assured us that one easily gets used to the idea of carrying one's *iqama* on you; and getting travel papers is a mere formality.

Next stop: sign up for aerobics. Fourteen classes being offered throughout the month of May at 15 riyals a class (*$4.00*.) You can sign up for any number of classes. When he asked me how many classes I was signing up for, I wanted to say: all fourteen.

Khalid came home and said we were invited out to dinner that evening by one of his colleagues, who I will call Christine. She is an American, an oncologist, married to a Lebanese, a CPA with Arthur Anderson. They live in the Kingdom City Complex. She offered to send her driver, but I insisted that we take a cab. I had brought half a dozen coffee table photo books on New York City and a whole lot of gift bags. They are coming in handy. I should bill New York City's mayor for the free promotion.

Khalid called Haala Cab service. "We will be there in two minutes."

And there he was, in two minutes.

The Kingdom City Complex is at the far end of town, when the high-rises become low-rise and the land becomes bare and flat. Minarets dot the landscape, rising above the domes of the mosques, illuminating the landscape and glowing against the gray sky. We approached what appeared to an exclusive compound. The fancy gates were shut, and the guard approached us with a mirror attached to a long handle. We gave him our names, who we were visiting, and the address. He called our hosts, came back, had us sign in, and asked for Khalid's ID. The only acceptable ID Khalid had was his passport, which he took away, to be returned when we leave the compound, after we give him the form signed by our host. *Gee!* Then he scanned the underside of the car, looking for bombs, flashlight in hand.

Goodness! Only then did the gates part, and we drove into a complex that took my breath away.

My eyes popped out at the exotic landscaping, designer-look houses with curving walkways. Christine and her husband were waiting at the door. Petite and slim, blonde hair permed, and wearing a mini pale-blue skirt, she was all smiles. Her husband, wearing dress slacks and a white-collar shirt, extended his hand, "I am Fahad."

I started complaining the minute I stepped out of the car.

"They took our *passports*!"

Christine gave me this serene look that seemed to say *I can see that it bothered you.* Seeing how matter-of-fact they were made me wonder whether I was overreacting. Perhaps this is business as usual here, and if this American woman isn't bothered about it, maybe I shouldn't be either. Like them, it's possible I will get used to it too. But it's my *passport.*

Their home was furnished in soft neutral colors, with a welcoming feel, artwork on the walls, and sparkling crystal on the buffet. Christine and Fahad took us for a barbecue dinner at a poolside restaurant in the compound, landscaped with artificial giant rocks and waterfalls. I tried to be an attentive guest to this charming couple, but the setting was distracting.

This compound rents only to expatriates. No Saudis. The purpose is to keep the cultures separate so that the expatriates can live according to the lifestyle they are used to. It also helps in recruiting and retaining expats by providing them with tennis courts, gym, piano lessons, school up to grade 5, you name it. I saw no abayas.

Fahad filled us in on the banking system in Saudi Arabia. Being an Islamic country, it is an interest-free economy, one of the few Islamic countries with this system. No mortgages, and loans are interest-free. How about that!

I asked Christine if she had any household help.

"An abundance," she said. "A maid, a nanny, and a driver."

The nanny is a live-in. Most people who own cars have a full-time chauffer. He drives the lady of the house to work and the children to school or their other activities, and in our case, the dinner guests to their homes.

I asked about the heightened security at the gate. She explained that it is all preventive; it holds the residents accountable for their guests (not more than two guests per family in the pool), keeps rowdy teenagers to a minimum, and keeps the place safe, not that they have had any bomb incidents. I guess it was my first encounter with the mirror scanner and I was intimidated. Come to think of it, how is it different from the security at the airport, where our baggage goes through an X-ray device and our person through a metal detector? And I shouldn't be surprised at the passport incident either—that's the norm here. Hotels routinely hold passports of guests (in lieu of your Visa card number) and release them at check-out.

Before their driver drove us back, we handed in the form and got our passports returned. *Phew!* Tomorrow is Thursday, beginning of a weekend. It feels odd.

Laura Bush is being interviewed by Larry King on CNN. I like her smile.

All the best,
Sabeeha

Religious Police

April 20
Subject: Days 7–10

Dear All,

Day 7
I have been here just about a week. Khalid has gone for *Jumma*,* the Friday prayers. At my former job as compliance officer at University of Medicine and Dentistry of New Jersey (UMDNJ), *Jumma* prayers were held in the chapel across from my office. Here, the hospital has its own mosque.

---

* Obligatory congregational Friday noon prayers held in the mosque. It includes a sermon by an imam, followed by two units of prayer. Traditionally, only men attend *Jumma*, and women stay home to take care of the children.

Yesterday I had my first *mutawwa* incident. They are the morality police that enforce moral and religious rules. People fear them because they are accompanied by a cop who has the authority to arrest and put you in jail. Whether it's the Office of the Inspector General in the States—a compliance officer's worst nightmare—or the *mutawwa* in Riyadh, I can't seem to be able to get away from "the most dreaded."

It was Thursday evening—a weekend—and we had gone to the Faisaliah Mall to pick up a few items and get a bite to eat. No one had invited us for dinner that night, so we had to fend for ourselves—what an outrage! We left home after *Maghrib* prayers, knowing well that it would be *Isha* time while we were at the mall. Neither of us was sure how that would work out, but we decided to find out. Sure enough, at 7:45 p.m., we heard the *adhan* call to prayer resonate through the mall. What a pleasing sound!

What is distinctive about the recital of the Qur'an is the sound. It is musical, mystical, and poetic. But to achieve that quality of sound, it must be recited with the correct Arabic pronunciation (not in my hopeless Urdu/English-accented version). The impact of the *adhan* resonating from the Kaaba or other mosques in Arab countries is mesmerizing. The sound, and its echo throughout the mall, brought tears to my eyes, which always happens because it reminds me of when I first heard the *adhan* in the Kaaba in Mecca. All at once the shutters of the stores started coming down slowly and noiselessly, as if bowing in submission to prayer time, and I marveled at the good fortune of this nation. Businesses were closing, for just a little while, so that employees could fulfill their obligatory prayers.

Little did I know what awaited me.

We decided that Khalid would go to the mosque, which was next to the parking garage on the lower level, and I would wait for him in the family dining area of the food court. I had not seen a ladies prayer area and figured that the mosque was for men only.* Besides, I prefer

---

* Most mosques have a male attendance only, and in mosques where women are part of the congregation, the genders are segregated.

to say my *Isha* prayers as the last thing before I go to bed. Does that sound defensive?

"Will you be OK alone?" Khalid said.

"Sure, don't worry about me."

Little did I know.

"No. Let me walk you back to the food court."

So, Khalid walked me to the food court, sat me down in the family area, which was teeming with families eating, and walked to the mosque. I settled down with my notepad to make my journal entries. On the left was the men's seating area, with no visual barrier, and on the right, another family area fenced off by a glass-brick wall.

Suddenly, I heard this loud voice—a man's voice. Looking up I saw a tall, long-bearded man wearing a brown robe, a scarf draped over his head, hanging from both sides. He was accompanied by a skinny police officer in khaki uniform—shirt and pants. They were walking through the men's eating area, and the man in the long robe was waving his hands and speaking in Arabic in a loud voice that sounded angry and commanding. The men quietly got up from their seats and started leaving the eating area. I was startled. Why had the men left? Where did they go? He couldn't have asked them to go for prayers, because many of them might not be Muslims, and one cannot impose prayers on a non-Muslim. Then he and the cop were gone.

I was still recovering from my confusion when he walked into the family area and started addressing the crowd in Arabic, waving his hands. It sounded angry but that may just be his style; it's hard to tell, not knowing the language. What was he saying? What did he want us to do? What were we doing wrong? I looked around and saw people looking nervous. Some women covered their faces with the veil. Then I saw everyone get up and start walking out of the area. I followed and stayed close to the crowd. While we were walking out, I spotted a Filipino woman. I inched close to her.

"What is he saying?" I asked.

"I have no idea." She didn't seem nervous.

"So why is everyone walking out?"

"I have no idea."

"I see. Just follow the crowd? They must be doing something right?"

"Yes," she said calmly.

And then the crowd walked into the other family area adjacent to where we had been sitting, behind the glass wall. That place was already packed, and next to it was a children's play area packed with kids laughing and squealing. I looked around for an empty seat—I didn't want to be noticeable by standing.

"May I have this seat?" I asked, using hand gestures, not knowing if the family sitting at a table spoke English. The woman nodded, and I pulled the chair just a little aside, to allow them privacy and yet not appear to be alone. Still recovering, I heard him again. He had entered *this* area and was walking through, waving his hands, talking in a raised voice and again sounding angry—I think. People looked less nervous, but no one moved. Then I saw him point at a woman, a blonde, and gestured that she cover her hair. She made no move to comply. But he had moved on, unaware of her defiance. I wouldn't have taken that chance if I were she. Then he walked out the other end. No one had moved, no one had left, nothing had changed. Everyone went back to the business of eating.

I didn't know what to make of it. I noticed two European girls standing against the wall. It's amazing how one can tell the difference between a European and an American. It's something about their look. They both looked nervous. I walked up to them.

"What was that all about?" I asked.

"That was the *mutawwa*," one of them said.

"That I figured out. But what was he saying?"

"I don't know. Probably that people should leave during prayer time."

"And go where?"

"Outside."

"Outside where?"

"Outside the mall."

"Then why didn't anyone leave? Why did everyone move from one family area to the other?" I asked.

"I don't know. Maybe he wanted people to go for prayer."

"I don't think so. There could be several non-Muslims here. And besides, where are women supposed to pray?"

"There is a women's prayer area on the third floor."

I didn't know that.

"With the *mutawwa*, you should do as they say or they will put you in jail. If they tell you to cover your hair, do it. Don't fight them," she said.

"I don't have a problem with that. If that is the law of the land, and we came here by choice, then we live by the law. They tell me to cover my hair, I'll cover my hair. What *is* a problem is not knowing what you are being asked to do."

"Well, if they ever confront you personally, just say, 'I only speak English,' and they will know that you don't understand Arabic."

One of them was Irish, the other Scottish. Both nurses who had been here only a month and were as unnerved as I was. I felt puzzled, threatened, and intimidated. It was *not* knowing that bothered me.

Did I give Khalid an earful when he returned!

Next day I tried to make informal inquiries. I wanted to be sure I was conducting myself in accordance with the rules. At the residential compound, I went to the pool expecting to find ladies willing to converse. A woman in a bikini was sunbathing with a book in hand. I decided not to interrupt. Another lady was conducting swimming classes. That's out. I spotted two women in the abaya with shades on, watching their children take lessons. I hovered around them to get a sense of who they might be. They looked at me for a minute and then went about their business of minding the children. I was wearing a long denim dress, shades, and my head was covered with a bright colored scarf to protect myself from the strong sun. From their accent, the two women seemed Pakistani. Then one of them spoke to the children in Urdu, and I knew for sure. I walked up to them and introduced myself.

"Oh, you are Dr. Rehman's wife. We know you. We had met you at Razia's house in November. I didn't recognize you in this dress."

"I thought you were Lebanese," said the other.

In a minute we were chatting away. They invited me to their home, took my phone number, offered all the help in the world, and then I asked my burning question.

"What was that *mutawwa* incident all about?" I gave them the whole story.

"Oh, don't worry about that," one of them waved her hand dismissively. "As long as you are sitting in a waiting area, it's not a problem."

"But, but . . . "

"Don't worry. You were just fine."

They took it so lightly. Well, I don't feel so lightly about it, so I am going to be on my guard.

Perhaps Sangeeta can explain.

"What was that all about?" I knocked on her door and poured my heart out.

Sensing my agitation, she sat me down, assured me that waiting in the family area is exactly what is expected of mall shoppers during prayer time, so I shouldn't agonize over it.

Well, for now, I have decided to follow my instincts and not take any chances. No more frequenting public places during prayer time until I am sure about the rules.

Day 8

It is Saturday, April 21. I called on Nasreen, my neighbor, and invited her over.

"No, no, you should come over," she said.

Since I am new, it is customary to be invited before one invites old-timers. With a big smile she welcomed me into her oh-so-large apartment. Families with children get a three-bedroom apartment, with a living/dining the size of a four-car garage. After the formalities and small talk was over, I brought up the *mutawwa* incident.

"Newcomers get very distressed when they first encounter the *mutawwa*. But over time, you will feel less concerned. As long as you are wearing the abaya and are not wandering around during prayer time, you are OK."

"What do you do when you are out on the mall and it's prayer time?" I asked.

"It happens to us all the time because we always go in the evening after work. We get in the restaurant before the *adhan*. Once the *adhan* is called, you won't be allowed in because the kitchen closes and the attendants go for prayer. But you can walk into a food court at any time. We have gotten the hang of it and know exactly when to stop shopping and head toward the food court. Once there, you are OK. If the *mutawwa* comes in, don't worry."

"I see."

I think I do.

Here is my theory. This incident was an aberration—just my luck. When he came into the men's eating area, he was probably saying, "What are you men doing here during prayer time?" and they quietly left the mall. Then he came to the family area and probably asked people to move into the secluded, less visible family area with glassbrick walls (we were sitting in the area very visible from the mall with no visual barriers). Once there, he moved through the area reminding people of their obligations, and left, which is why everyone stayed put. This is purely conjecture on my part.

What do you think?

All the best,
Sabeeha

* * *

Recycled Pillows

Sunday, April 22
Subject: Back to Day 9

Dear All,

I woke up with the worst back pain and a pain in the neck—literally. It was the mattress. I had been experiencing this problem from day one and thought I could weather it since we were in temporary accommodations. But this can't go on. Besides, Nasreen had advised me to call the Housing Department for every problem. So, I decided to set aside my entire day today for housing issues. I had my grievance list and was going to make calls, wait for people to return my calls, be around when they said, "We will be there between nine and five"—in this case between eight and six.

The Housing Department of the hospital has a nice glossy telephone directory with all the offices listed. I first called the furniture replacement office.

"Hello, this is Mrs. Rehman in KAC number 120, and I need a new mattress."

"For mattresses, call extension 6."

A mattress extension! Wonder how many mattress calls they receive to have an entire extension devoted to mattresses. I dialed.

"Mattresses, good morning. How may I help you?" a man answered.

"Hello, this is Mrs. Rehman in KAC number 120, and I need a new mattress."

"What size, and how long have you been here?"

"Queen size, and one week."

"My men will be there in ten minutes."

"OK. But how long will it be before I can have new mattress?" I assumed that their men were coming to assess the lumpiness, write up a work order, or some other bureaucratic stuff.

"In ten minutes," he said. "To bring you a new mattress and box spring."

My jaw *did* drop.

"Oh! Oh . . . thank you very much, sir," was all I could muster. Is that all I had to do—just ask?

"Sir, I also need new pillows."

"For pillows, call extension 4."

A pillow extension! So, I dialed.

"Sir, this is Mrs. Rehman from KAC number 120. I need four new pillows, and I have been here one week."

"Are you sure you need *new* pillows?"

"Yes. My neck hurts."

Why the question on "new"? Read on.

"My man will be there in ten minutes."

Why should *they* be left behind!

Keep going.

I called Maintenance. They owed me an icebox for the freezer.

"Sir, this is Mrs. Rehman in KAC number 120. I need a new icebox."

"My man will be there in ten minutes."

Of course, what else. I wondered if they would be tripping over each other in the race to get to my apartment in ten minutes.

"I also want my kitchen inventory replenished." I had just discovered after visiting Nasreen's kitchen that I was entitled to an extensive array of housewares.

"For kitchen inventory, page Mr. Shauki at extension 5420."

"I also want my sofa upholstery shampooed."

"For sofas, call extension 7." I dialed.

"Sir, this is Mrs. Rehman from KAC number 120. I want my sofas shampooed."

"My men can be there at 9 a.m. tomorrow morning. Will you be available?"

Not in ten minutes? It's an outrage!

"Yes, yes, 9 a.m. is fine. See you then."

I keyed in Mr. Shauki's pager number in the phone—the sofa pager number.

Now, how long has it taken you to read all my telephone conversations? That is exactly how long it was before the doorbell rang.

Two smiling Filipino men, with a new mattress (wrapped in cellophane) and a box spring, on a trolley. Aha! So they *had* a trolley. Wish we had this when we moved in. I showed them into the bedroom, and as I was peeling off the linen, the doorbell rang. It was the icebox men—two Filipinos! One had the icebox, the other held a screwdriver. I showed them into the kitchen, and they got to work.

The doorbell rang. A Filipino young man in his twenties, with spectacles and a smile on his face, stood with a large bag.

"I apologize. I am not sure this is what you want, but we don't have new pillows. These are recycled pillows."

So that is why he asked if I really wanted new pillows.

"Oh, I don't know," I said as I started feeling them. I had never heard of recycled pillows. "Let me see—"

The phone rang. "Hello, this is Shauki. You paged me?"

"Yes. I need my kitchen inventory to be replenished—"

The mattress man held out a receipt for me to sign. I waved him to hold on. "And I want to know when you can restock the kitchen," I said to Mr. Shauki on the phone. The icebox men waved at me; they were done and wanted to leave; I waved back and they left.

"I am sorry," I spoke into the telephone. "OK, so when can you take care of that?"

The mattress man pushed the paper at me again. I waved him away again.

"OK, Shauki," I spoke into the phone, "so when—"

The pillow boy waved at me, "Should I leave these pillows for you?"

I waved back, Yes.

"I am sorry, so when—" I spoke again in the phone.

"I will be over after 5 today when my shift starts, and will go over the items," Mr. Shauki said.

"Fine, fine, I'll see you after 5," and I hung up.

Now, what do I need to sign? OK, all signed, thank you, goodbye, and I closed the door as the last of the men left. All gone. The house was quiet. Phew! I can't deal with this level of efficiency. And to think that I had set aside my whole day!

Day 10
I have gleaming clean upholstery.

Day 11
Still waiting for Mr. Shauki. And I am going out shopping today to buy new pillows. Not recycled.

All the best,
Sabeeha

What Brings Expats Here and Lay of the Land

April 25
Subject: Days 12 & 13

Dear All,

Day 12
I am getting more calls from the Pakistani community. Word has gotten out that there is a new arrival. Often Khalid walks into the apartment and finds a house full of ladies.

Yesterday Razia had invited us to her house for dinner for a gathering of families from Pakistan. Or, I should say, of Pakistani origin in the diaspora. I met two other families who had also moved from the US. Did I mention that men and women self-segregate into different living rooms?

Why had these families relocated? A woman from New Jersey moved because she had grown up in Saudi Arabia and wanted to come back so that her son could become a *hafiz* (one who has memorized the Qur'an). He is now nine and is a *hafiz. Mashallah* (Praise be to God).

A lady from Pittsburgh told me that her in-laws live in India and are now too old and feeble to travel to the US to visit; her husband is the only son, and they felt that if they moved closer to India, they could just hop over when needed.

Today I spent some time at the poolside reading a book. A western woman was conducting swimming classes as mothers and nannies looked on. The little girls wore bathing suits that I would say are shari'a compliant, with tights that ended just above the knee—like a wet suit, but the top was made of regular bathing suit fabric. Some of the girls wore tops that were tailored as short-sleeve dresses, and then tights along with it. The boys wore a tee shirt over the bathing suit. Even the instructor was wearing a tank-top over her bathing suit. I saw all nationalities there—Saudi mothers in the abaya and veil, Filipinos in tee shirts and jeans, and Pakistanis and Indians in shalwar kameez. I don't think you would find bikinis in the Saudi stores.* The bikini-clad women I saw earlier probably brought their bathing suits from back home.

Day 13
We've signed up for Arabic classes at the American Community Services (ACS). It is operated by the American embassy. Evening classes are held twice a week, and the focus is on spoken Arabic. Such security! They looked in the trunk of the car, the engine, under the car, etc. before letting us in. The ACS has tours, a book club, classes, July 4 celebration, campouts, and a library. Our classes begin in May and last a month. Let's see how we do.

I want to study the Qur'an in its original language. These ten classes of spoken Arabic won't get us there, but it's a beginning.

My impressions of Saudis so far: They are low-key, quiet, reserved, keep to themselves, and are respectful and courteous. Judging from their appearance, the men are very, very clean. Their white robes—thobe—look as if they were just laundered. No matter where you see them, at work, in the stores, on the streets, this is what you see—gleaming white thobes. How they keep white robes so clean is beyond me. And all men wear the same garb, thobe with sandals. You cannot make out anyone's socioeconomic status by the look of their clothing. It conveys an image of equality. The public persona of women is the same: they all wear black. It if wasn't for the expatriate men, who add the

---

* Turned out to be true.

variety with jeans and knit shirts, all one would see is black and white. Takes care of the ego and vanity. And it constantly reminds me of Prophet Muhammad's last sermon: "all men are equal in the eyes of God," not to mention the Declaration of Independence or the poet Iqbal, for that matter. By the way, I read in the Fingertip Guide to Riyadh—a book Christine gave me—that western women are allowed to wear colored abayas. That explains why the blonde in the shopping bus was wearing dusty rose. Now, tell me how you define a Western woman? If I wanted to beat the summer heat and wore dusty rose or lavender, would I get apprehended? I am an American citizen, a registered voter, have lived in US for more than half my life, thirty years almost, but I have dark hair and wear a perpetual tan.

Let me know what you think.

All the best,
Sabeeha

Cantaloupes

May 1
Subject: Day 18

Dear All,

Today it is 95 degrees F.

I have been reading, writing, and entertaining. In the evening Khalid and I walked down after *Isha* prayers to pick up some groceries. That seems to be the best solution for us (i.e., to go shopping after the last prayer of the day). We first stopped at McDonald's to grab an ice cream cone at $0.20 apiece (can't pass up the bargain) and then headed on to serious shopping.

We had miscalculated when we first went grocery shopping to Al-Azizia a week ago. We went during the one-hour gap between *Maghrib* and *Isha* prayers, thinking we could get our shopping done quickly. Well, it didn't work out. We didn't know our way around the aisles, and despite splitting up and keeping our list to a minimum, we were still shopping when the lights dimmed and an announcement was made that the store would soon be closing for thirty minutes for *Isha*. We headed for the checkout line. Too late. We knew that by the time we got through the long line, we were going to end up on the curb with no cabs to get us home. Better to wait inside the air-conditioned store. So we got out of the checkout line. And then we heard the *adhan*. I just stop in my tracks when I hear that beautiful sound. All of a sudden, the men left to go to the mosque attached to the supermarket. I told Khalid to go ahead while I hung around. I assumed that like Pakistan, the mosque was for men only.

All business stopped, the checkout counters closed, and it became quiet. There were many ladies still inside who continued to shop quietly. Then I saw women beginning to line up at the empty checkout counter. I followed suit. And exactly thirty minutes later, the lights brightened and an announcement was made: "Prayer time is over. Staff, please return to your stations." All of a sudden, people came out from who-knows-where, checkout counters opened, and the place came alive with the sounds of chatter. The next instant Khalid was beside me and we were putting our groceries on the conveyor belt. Amazing! I give this nation a lot of credit. They stand up for their beliefs and have made their faith a part of their day-to-day operations. I was in awe.

But the experience of being inside the supermarket during prayer time did not feel right. Although one can perform one's *Isha* prayer anytime before midnight, if everyone around you has taken the time to face Mecca and say their prayers, why should I be shopping? It felt disrespectful. So we both agreed that from then on, we would not be out when the *adhan* is called.

But here is the best part. I had picked up a cantaloupe at the store. When we got home and started putting away the groceries, Khalid exclaimed, "Sixteen dollars for a cantaloupe!"

"Really?"

"It says right here."

"Must be a mistake." I was feeling guilty for not having paid attention.

"Doesn't look like a mistake. See, it's printed on the receipt."

Now that is outrageous. Sixteen dollars for a cantaloupe! So guess what Khalid did. He picked up the cantaloupe, walked back to the store, went to customer service, and complained that the cantaloupe was overpriced. They promptly gave him a refund.

"It's imported," the attendant said.

So is almost everything else in the store. Anyhow we are now sixteen dollars richer minus the cantaloupe.

Go figure!

All the best,
Sabeeha

Male Guardian Required

May 2
Subject: Day 19

Dear All,

The other day Khalid and I ended up in a Lebanese restaurant. It was what we in the US would call "fine dining." The restaurant displayed a sign that read: a woman must be accompanied by a *mahram*. Let me explain: A *mahram* is a woman's male family member, defined as her husband, father, son, brother, uncle, son-in-law, stepfather, grandfather, or her sister's husband. It is acceptable for a woman to be in the company of a *mahram*, who serves as her escort. Got it? In the case of the restaurant, it translates into: no dating couples, and no all-girl groups. This is the first time I had seen such a sign. There was no such requirement in the food court at the mall or fast food outlets. But then as I entered, I noticed that this restaurant had a much more private setup. The family room had screened-off cubicles, making the tables intimate and private, with room for mischief. *But why no all-girl groups?* I started thinking:

in the US, it wasn't too long ago when it wasn't considered proper for a lady to go unescorted to a white linen restaurant. *I guess Saudis are just on a different timeline.*

Here is what else I learned: A woman can sit in the front seat of the car if it is being driven by a *mahram*; otherwise, she must sit in the back or risk being put in jail. A man cannot transport a woman in his car unless she is chaperoned by a *mahram*. However, a woman can ride alone in a cab with a stranger driving, as long as she sits in the back seat. Go figure!

I had read in the *Fingertip Guide to Riyadh* that wearing of shorts (by men, of course) is not permitted under any circumstances. The other day Khalid and I were grocery shopping when I saw a tall blond man walk right through the checkout area wearing shorts. I tugged at Khalid's sleeve, "Did you see that? A man in SHORTS!" He was definitely taking chances, and summer hasn't even begun. I felt that it signified lack of respect for the cultural sensibilities of the locals.

My initial impression was that wearing a scarf over the hair was optional, since most of the expatriate women shoppers walk around with their hair uncovered. But now I'm confused. The book I'm reading says that women *should* wear a scarf. The same day in Al-Azizia, an elderly Saudi man gestured to me to cover my hair, which I immediately did—I had let it slip to enable Khalid to find me. This is their custom, and we are their guests, and it is only proper that we do not offend.

The other day we were shopping in Ikea for pillows (non-recycled), and Sangeeta and I walked off to scout the area when I heard Khalid calling me. I looked back and saw him and Dr. Pai smiling at the two of us.

"This is not America. You can't just take off like that. Stay close to us," Khalid said.

"How about you two keeping pace with us, if you want to keep us girls out of trouble," I said.

In my understanding, it seems that the lines blur between what constitutes a legal requirement and what tradition calls for. I am still learning and don't have the answers. Until then, we just follow the norms: when in public, cover your hair and keep your husband close.

All the best,
Sabeeha

◆ ◆ ◆

Friday, May 5
Subject: *Jumma*

Dear All,

I have just experienced the wonder of *Jumma* prayer at the Prophet's Mosque in Medina. And I wasn't even there. It was noon, and Khalid had left for *Jumma* prayers when I decided to see if *Jumma* prayer was being telecast. Sure enough, on Channel 2 a young Saudi announced the beginning of the program by the recitation of the Holy Qur'an. The chapter of Saba was recited with each sentence flying into the screen in a melodious *qirat* (recital). It was followed by the English translation. Then another young man in clerical robes gave a brief sermon in English on the virtues of congregational prayers in the mosque (vs. individually at home). He spoke with an American accent but looked Saudi.

Then came the actual *Jumma* prayers. The camera first scanned the horizon, the green dome, the tall minarets, and the barren hills against the bright blue sky. Then it took us inside the mosque where the faithful were gathering for prayer, and to the front row where the *muezzin* had taken his place. As he raised his hands to his ears and began the *adhan*, "Allahu Akbar" (God is Great), I felt goose bumps all over and my eyes welled up. And as the *adhan* rang out, the camera took us on a panoramic view outside the mosque and you could see the faithful making their way across the plaza, the *adhan* resonating through the town. Zoom in to the doorway, and they were removing their shoes and entering. "Hasten to prayer, hasten to success," the *muezzin* was calling.

As the mosque started to fill up, the *muezzin* called the second *adhan*. His melodious voice and the photography accentuated that feeling of awe and wonder bringing me in to a state of absolute stillness. The head imam took his place on the *mimbar* (pulpit) and began his sermon in Arabic. The congregation sat on the red-and-gold carpet and listened in silence. I have had the good fortune of praying in the Prophet's Mosque several times, but I never had a close-up view of all these details—few people have. Although nothing can match the feeling of being physically present, the cameraman sure tried to compensate for it. And although I couldn't understand what the imam was saying, his delivery was so pleasing to the senses that both Khalid and I were mesmerized. (Khalid had just walked in as the sermon began, *Jumma* starting later in Medina in the north due to difference in latitude, as the sun passes its zenith later.)

Then just as soon as he had finished his sermon, the congregation raised their hands in prayer, in unison, each silently asking God for His mercy. The *iqama* was called (all rise to prayer), and you got a bird's-eye view of people lining up, side by side, shoulder to shoulder, all distinctions of rank erased, all equal in the eyes of God. And as always, the imam instructed the congregation to straighten their rows. His voice resonated through the mosque, and all was silent as he began the prayer in Arabic, and in unison the congregation bowed in submission to God Almighty. The two units of prayer were over in ten minutes and as the congregation started filing out of the mosque, with no sound and in complete silence, the camera moved ever so slowly as it took us through the arched walkways, and the infinite rows of arches checkered in ivory and black, supported by white pillars topped with gold casing, row after row, white and gold. It scanned over the blue chandeliers with etchings of Qur'anic verses, the beautiful ceilings, and the endless arches and pillars again and again, ever so slowly, in silence. Breathtaking! I was left with a feeling of utmost peace. And as the camera zoomed out of the mosque, out of the plaza, and out of Medina, it took us back to the studio and the young announcer.

"And we now take you to our children's program, your favorite cartoons followed by Sesame Street."

All the best,
Sabeeha

US Embassy

Sunday, May 6
Subject: Day 23

Dear All,

What a letdown!

Today we visited the American embassy and registered as residents of the Kingdom. The security here was like nothing I have ever seen. But that was just one part of it. First, I had to find out their days of operation. Each time I called, I got a recording: "This is the American embassy . . . press 1, 2 . . . " and not finding my option, I would hold for the operator, who would come on and say, "Hello," put me through to the counselor's office, and I would get voicemail. My calls were not returned.

I called the American Community Services (ACS), and they informed me that the embassy was open Saturday through Wednesday (Saudi working hours), but each office had its own operating hours and I had to call directly. On Sunday morning I called the embassy again, and this time I got a live person: "May I help you?"

"I want to come in to register and need to know your hours."

I was again put through to the counselor's office and yes, again got voicemail. Called the operator again, "Please do not connect me to the counselor's office because I get voicemail. Just tell me the hours for registration."

"We are open till 5 p.m. today."

I called Khalid, he took off from work, and we took a cab to the parking lot of the embassy. As we stepped out, we found ourselves in a desolate, unpaved, dusty parking field, encircled by concrete roadblocks. Beyond the roadblocks was another open field and beyond that, far away in the distance, was the embassy, looming large and imposing, rising above the terraces dotted with palm trees. This was going to be a long walk, and already at 10 a.m. the sun was strong as the mercury reached ninety degrees. The isolation of the parking lot just hits you. Then you see these sandstone barricades, then open barren fields, then sandstone terraces, then the walls rising, then the massive structure of the embassy, rising above you. It felt like a forbidden city.

We began our walk. The barricades had flowerbeds, the terraces were landscaped with flowers and bushes, and as you got closer, the vegetation and palm trees got lusher and greener. Now we were in front of the embassy. An immensely large wrought-iron gate, barricaded inside and outside by concrete blocks, welcomed us. We were greeted at the window by a Saudi.

"We are here to register," Khalid said.

"Registration closes at 4:00 p.m. I am sorry." His tone was polite.

That just *did* it.

"But we called . . . but we spoke to someone . . . we were told . . . "

Both Khalid and I were protesting, talking at the same time and getting agitated. Khalid showed him the form we had filled out.

"We are American citizens. All we want to do is register. We called . . . we were told . . . "

"I will call the office." He picked up the phone. "I have Mr. Khalid Rehman here who is a US citizen and wants to register, and he called this morning and was told to come in anytime before five."

He hung up the phone.

"You may go in, sir," he said, and he gestured toward the door.

Wow! Relieved, grateful, and with a lingering sense of embarrassment over our outburst, we went in. We were greeted by a security check—an Indian/Pakistani-looking guard. We were asked to turn in our electronic devices. Then we went inside the embassy compound. The open-air atrium was spectacular, beams rising overhead in a triangular crisscross, letting in air and light; marble flooring and fountains perfectly blending into the natural landscape. But it was sterile and empty.

We walked through to a large lobby. Empty. Then a second security check. A Saudi man greeted us. Going through the metal detectors again, we were directed down a corridor—empty—with a security person standing halfway down the hall. Offices on our left and right were devoid of human existence. Almost as if word had gone out: "The Rehmans are coming through. Take cover." When we reached the guard—an Indian/Pakistani—he ushered us into an empty, dimly lit waiting room.

At the end of the room were windows with signs: registration, passports, etc. All closed.

"We just wait?" Khalid said.

"They have been informed of your arrival and are coming."

We had barely taken a seat when one of the windows opened. A Saudi man appeared, smiled, and beckoned to us. He was so polite, friendly, helpful, humble, so everything nice that we were immediately appeased. I had walked in with my list of grievances, and he so disarmed us that all my indignation vaporized. He gave us a briefing package. We thanked him again, and truly, we appreciated that they had bent the rules and had specially opened their office for us. They could have turned us away. But they took responsibility for the miscommunication.

When we walked out, our electronic toys were handed back to us. We couldn't help but overhear a Saudi at the window making inquiries. "The princess and her entourage are visiting the United States. What is the procedure for visas?" A princess!

We left with a sense of unfinished business. I had not met anyone from the home country—correction—I had not even *seen* anyone. This is *our* embassy, an extension of the United States, the agency that assures security for its citizens in a foreign country, and yet we didn't get that feeling while we were there. No greetings, no welcome, no "we are here for you." I had wanted to meet our representatives and have a personal contact. I understand that security is paramount, and I am not sure if there is a right balance, but it sure is evident that each time you add a layer of security, it chips away at hospitality.

And now, let me change the subject.

I read the briefing package that evening and went into a state of semi-shock. If I had read this package before coming to Saudi Arabia, I might not have come. *"You can lose your head. . . . You can lose your hand. . . . You can be thrown in jail. . . . You can be deported . . . . You can be charged with prostitution."* Good God! It *is* the embassy's obligation to warn their citizens of the worst-case scenarios, and sometimes shock treatment is an effective way to bring about change in behavior, yet the impact is terrifying.

I recalled a similar feeling when many years ago I was driving to work and listening to the news on the radio. A study had just reported that Newark, the city I work in, was the most dangerous city in the US. The announcer started listing all the crime statistics. As I listened, I said to myself, "It's a good thing I didn't hear this when I was deciding whether to accept a job here, or I never would have." I had been driving to work for many years, had never had an incident, thank God, but more than that, I had never *felt* unsafe. And that was true for most of us who worked there, if not all. Of course, we took more than the usual precautions that quickly became second nature, but we never felt unsafe. Yet any outsider hearing the report would have felt they should stay away. I don't feel unsafe in Saudi either. In fact, I feel very safe.

I pray that we remain safe, all of us—you, me, our family, our friends, everyone, everywhere. Amen.

All the best,
Sabeeha

Female Guardian Required

May 6
Subject: Day 23

Dear All,

There is a sign outside the Faisaliah Mall and Al-Azizia which says: young men not allowed.

Shopping centers bar boys under the age of twenty-one after *Isha* prayers. If you had read the article that appeared in the *New York Times* several months ago, it reported that malls in Saudi Arabia were becoming a place where teenage boys attempt to look up young girls. This rule is to prevent that. And of course, prime time is after *Isha* prayers. So, no young boys allowed in prime time unless accompanied by an escort, as in a parent, mother, or sister.

The mannequins are headless. And I hadn't even noticed until Khalid pointed it out to me just the other day. Now, I have been to four malls in three weeks, most of the stores are clothing stores, and all these stores have mannequins in the window, yet we had both missed that. You know why that is—headless mannequins, that is? It goes back to the association of statues with idol worship, hence an absence of statues in any setting. So the mannequin starts with the neck, which is capped, and it looks just fine. And that is just one more example of how they incorporate their beliefs in their day-to-day lives.

When I come back to the States, I am bringing date candy, date pastry, date baklava, you name it. Sweet and sticky and delicious! These are bite-size mini pastries with date filling. Some have pistachio filling, some are chocolate covered with coconut filling, some look like triangular cookies with almond and date filling, some with date and cream cheese filling. They are in all kinds of creative shapes and designs, looking so exotic. And when you go up to the dates counter, the attendant immediately hands you a sample. Khalid is always reluctant to take a bite because he doesn't want to impose. So I take a bite (well, someone has to), and it is always so good that we inevitably end up buying an assortment. Then there is the *halawa*, like a cotton candy in the form of strands or a block, made out of ground sesame seeds. It melts in your mouth before solidifying, and then melts again. Pure yummy sugar.

Yesterday Khalid and I went to have dinner at the Hotel Intercontinental. Of course, it's a five-star hotel, so it's gorgeous, with all the exotic landscaping, but what struck me when we walked into the restaurant was that it was not segregated. What surprised me next was that I found it striking. See how one adapts! Two couples walked in, the women in abayas. After taking their seats, they removed their abayas before going for the buffet. I gasped! Apparently, being abaya-less is acceptable in a five-star hotel.

It seems like the main staple in the Saudi diet is cheese. The supermarkets have a cheese deli right in the center of the store—prime location—with every kind of cheese in all shapes and forms, some I am familiar with, and others completely new. And cream cheese in all forms all over the store, in case you missed it. Then there is the olive deli with barrels full of every kind of olive. It does show up on the waistline; those gorgeous children are chubby.

All the best,
Sabeeha

Month of Honey

May 8
Subject: Day 24

Dear All,

Yesterday Khalid and I attended our first Arabic class. Our teacher is a Sudanese gentleman and looks like Anwar Sadat, late president of Egypt. We have ten students in our class, all American. We enjoyed this class immensely, hooked up with another student from the hospital, and will be cab-pooling with her. Joan—not a Muslim— is an echo technician from Colorado.

Sitting through the first class, it is apparent that I have been reading some words of the Qur'an incorrectly. Let me backtrack. In Pakistan, we learned to read Arabic and had completed the reading of the entire Qur'an, a rite of passage for children. But we did not understand the language. Due to the similarities in the Urdu and Arabic alphabet, I had been pronouncing some of the Arabic alphabet in the Urdu version. Well, it's never too late to make amends.

If you are interested in knowing more about the language, read on. If not, go no further, but then you are going to miss out on the story title.

Classical Arabic is the language of the Qur'an. It is also the spoken language of the land, with some mingling of colloquial Arabic, the dialect varying from region to region. As communication between the three Saudi regions has increased, a standardized version is emerging, but all have their roots in Classical Arabic.

Arabic doesn't contain the equivalent of the letter *P*. When brand names such as Pepsi-Cola are written in Arabic script, the letter *B* is used, making the word sound like *Bebsi Cola*. Paul will be *Baul*. When the Saudis speak English, you wouldn't know that their mother tongue does not include the sound of *P*, for they are able to pronounce it with ease. The Arabic sounds are heavy, and you have to exert yourself. Some sounds are guttural, coming deep from the throat, some require a certain manipulation of the vocal cords. I continue to revert to the Urdu version, which is much softer, while other students are already producing the right sounds.

We now have fifty words in our vocabulary. I am getting the hang of the most frequently used two-letter sentence: *maafi mushkila* (i.e., "no problem").

<u>May 8</u>
Today during class, our teacher put a word on the blackboard: *Asal*. "It means 'honey,'" he said.

Noted.

"*Shahr*," he wrote. "It means 'month.'"

Noted.

"*Shahr Al Asal*," he wrote. "What does this mean?"

Silence.

Now I am thinking . . . *Shahr* means "month," *Al* means "the" or "of," *Asal* means "honey" . . .

"Month of Honey?" That was me, sounding very uncertain. It didn't make sense, but isn't that what each word meant?

No one spoke.

The teacher smiled benevolently, paused, and said, "It means honeymoon."

Chuckles!

Everyone turned around to get a good look at me. More chuckles.

All the best,
Sabeeha

CHAPTER 3

On the Job

Subject: Personnel Encounters

Dear All,

Today I called Samir and accepted the job in the Quality Resource Management Department, as the Utilization Review Specialist. What appeals to me is that this is a new position and, as in my previous two jobs in the US, I can start with a clean slate and shape the job as I see it. My job will be to ensure that only medically necessary tests are done on patients, in a timely manner, and patients are not kept in the hospital longer than necessary, thus freeing up the bed for critically ill patients. Samir also comes across as someone I can work well with and that became the deciding factor. The salary is half of what I was earning in the US, but when adjusted for tax benefits and cost of living, it's fine. Besides, I didn't really have much of a choice.

Now we just have to do the paperwork.

"Here is the application form. We'll need a photograph," Sarah in Personnel said. You remember Sarah from my earlier email, right?

I didn't know they would need a photograph. Now I have to go all the way back to the apartment, unless Khalid has one on him. He did.

"And we'll need your original master's degree."

I didn't know that they needed an original.

"I have a *copy* of my masters degree, but not the original." I handed it to her.

"Is it a certified copy?"

"No."

"Then who copied your degree?"

"I did!"

"You copied it *yourself*?" she asked, incredulous.

"Yes," I said, incredulous.

"Then you need to sign this affidavit stating that you will provide the original within ninety days after starting employment."

I was upset with myself. Why didn't I bring my originals? What was the point in leaving them neatly filed away on the other side of the Atlantic? Now I have to call dear Asim and ask him to mail it, and then hope it gets here.

"And here is another form for your husband to sign."

"What is this?" I asked, taking the form from her.

"It is a No Objection Form. Your husband has to state that he has no objection to your working."

Straight face, straight face.

I paged Khalid.

"What's up?"

"Where are you? I need to bring over a Personnel form for you to sign."

"I have to sign *your* Personnel form?"

"Yep. You have to give me permission to work." I giggled.

"What's in it for me?" Khalid chuckled.

All the best,
Sabeeha

◆◆◆

Subject: A Dependent

Dear All,

Being a dependent has its advantages. One is not entitled to annual leave during the first six months of employment. We plan to go to the US in October. Khalid's six months will be up by then, but mine will not. When I raised this issue with Samir, he told me that since I am being hired as my husband's dependent, I am entitled to the same time off irrespective of whether I have met the six-month requirement. Likewise, if he goes off on business leave to attend a seminar, I get to go, if I so choose. For that reason, many departments do not like to hire dependents.

Most of the female staff here—nurses and secretaries—are hired as an "independent," for lack of a better word. In fact, single females account for the highest volume of expatriates at the hospital. These women get visas based on their own contract, have their own *iqama*. In fact, there are so many of these "independent" women, that apartments for single women account for the largest block of housing units. Their housing is located on a sprawling complex dotted with palm trees and red bougainvillea, with a guarded gate, and is right across the street from the hospital; and there are four additional complexes on hospital grounds with all the recreational amenities, such as pool, gym, etc. Now, if a woman gets a contract to work here as an independent and wants to bring her husband along, he has to come on her *iqama* and get a visa based on *her* contract. Is he classified as a dependent? Who signs his No Objection form? I don't know, but I am trying to find out.

Today Khalid received his *iqama* and had to turn in our passports to the hospital. When we travel outside the country, they will give us back our passports and take the *iqama*. That means that you must inform your employer of your intention to leave. For emergencies, the office is open twenty-four hours a day, and the paperwork is handled immediately. It is illegal to have both the *iqama* and the passport on you. Muslims get a green-colored *iqama*, non-Muslims a brown one.

I am told that if a man with a green *iqama* is found wandering the streets during prayer time (versus being in a mosque), he can get into trouble. No such requirements for Muslim women.

All the best,
Sabeeha

Putting Out Fires

Subject: Orientation Day 1

Dear All,

Today I had my first day of orientation. There were forty-five of us, and apart from three or four people, all were expatriates. Canadians and Filipinos were by far the dominant group, with the rest from South Africa, Australia, New Zealand, India, and the United States. All but a few were fresh off the boat—sorry—plane. We quickly bonded, starting with dinner last night. The highlight today was learning how to put out fires—literally. We were given a briefing on fire safety and then they put the first twenty-five of us in a bus and took us to a field where they had lined up twenty-five fire extinguishers. A young American man in a fire marshal's uniform gave a demonstration. Twenty feet across from us was a large metal container, shaped like a bathtub and filled with water. A man wearing gloves and a face mask went up to the container and poured flammable liquid in it. Another man, also wearing gloves and a mask, lit the end of a long rod that he dropped into the container. The container burst into flames. He proceeded to demonstrate how to unlock the fire extinguisher, test it for pressure, and then, escorted by the third man, went to within ten feet of the fire and, using the extinguisher, put the fire out. Then a fourth man went up and sprayed water on the cauldron.

One by one, the twenty-five of us, twenty-five times: fire lit, fire put out, cauldron sprayed. Who cared if we were standing in the blazing

100-degree heat; the excitement of all that fire was overwhelming. Never in the US did my orientation include such hands-on training. I wonder if it's because fire is a serious threat here or because fires seldom happen.

Later, in the auditorium, presenter after presenter walked us through "all you need to know." An eighty-page *Orientation Guide* on how to navigate the hospital and the city, directories, schedules, maps, you name it. There was one presentation on recreation alone, with the schedule for the upcoming month for city tours, national tours, international tours, swimming classes, ladies' fitness, tennis, taekwondo, horseback riding, ice skating . . . ice skating!

Policy and Procedure: Dress and Appearance Code explained that employees and dependents should dress in a manner that shows respect for the culture of the Kingdom of Saudi Arabia. (Culture, not law). Women are to dress modestly, hemlines below mid-calf. Dresses or skirts with slits are not allowed. (I had noticed many of the women walking around with slits.) Blouses and dresses should be properly buttoned. Sleeveless or sheer material is not allowed. Blue jeans and tee shirts not allowed during working hours. Trousers should not be tight-fitting and should be covered with a tunic top or long jacket. Male employees in Western clothing should wear a shirt and necktie, properly button the shirt, and not wear tee shirts or shirts with eye-catching phrases.

If you want to take photographs of the hospital, you need to get permission. Photography is a sensitive issue, and you don't see people with cameras in hand.

This is what the *Orientation Guide* said about prayer time: "If you are in a shop when *salah* [prayer] is called or notice the *mutawwa* signaling merchants to close shop, you should leave. If you stay inside the shop, the merchant can get into trouble, which may include revocation of his license."

The schedule of orientation was in military time. English is the official language of the hospital. The hospital follows the Hijra calendar (Muslim calendar—starting from the date the Prophet Muhammad

(Peace be upon him) migrated from Mecca to Medina). However, the Gregorian and Hijra calendar are printed side by side on all documents (i.e., Safar 5, 1422 AH/April 29, 2001). Salary is stated in terms of monthly salary rather than annual. Paychecks are issued monthly rather than biweekly and according to the Hijra calendar. Since the Hijra calendar is ten days shorter than the Gregorian calendar, being on the lunar schedule, in three Gregorian years you get an extra paycheck (i.e., thirty-seven paychecks versus thirty-six). Let's do the math: if your monthly salary is $10,000, your annual is $120,000, but over three years, instead of $360,000, you end up with $370,000. Got it? I won't complicate it further by telling you that here you get paid in Saudi riyals.

That evening Sangeeta called and suggested that we all go to the Jarir bookstore. Great! I get to pick out books on Saudi law and regulations and get the answers to my questions. The store was a combination of a Barnes & Noble and Staples only three times the size, but not unmanageable. The first floor had computer and office supplies, and upstairs was the bookstore. I went straight to the information desk.

"Sir, I need a map of Riyadh, and books on the history of Riyadh and the laws of Saudi Arabia."

"I will show you where the maps are, but all we have on the history of Riyadh is the photo books."

"And books on law?" I asked.

"The books on law are in Arabic only. English books on law are banned," he said with a straight face. I think what that means is that books written by outsiders on the law of Saudi Arabia must meet approval of the authorities. Just guessing. Well, that didn't help. So I selected a book on "Customs and Etiquettes of Saudi Arabia," written by Kathy Cuddihy, a Canadian writer. It wasn't what I was looking for, but by now it was beginning to appear that customs were equally important, if not more. Still learning. In the English-language section, the store had all the Oprah Book Club selections: Tom Clancy, Mary Higgins Clark, Danielle Steele, *Brethren* by John Grisham, and my recent favorite, *The Poisonwood Bible*. But no books on law.

When we stepped out, the town was drenched. It had rained, and it smelled good. There is something about the fragrance of water on dust, or maybe sand—there is no dust here—that is invigorating.

All the best,
Sabeeha

Mutawwa Question Answered

Subject: Orientation Day 2

Hello again:

Today's sessions were about Saudi culture. We learned that Riyadh has a population of 3.5 million. I had thought it was a lot less. Due to the intense heat, people stay indoors during the day. When downtown, the speaker advised, a woman should wear an abaya and cover her head. *Hmmm! So no abaya elsewhere?* As for behavior, he advised that men and women not express intimacy in public and not laugh loudly, especially downtown. Saudi has the lowest crime rate in the world, as evident from recent studies. In Saudi, the Islamic penal code applies. Killing is punishable by death. Executions take place in public. Death by car accident or killing in self-defense does not constitute killing. Trials are swift and conviction requires a clear confession or four witnesses to the killing. There are no psychiatrists or lawyers involved. He added that the O. J. Simpson case would have been resolved in two days. For me, the idea of swift trials in murder cases and public executions was unsettling.

Then he went straight to shopping tips and travel requirements. It is a legal requirement that when we enter the country, our sponsor receive us at the airport.

Saudis have a great deal of respect for elders and do not call anyone who is older than themselves by their name. Instead, they refer to them as father of so-and-so or mother of so-and-so, so-and-so being the oldest child. *I guess that makes me Um Saqib.* Married women do not adopt their husband's names; they maintain their father's name.

"If you are in the shopping mall and the call for prayer is announced, what is expected of us, both men and women?" I asked my burning question.

"Shops are supposed to close for thirty minutes. And you don't have to do anything. You can walk around," he responded.

"Who is the *mutawwa*?" asked Shelly, one of the new hires from Canada.

"*Mutawwa* is the body that monitors rules of behavior and security. They are volunteers or officials. The *mutawwa* has good and bad. The good is that they are more sincere about their job than appointed officials and take quick action. If the regular police have to take action, they first take you to the police station, book you, go through all the process, and that takes time. The *mutawwa* can arrest people and put them in jail. Their main concern is drugs, alcohol, men's behavior toward women, and for that matter, women's behavior toward men, and women's dress. The negative side is that they have no written policy. Each person exercises his own judgment. Whenever they have been asked to have a written policy, for example on women's dress code, they say, 'How can we write what is right and what is wrong when the women's fashions keep changing?'" Laughter.

I had my answer.

"In public, does a woman have to cover her hair?" I asked.

"The veil, covering of the face, is not an Islamic requirement. Those who cover their faces, do so based on the belief of their sect or personal preference."

I guess my question had not gotten across.

"Is the abaya a requirement?" asked someone.

"The abaya is not an Islamic requirement. It originated from the Turks. It is the best way to dress modestly, but it is not a requirement. But it is better if you wear it in downtown. Clothes should be clean, and one should dress modestly, that is, no see-through or tight-fitting clothes."

"Can we wear shorts?" asked a gentleman.

"You can wear anything you like or not wear anything you don't like, but if you wear shorts, it would be disrespectful."

Can a woman walk alone on the streets?" I asked.

"Yes, she can. But it is better if you are accompanied."

"Why are you wearing a white head scarf and not the checkered scarf?" asked Anna. *Bold!*

"What we wear is based on our environment. It is getting hot, and white is better for the heat." At this he started disassembling his head gear, demonstrating its various pieces.

"This is the black cord that keeps the scarf in place," he said removing the round cord. Then he removed the scarf and pointed to his skull cap.

"The skull cap keeps the hair in place," he proceeded to remove his skull cap to reveal his hair. "And you can wear the scarf in ten different ways. When there is a sandstorm or hot air, you cover your face with it," he covered his face in the Lawrence of Arabia style. "When you are at official functions, you let it fall loose"—it fell loose in the King Fahd style—"or you can . . . ," and he continued to demonstrate all the styles and had the audience mesmerized.

I came home and scanned my book on Saudi customs. Nothing on prayer time requirements; and dress code is stated as a custom in terms of "this is what women wear," not this is what one *should* wear. But it had good information on the *mutawwa*: "The guardians of moral standards are called *mutawwa*. Conflicts frequently arise over what constitutes the official policy and what is correct behavior according to an individual *mutawwa*. Numerous unsuspecting individuals are caught in the crossfire and brought to special *mutawwa* jails for offenses . . . . Release is usually dependent on the guilty party signing a paper swearing not to commit the same offense again. Women are not released until their husbands or sponsors collect them. A *mutawwa* cannot make an arrest unless a civic policeman is in attendance."

This confirmed what I understood from orientation. I had been looking for the legal requirement, my mindset shaped by my former job as Compliance Officer. Here, the answer lies in the customs and traditions as well as the law. Wear the abaya in public, cover your hair in public, and refrain from being in public places at prayer time; show respect for the culture and traditions and take the path of least resistance. Anybody could have told me that. Oh well!

Another incident took place today during orientation. We had been given a lunch break, and Shelly, Anna, Brilly, and I went to the cafeteria. I was ahead in the tray line and went into the seating area, sitting down at a table for four. I noticed that a group of Filipino young men sitting at the next table were giving me this strange look. Just then a Western-looking gentleman at the next table called out to me. "This is the men's seating area."

Whoops!

PS: After orientation I stopped by the office to see Samir, my boss. He looked up from his desk and, with a smile on his face, said, "So, how was orientation? I hear you have been asking a lot of questions."

Stumped. Who at orientation knew who I was, who I was going to be working for, and lost no time in reporting to Samir on his nosey new hire? Gee!

All the best,
Sabeeha

◆ ◆ ◆

Subject: Practice of Medicine

Dear All,

Here are some observations on the practice of medicine in a Saudi culture.

A male relative always accompanies a female patient. The male guardian has to be a *mahram* (husband, father, brother, son). No cousins. In the Islamic faith, you can marry your cousin; therefore, cousins are segregated. He is given paid time off from work to accompany his female relative.

Patient rooms are private, for the most part, and doors are kept closed for privacy. Officially designated live-in sitters are the norm, and every inpatient room has a bed for the family member.

There are no real barriers to a male doctor examining a female patient or female doctor examining a male patient. The chief of Gynecology is male. Some women will not expose their face but will bare their chest and the abdomen without protest. They will uncover their face only if the physician insists, some under protest, if the face must be examined. And then there are some elderly female patients who will absolutely refuse to be examined by a male physician.

This paragraph is rated R. Khalid tells me that when he came here for a locum, he was startled when he walked into the exam room and saw the female patient sitting on the exam table, her face veiled, but her chest uncovered. A female nurse stood by for translation. Khalid mentioned it to the chairman—an American—who said, "In Bedouin culture, breast is not a sexual organ." Did Khalid choke?

Most patients do not speak English. Many nurses are bilingual and always accompany the doctor for translation purposes. Khalid has not found communication with patients to be a problem.

The cancer pathology in this population is different from in the US. Breast cancer, lymphoma, and throat cancer are the most common cancers. Prevalence of cancer of the placenta (during pregnancy), rare in the US, is rather high here. Khalid sees two such cases a day. Cancer also afflicts the young in much greater proportion than in the US. Patients are accepting of their condition, even when it is terminal. They are calm and accept their diagnosis without any display of fear, denial, anger, anxiety, or apprehension. As patients, they are compliant. It must be culture.

The mission of the hospital is to be the tertiary healthcare provider for all Saudis in the Kingdom. It is also the primary, secondary, and tertiary care provider for all VIPs. The latter of course is unwritten. The hospital was established around 1970 so that the extended royal family would not have to go to the Mayo and Cleveland Clinic. It also caters to the impoverished population of the Kingdom.

The hospital has six hundred beds and a staff of over six thousand, comprising fifty-eight different nationalities. Forty-four percent of the medical staff are expatriates including 16 percent US/Canadian. Nurses are recruited from across the globe. The CEO is appointed by King Fahd Ibn Abdul Aziz Al-Saud. The hospital's Bone Marrow Transplant Program is one of the world's largest programs of the allogenic (human donor) type.

What surprised me was the number of female Saudi doctors, and in high positions too, in specialties beyond pediatrics and OB/GYN. How about surgery! They sit on committees, make policy decisions, and are pretty vocal. Male patients are OK with being treated by a woman, veiled or otherwise.

Everyone wants to come *here* for treatment; therefore, the hospital has very specific criteria and process for accepting patients.

Here is how it works: If a doctor at another hospital determines that his/her patient should be treated at King Faisal's, a request is sent to the accepting physician. Based on the criteria for tertiary care, the accepting physician at King Faisal accepts or denies the case and has complete authority in this matter. If accepted, the government pays the entire cost of care, including prescription drugs, travel, and lodging. Impoverished patients, most of whom live in outlying areas in the desert, account for a high volume. If the patient is employed, the employer must give paid time off. If the patient is female, the male relative accompanying the patient is not only given paid time off, but all travel and lodging expenses are covered. The accepting physician must certify that the patient needs x number of days of care and thus the male relative must be given time off for an equal number of days. The facility accepts Saudi citizens only. The exceptions are hospital employees and their families, who are provided complete healthcare.

This institution is so coveted that patients wait sometimes for months to get in. Once they get in, they don't want to leave, and discharging them is a major challenge. This is one of the most difficult problems the institution is facing, because waiting lists are long, post-hospital care is in its early stages, and the monetary incentives are not there for the patients to leave. There is a move toward an insurance-based system, but that will take time. Services such as long-term care and chronic rehabilitation are just beginning to evolve.

Cases involving potential termination of pregnancies are handled within the context of religious beliefs and prudent medical practice. For example, if a case involves a woman who is close to the end of her first trimester, has been diagnosed with cancer, and needs treatment, the following options would be considered, irrespective of the patient's faith:

a. Terminate the pregnancy, since chemotherapy will cause irreparable harm to the fetus at this stage, and treatment is necessary to save the life of the mother.
b. Delay chemotherapy and do not terminate the pregnancy. This will save both lives, and the delay would not have significant effects.
c. Get a fatwa: a religious decree from a religious authority.
d. Delay chemotherapy, do not terminate, and involve the mother in the decision.

The recommended option is d.

This is a paternalistic society; its traditions and values are embedded in day-to-day life for centuries. When physicians discuss diagnosis and treatment options, the male guardian makes the decisions. Many American physicians have difficulty adjusting to this form of decision-making. Some doctors accept it, and others challenge it. But this is their culture, and women go along with it.

Then there is the issue of consent. Legally, a female patient can sign her own consent for treatment, but culturally the female patient delegates this to the male guardian. The hospital worked with Joint Commission on International Accreditation (JCIA) to design a patient rights formula that met the Joint Commission standards and was also culturally sensitive. Here is what they came up with: the physician explains the diagnosis and treatment to both the patient and the guardian and documents it, stating that the patient has delegated this right to her male guardian.

The clerical staff is amazing. Most of them are Saudi women, all of whom wear the veil. Their eyes through slits in the veil are all one can see. They handle all the paperwork, the transcription of physician orders into the order-entry system, and if paperwork is missing, they are knocking down his/her door. And they are smart. The other day Khalid went to the *Iqama* office. He approached the woman at the desk, a Saudi, introduced himself, and asked if his *iqama* was ready. In a flash, she looked at the PC and said that it was not ready. Khalid did not even see her enter any data, yet when he glanced at the screen, his ID number, name, and related info was there. She had probably read his ID number off his badge as he was speaking to her, had keyed it in while he was talking, and by the time he finished his sentence, the information had flashed on the screen. They are all bilingual (i.e., English and Arabic), and are dealing with all kinds of English accents—Australian, British, American, Canadian, Pakistani, Indian, Sudanese, Filipino. . . . And back home when I would see a photograph of a woman in the veil, it created such a different impression.

Reality vs. perception.

More to come!
Sabeeha

A Prelude to My Next Email

Remember my encounter with the Personnel Department, asking for the original version of my master's degree? Well, later that day, I placed a call to our son Asim and asked him to retrieve my master's degree and mail it to me. It arrived within a week, and I took it over to the Personnel Office and showed it to Sarah. She looked at it and handed it back to me with a thank you. And that was it. I didn't see her make a note of it, make a copy, or pull out my file.

Later that day, I mentioned the episode to Samir. He gave me this knowing smile, "If you had told me about this when they first asked you for the original, I would have told you to get the degree but don't give it to them. Let's see if they remind you."

I guess he had been there long enough to know the cracks in the system.

♦ ♦ ♦

Subject: Day 1 at the Job

Dear All,

I started work on Saturday, the 18th of Safar, corresponding to the Gregorian date of May 12.

Our offices are in the administrative building. It has a circular lobby with glass walls rising all the way up to the fourth floor, well-lit and pleasing and next to the main hospital building. In two weeks, I am to develop an outline of a plan for optimizing inpatient bed utilization, and in one month, the Plan itself. I am to meet with eighteen members of the management staff one-on-one and expand that list if I choose to. My Day One assignment was to read all departmental policies and procedures, personnel policies, official memorandums for general distribution, and administrative policies on the web.

By the end of the day, my eyes were glazing over, and I was intrigued. The policies are very detailed, more so than any I have ever seen. I don't understand the necessity for that level of detail. Even the issuance of memorandums has a policy and is very formal. I was issued a guest number to access the internet, and boy was I impressed! The amount of information they have on their website is staggering—you don't have to go calling for data or refer to manuals that may be out of date. Statistics, databases, performance improvement tools, and even the leave schedule of all the physicians are all up there. Compared to this place, my previous hospital in New Jersey is way behind.

Other than Samir, I am the only non-nurse in the department. Most of the staff in the office is American with three exceptions: the secretary, who I will call Susan, is from Australia; one of the quality improvement analysts, a male nurse, is from Jordan; and there's a female nurse from Germany.

By midday my contract was ready. This is the first time in my career that I've had to sign a contract. I had so many questions when I first read it, and both Personnel and Samir took the time to explain. I wanted to know why I was hired at a particular step. The answer: The step, which determines salary level, is based on the geographic origin of hire (i.e., Saudi, Asian, European, Canada, or US). US hires have the highest steps, and I was being employed as a US hire. I had no objection to that. Then I called Khalid and went over the details with him, said a prayer, and signed it. It felt like a big moment. Now I am locked in for two years. I hope it is a good two years.

And here is the best part. Khalid called me at noon and said, "Want to have lunch?" Now, since I began my career nineteen years ago, we have never worked in the same hospital. The sheer thought that now we can have lunch together as often as we want made us both feel good. But here is the problem—you guessed it—segregated seating. Next to the hospital cafeteria is the family dining room, a fancy and elegant setup, elaborate menu, buffet-style with all the trimmings, waiters; but it is relatively expensive. Not a place where one would eat every day. Then there is a small shopping center on campus that has a restaurant, bowling alley, gift shop, deli, music shop, Dunkin' Donuts, Baskin-Robbins, video rental; you get the picture. The restaurant, which is privately owned, has open seating. Its prices are mid-range so it's very popular. That is where we went.

I gave Khalid a call, met him in the lobby, and we walked home together. Nice.

All the best,
Sabeeha

Act American

"You have to project an image of an American," a senior Saudi said to me during my first week on the job.

For a moment I wasn't sure what he meant.

"Here, we look up to Americans. If you are seen as an American, people will listen to you. None of this Muslim business." He was saying: *Don't tap into the "I am a Muslim just like you" sentiment.*

Either my jaw must have dropped or my eyes popped wide, because he added: "I know how this sounds, but this is how it is. You will have credibility and respect if you act American."

Got it. Actually, I don't. How am I supposed to know what is "acting American" and what is "whatever else"?

But I appreciated his candor and advice and made a mental note of it.

"And speak up. You have six months to make an impression. After that, no one will listen to you."

I am grateful for that guidance, because in the past, my approach in my first few weeks on a new job had been to first listen, take it all in, get the lay of the land, and then start making my voice heard.

He was right on both counts. I was in a meeting and one of the American attendees said, "In the States, this is how we do it." Heads turned, and the chairman asked him to elaborate while everyone nodded in affirmation. The buzz around the table was: "If this is what they do in the States, then it must be the right way." I don't recall what the issue was, but this phenomenon repeated itself in many a meeting, and the mantra was, "American standards are the gold standard." At first, I was too shy to flaunt my American credentials, but it didn't take long for me to overcome my inhibition.

It didn't matter that at times I was the only woman at the table, surrounded by Saudi men in their traditional garb. When I spoke, the high-powered executives around the table listened. I didn't have to fight for my voice to be heard (unlike in corporate America), and I was not brushed aside with a dismissive "thank you, let's move on" gesture. I got bolder. The Saudi men were respectful, professional in their conduct, humble in their demeanor, yet would rightfully question and challenge my assumptions and hear me out. I would leave a meeting feeling that I was heard. If I did not get the outcome I wanted, it was for a good reason and had nothing to do with me being a woman.

Getting back to Americans. They were at a premium, particularly the nurses. And if they were white, premium-plus. I first heard that from another Saudi colleague. There was some rumbling that one of the staff in a department might be leaving.

"We have to hold on to him," he said to me. "He is white."

This American must have jolted in her seat, because he said, "I know how this sounds, but that is how things are. Having white people on our staff lends credibility to our department. People pay attention to our recommendations if it comes from a white person."

My expression must have said, *Really!*

"When a doctor challenges a white nurse, she pushes back"—he gestured, pushing himself forward—"but if it's a Filipino nurse, she backs off," and he gestured again, pulling back.

I was getting the lay of the land.

It goes one step further. The hospital has a Royal Wing for members of the royal family. Over lunch, one of the nurses told me that these patients prefer—demand—that they be assigned a white nurse from a western country. In other words, not a white-skinned Lebanese or Syrian nurse but an American, Canadian, or the like. Now, one would think that the patients would be more comfortable being nursed by their own kind, someone who speaks the language and is familiar with their cultural considerations. This nurse explained that one reason is that western nurses are considered more skilled; the other being that an Arab nurse is considered too close for comfort. Saudis are private people and the royal family more so. They find security in the distance that an outsider provides, and they tend to trust their discretion. *Hmmm!*

"The white nurses are arrogant," she said. "They know how much they are valued, and it goes to their head." She was white.

A physical therapist I was talking to said to me that she had accepted a managerial position in one of the gulf states, an upward move in her career. "I have the right color."

Khalid tells this story: A cancer patient—a wealthy person—asked that he be assigned an American doctor. When Khalid walked into the exam room, the patient protested, saying to the female nurse in Arabic that he had asked to be treated by an American doctor.

"He *is* an American," the nurse said to him in Arabic, and then translated it to Khalid.

Khalid shrugged.

"But he is not an American," the patient said to her in Arabic.

The patient canceled his appointment and took the matter up to Khalid's boss, who told him in so many words that he could take it or leave it. He decided to leave it and took a flight to America.

Months later, we heard that he had gone to the Cleveland Clinic, was admitted to the hospital, and then promptly discharged himself, returning to Saudi exasperated: "*Kullo Indian ductoor.*" Translated: "All the doctors were Indian."

Another story, also by a colleague: The hospital had hired a Dr. Brown from Canada. There was a lot of excitement about his Canadian credentials. The welcome party went to receive him at the airport, and when the passengers arrived, Dr. Brown was nowhere to be seen. They looked around until all the passengers had left the terminal. There by baggage claim stood a Haitian-looking man. Noticing that they were holding the hospital's sign, he came up to them and asked, "Are you here to receive Dr. Brown?"

"Yes."

"I am Dr. Brown."

"You? But . . . "

Arabic, the Thobe & Socializing

Samir and I had just concluded a meeting when, in an effort to impress, I said, "I plan to learn Arabic."

"There is no need." He waved his hand dismissively. "Everyone speaks English."

"I know everyone speaks English, but I want to learn it for the sake of learning the language. I also want to be able to understand the Qur'an in its original language."

"It's a very difficult language. Very hard to learn."

I had thought Samir, or any Saudi for that matter, would encourage an expat to learn their language, have a sense of pride in knowing that others are interested in studying Arabic. I would later learn that Samir's was a universal attitude among Saudis. Once I started taking Arabic classes, I would attempt to make conversation in Arabic with my Saudi colleagues, but they would respond in English. I could never get past my opening sentence. Very soon I realized that this was unique to Saudis only. Other Arab men and women—Lebanese, Jordanian, Syrian—would not only encourage me to converse in Arabic, but they also became my teachers. I started recruiting them to coach me over lunch, and they gladly obliged.

When I mentioned this observation to a Pakistani doctor, he pointed out: "Have you noticed that none of the expat men wear the Saudi thobe and *ghutra*?"

I hadn't noticed. But now that he mentioned it, yes, come to think of it.

"Saudis don't like expats to wear their dress."

After that I *did* notice.

There was something else I learned. I was interacting with Saudis in the workplace for the better part of the day, and all encounters were highly professional, yet there were boundaries. Religion and politics were off the table—so what else is new—but so was personal life—not unusual either, but yours truly was accustomed to inviting her colleagues to her home for a meal. That never happened with Saudis. I just knew that extending an invitation was outside the boundaries. And the few times I did invite colleagues or neighbors, with one exception, they all politely declined. I would fill my living room with Lebanese, Syrian, and Jordanians, and I am still in touch with them. If there is one experience I missed, it was socializing with the Saudis. I wanted to get to know the lovely Norah one-to-one as well as the vivacious Abeer or the chatty Huda.

I would continue to study Arabic, first at the ACS, then hiring a Syrian tutor for five years, and then joining an Arabic language school for expats for another year. But I never learned to speak the language because I had no one to converse with. Upon returning to the States, I tried to keep up whatever I had learned by studying every morning, but after a year, I gave up. I have lost most of what I learned.

♦ ♦ ♦

Subject: First three weeks on the job

Dear All,

My overall impression of the workplace: I am impressed.

As I made my rounds, meeting colleagues for the first time, three things struck me as noteworthy.

First, the culture of customer service. Front-line people in particular are polite and will walk the extra mile to help you. I am not a known entity, and anyone at the front desk could easily give me the brush-off or pass the buck, but when I stop by to make an inquiry, e.g., if I am asking for directions, they will leave their desk, show me the way, and then rush back to their station. If they cannot help me, they will apologize, try to find an alternative, and compensate. Most of the front-line people are Saudis.

Second, the hi-tech environment. They are definitely in the twenty-first century, and it permeates the institution. Just the laboratory alone has every conceivable capability. Radiology? It's the upper limit. They even manufacture their own radiopharmaceuticals for nuclear medicine and PET Scanning. They have their own Cyclotrone.

Information Systems: Everyone has a PC* or has access to one except for those whose function does not absolutely require it, e.g., the gardener, the painter. All these people are computer-proficient and evidently are using their skill to its maximum potential. Communications are electronic. I can make an appointment for a doctor's visit or request a record through the intranet.† General staff meetings are held in one auditorium and relayed live in other auditoriums to enable maximum participation. We didn't have any of this at UMDNJ, a tertiary care major teaching hospital in New Jersey; not even a hospital website.

Telemedicine is the norm between the sister hospitals in both Riyadh and Jeddah. Can't help comparing, but telemedicine has not yet begun at UMDNJ. Just received notice for an eight-hour seminar by Steven Covey beamed live from the US. Almost every department has its own website. The phone directory and all such reference documents are on the web. But more than that, the staff has developed the mindset of electronic vs. paper and that, for information, they go to website. There is very little paper going around.‡ All the presentations at meetings that I have seen are slick, PowerPointed to the limit—and these are all in-house productions.

That brings me to the third thing that impressed me: the caliber of the staff. The hospital has some of the best talent that money can buy. As I made my rounds meeting people on a one-on-one, it continued to strike me. One of the people I met was a middle manager within one of the ancillary departments, a Saudi. Each time I would ask him a

---

* Of course it is not a big deal today, but remember, this was 2001. In the US hospital where I worked, PCs were a luxury and shared. Department heads had to fight to get a PC for their staff.

† That didn't surprise you either, Dear Reader, but twenty years ago, this practice was nonexistent in the US. It didn't get operationalized in US medical practices until in the most recent decade or so. So, what is King Faisal like in 2022? Imagine the state-of-the-art in the US at premier hospitals today. That is what you will find at King Faisal Hospital now.

‡ When I returned to the US in 2007, at my office in New York, we were still huddling around the copying machine. That is where we held our water-cooler conversations as we waited in line.

question, he would jump out of his seat, leap over to the shelf, pull out a document, and hand it to me. "This is the study I did on ... This is your copy." Or he would press the button on his PC, lean under the table, pull out a paper from his printer, and hand it to me, "These are the graphs and tables that show ... This is your copy." I asked him if he thought his department was being overutilized. He handed me a study he had done on his own initiative showing how very overutilized it was and how it was contributing to injuries on the job and staff turnover. The way he conducted the study was creative, but more than that, it showed how much he cared. I was so moved by his sincerity that I came back and told my boss that people like him should be cherished by the institution. I am most impressed by the Lebanese staff, men and women. They are talented, diligent, creative, and very friendly. Saudi women (in the veil) hold management positions in Finance, once a man's domain.

Performance improvement is a big deal throughout the hospital. Some departments have dedicated staff for this function alone. Most presentations focus on performance improvement, along with pre- and post-tests.

The administrative system is all American-based. It is interesting to see an American system juxtaposed with a Saudi culture. All cultural considerations are accommodated, and yet this is one of the four hospitals in the world that is accredited by the Joint Commission on International Accreditation of the US (JCIA). They received a 99.5 in the survey last November. I just finished reviewing the report and it is glowing with commendation.

The exterior of the hospital is covered by hand-hewn masonry with computer-determined angles on the stones to reduce glare. The irrigation system is designed to use recycled water from the hospital and is one of the most efficient watering systems in the world, I am told.

Like all professionals, I wear a white lab coat at work. I call it my *white abaya*. Life has become simple—no need to decide what to wear or whether to go on a diet. We are encouraged to have our lab coats laundered from the hospital's laundry service for quality control. The laundry window is on the main level. You get a receipt and pick it up the next day. We are issued four lab coats. I don't have to wear the abaya to cross the street from home to work; the lab coat is considered an acceptable substitute. What you see mostly around the hospital is people in white. Saudis who are not in lab coats are required to wear Saudi attire. In case you are wondering, I don't cover my hair.

The cafeteria has a menu that always includes an international menu: American (meatloaf), Pakistani (biryani), Middle Eastern (lamb kapsa), Filipino (spring rolls). It is so cheap, I actually feel bad walking away with a heaping plate for just a dollar.

The management staff is Saudi, Canadian, and American. The official language of the hospital is English. The Saudis speak English so fluently that, if it were not for accent, one could not tell that English was their second language; and they use the American lingo. I wonder where they picked that up from.

Saudi female nurses do not attend to men. It's interesting, since female doctors do attend to men. I wonder if it has to do with doctors having authority. King Saud University has a nursing school and is graduating both male and female nurses.

One of the first people I met with in my rounds was a Saudi woman who is a manager in one of the finance departments. She wears the veil. Her first question to me was, "What is the objective of your meeting?" As soon as I explained that to her, she came around the desk, sat next to me, and started walking me through the system. She kept her discourse focused on my needs and gave me all the information I wanted. Sharp as a whistle, she watched me take notes and, sitting opposite me, made corrections. Saudi men on her staff occasionally interrupted her to get a sign-off. I realized later in our discussion that she had done her homework about me and knew all my particulars. I could not make out her reaction to what I was saying. When I smiled, I didn't know if she smiled back. When I'd make a comment, I didn't know if she was amused or frowning. She was completely veiled, and with just those eyes looking at you, you cannot tell. I felt at a disadvantage. I was totally exposed, and she was completely masked. I realized that if I was to run into her in the hallway, she would recognize me and say hello, and I wouldn't have the foggiest as to who she is. I got the verbal answers I was looking for, but only that and no more. It was strictly business.

In two of the grand rounds that Khalid has attended, the presenter was a doctor in the veil. One, a radiologist who gave a lecture related to the PET Scan, was very knowledgeable in her area and articulate. She had published and was quoting world authorities right and left. I guess it is because of our perception of a woman in the veil that we are surprised.

The campus is so large that to get to meetings, I sometimes have to take a cab. Besides being a long walk, it's also hot. And the cab service is on hospital grounds.

The hospital has a beauty shop (with dark-tinted windows) where I got my hair cut, off hours of course. As for prayer time at work, I had a very convenient arrangement at my former job in New Jersey. The chapel was across the hall from my office and was equipped for prayers for all faiths. Here, there is a mosque, but it is for men only. There is a large prayer hall on the main level, and that too is for men only. So, I asked Samir if there was a prayer area for ladies. "Yes, there is one in this building." He picked up the phone, called someone, hung up and said, "There is a ladies prayer room on the second floor by the elevator." I am probably the first Muslim woman on his staff. Often in the prayer room, I would find women taking a nap.

My office area has a large kitchen, fully equipped. The first day I noticed a young Filipino man in uniform, a mustard-colored tunic and pants. Every time I went to the kitchen he was there. At times I would see him putting up the coffee, setting up the mint leaves, arranging the sugar and Coffeemate, and sometimes just sitting. One day while getting my coffee, my napkin fell on the floor. As I stooped to pick it up, he cried out, "No," leaped, and picked up the napkin and threw it in the garbage. Startled, but now beginning to figure it out, I stopped by to ask Susan, the secretary.

"Who is this young man in the kitchen?"

"He is the tea boy."

My vocabulary grows.

My ID card has information in both Arabic and English. It became a big deal because my position is new and Security couldn't print out my card because Personnel hadn't entered the Arabic definition of my title. The lady who handles this function was out on leave, so my ID had to wait.

The hospital's internet is blocked from personal use during peak hours. You cannot access Hotmail, Yahoo, or web addresses they consider non-professional between 8 a.m. and 12 p.m., and 2 p.m. and 5 p.m. Whereas people have internet service at home, it can become quite costly. At the hospital, it's free. So many people come to work early to get their private net surfing done before 8 a.m., and then of course during lunch hours and after hours.

Payday is once a month on the last date of the Hijra month. You are mandated to use the bank on premises, and it is direct deposit. When I got my first paycheck, it was unusual to see no deductions: the gross equaled the net. But we will have to file estimated taxes each quarter to the IRS. Inside the bank are no windows at the teller desks. The tellers are sitting there counting and handing out thousands, all out in the open. People cash in their entire paycheck—just like that. There is no fear of hold-ups. A colleague of ours had to buy a car. So he went to the bank, withdrew tens of thousands of riyals, went back to work, and after work took a cab to the dealer and bought the car.

One of the policies states that in Ramadan, the business hours are reduced to a six-hour day for Muslim employees. I wonder how that will work out.

There is a movement here called Saudization. Until twenty years ago, the workforce was comprised mostly of expatriates, government officials being the exception. Over the last decade, the trend to develop local manpower has taken hold. This hospital is a model. Gradually, as contracts expire, Saudis are replacing expatriates, which is good for the country. They have had their post-graduate training in North America, mostly in Canada. Many of the clinical chairmen are now Saudis, as is most of the senior management staff. They are highly qualified and professional in their conduct. I got assigned to a committee that has senior-level representation, most of them Saudi, and they follow Robert's Rules by the book.

I have noticed that it is customary to greet anyone you encounter with a salutation of peace, whether you know one another or not. If a Saudi enters a packed elevator, he or she will say *Salaam Alaikum*. If you walk by a Saudi in the hallway, he or she will say *Salaam Alaikum*. So unlike New York City. Now I find myself doing the same.

Let me end on a humorous note. I was sitting in my office the other day when a Saudi gentleman stopped by. He looked at me inquiringly.

"*Salaam Alaikum*," he said.

"*Wa Alaikum Assalam*," I said.

"Missayrrah?" he said.

"I am sorry, I don't speak Arabic."

My American colleague in the next office who had overheard the conversation stepped out and said to the gentleman: "I'll show you Miss Sarah's office."

All the best,
Sabeeha

Let It Ring

There was one exception to the efficiencies. Often when I would call an office, the phone would ring, ring, and ring. No answer, no voicemail. This I was not used to. You agree that in an office setup, it's unprofessional to let a phone go unanswered. Right? On one occasion after finally getting through, I said to the gentleman at the other end, "You know, each time I call, no one answers the phone."

"How long have you been here?"

"A week."

"You will get used to it."

Advice from Expatriates

I was having lunch with Michele one afternoon at the hospital cafeteria. An American, she was the administrator of a clinical department. She had been there for five years, and I felt the need to have a heart-to-heart with someone who knew their way around the corporate culture.

"You have to remember one thing," she said. "When holding a meeting with a Saudi, don't start the meeting by getting down to business. Make small talk, offer or accept a cup of tea, chat for a while, and then gradually bring up the topic of discussion. If you go straight to business talk, you will find your legs cut out from under you."

I am not exaggerating. This is precisely what she said, and I remember it clearly because it shook me up.

I never took her advice. I couldn't go against my approach to work, or my style if you will. Besides, I wouldn't know how to make small talk other than "How are you?" I couldn't even say, "Nice day!" because the days were always hot. So I continued to be Sabeeha Rehman, the *"Let's get down to business"* type. And tell you what! My legs stayed intact. So did my feet. Not only that, but I ended up making long strides for the next six years, stepping into big shoes.

Michele left right after 9/11, so I never got to share with her my tea-less encounters with the Saudis. I believe she had a one-time unpleasant experience and that left an indelible impression.

That was not my experience. I found my Saudi colleagues to be respectful in their demeanor and professional in their conduct. When I needed to discuss something, I made an appointment. That is what I prefer for myself rather than people dropping by when I am rushing to meet a deadline. "Do unto others . . . " I don't recall being asked if I would like a cup of tea. My meetings were always productive, no thanks to me; it goes both ways. If I went in to meet the chairman of surgery to go over his departmental scorecards, I would walk out with an agreed-upon plan to increase the scores and end up learning a thing or two about how the department functioned. At no time was I denied a second appointment.

By the way, the Saudi chairmen of the clinical departments were the cream of the crop. Well, most of them. Brilliant, strong work ethic, sound leadership skills, and forward thinking. They were often one step ahead of the curve. No matter what I or anyone else had to offer in terms of quality improvement practices, enhancing patient access to care, reducing medical errors, managing length of stay, they had already figured it out and were well on their way to making it part of their clinical operations.

◆ ◆ ◆

Subject: Saudi Nurses

Dear All,

Since the day I started work at King Faisal, I have been curious about the nursing profession. When I look at the profile of nurses, I mostly see western faces. Here "western" is a frequently used term and is related not to the geographic origin of the individual, but to the race (i.e., the features "blond, blue-eyed," be they from the USA in the west, Australia in the deep southeast, or South Africa in the south). Everyone uses this term, including westerners themselves. It is an integral part of the vocabulary of the land. I am resisting its use—although I just made reference to it in my opening lines. It must be rubbing off.

Getting back to nurses. I strained to see if I could identify any Saudi women on the nursing staff, and when I didn't come across any, I started asking. At first, I thought that the nursing profession was off the table for Saudi women. But then I was told that there *are* female Saudi staff nurses here, but just a few and only in Pediatrics and Obstetrics/Gynecology. I learned that there is a nursing school at the King Saud University and it graduates female nurses. So, where are they?

The other day an article appeared in the weekend edition of the newspaper *Arab News*. It was titled, *"Nursing slowly gaining acceptability."* One thing I have noticed in reading the local English paper is the freedom of press. I don't see evidence of censorship. They will publish articles that are critical of the culture and of the government, with humor, and articles written by women critical of general attitudes toward women. Anyhow, this article traced the history of the nursing profession in the Kingdom through the experiences of four nurses, three of whom worked at King Faisal and two who are still employed here. The article was written by a woman, Safinaz. She explained that "in the Kingdom, many people look upon nursing as inferior to other occupations. When it comes to women in nursing, the situation is even worse. Since nursing requires interaction with both sexes, many Saudis look upon women nurses as socially and culturally unaccept-able. Brave women, however, have struggled against these prejudices and have succeeded in winning acceptance for themselves and their profession. . . . Many who began to study nursing dropped out because of pressure from family and friends." She then goes on to tell the story of a nurse at King Faisal Specialist Hospital. At the time, she was the only Saudi among one thousand nurses, and many times she felt like a stranger in her own country. She went on to setting up a diabetes education clinic at the hospital, and, in her own words, "That clinic is what I am remembered for, even now." This nurse later obtained a master's degree from the University of Michigan and a doctorate from Yale, and is back in Saudi Arabia with her ideas and dreams. According to her, "One of my aims is to correct our community's misconception toward nursing. I believe strongly that a Saudi nurse communi-cates better with patients. She understands the patient's culture and psychological needs and so she is more effective in analyzing his or her condition."

The second story is of Dr. Sabah Abu Zinadah, the first Saudi nurse at King Abdul Aziz University Hospital in Jeddah. She fought to increase the grade level of nurses and after a two-year struggle secured the change. She then pushed for the establishment of a post-graduate degree in nursing at the College of Applied Medicine in Riyadh and was among the first to graduate. Later she obtained her doctorate from the US. Dr. Sabah Abu Zinadah is currently assistant chief of nursing affairs at King Faisal Specialist Hospital. She is proud to be the first Saudi nurse to hold this position and is known for her Saudization plans.

And the stories continue: "When Zulfa Al-Dar decided to register at the Nursing Institute at the Eastern Province, her parents literally locked her in a room to change her mind. Like many others, her parents wanted her to be a doctor. . . . Zulfa's father finally gave his approval, and she graduated from the institute. . . . She traveled to the US and spent a year there to improve her English. 'I believe the good reputation we Saudi nurses build is the first step in changing people's ideas and prejudices.'"

This article answered all my questions. The next day, Khalid photocopied it and took it to work to show it to the nurses. Of course, they had all seen it over the weekend.

All the best,
Sabeeha

♦♦♦

Subject: Housing in Diplomatic Quarter

Dear All,

As you know, we were placed on the waiting list for housing in the Diplomatic Quarters (DQ). One's place in line is based on a point system; the number of points are based on position grade, years of service, date of arrival, and position grade of spouse if he/she works in the same hospital. We were number sixteen on the waiting list. As soon as I got the job, we jumped up the list to number three, and two weeks later, number one. This week we got a call that a villa was available—these accommodations are called villas—would we like to see it? YES. A staff person from Housing Department drove us there. We just loved it: new and modern look, a patio and garden, great layout, lot of natural light, newer furniture, tiled floors, and enough room. We grabbed it.

Housekeeping will get it cleaned, painted, stocked, and then they will move us, *In sha Allah*. That may take a while because the system moves slow. So Khalid is on top of them. Hope it all works out well.

All the best,
Sabeeha

◆◆◆

Well, it took more than a while. A Pakistani/Indian gentleman, who was in charge, essentially told Khalid that he will move us when he is ready. At one point I started wondering if there was more to the delay. I mentioned it to an American colleague.

"Speak to Samir. He knows everyone. He will get it done."
Really? I have to pull rank.

I spoke to Samir. He smiled, picked up the phone, called whomever, spoke in Arabic, hung up, and turned to me. "They will call Dr. Khalid today and move you on Saturday. You get half a day off for moving."

Counting Our Pennies

There wasn't much to count. I don't mean that we didn't get paid well. Actually, I take that back. Our comparatively lower salaries were offset by minimal expenses. First, there were no local taxes. Second, whereas we had to file taxes with the IRS, there were exemptions on foreign earned income. Then there were the benefits. The hospital paid for our housing, utilities, inventory (kitchen supplies, linens, TV, etc.), gardener, maintenance, shuttle bus service, plus more. Khalid decided that he didn't want to own a car; shuttle takes us to work and the hospital's Haala Cab is affordable. Food was cheap—other than imported cantaloupes. There was no entertainment, as in movies, concerts, shows, etc. No insurance—our healthcare was covered by the hospital. So our monthly expenses seldom exceeded $150. Unless we traveled, which we did. All the rest was savings. I was told that many of the nurses had paid off their mortgages back home.

Spouses or Colleagues?

Often Khalid and I would end up on the same committees. On one hand, I felt proud watching my colleagues admire him as he asked intelligent questions and offered creative solutions; on the other hand, I had to navigate this awkward balance of disassociating myself as his wife and relating to him as a colleague. At times I was miffed if someone didn't rush to embrace his ideas and had to remind myself to act professional. My take: husband and wife should not work in the same setting.

Arabic Alphabet

I knew even before coming to Saudi that the Arabic alphabet does not have the equivalent of the letter *P*. Over time, I learned that it also doesn't have the letter *V*. Nor does it have the "ch" sound as in *change* or *chewing gum*.

I was chatting with Abeer, my Lebanese colleague, when she said to me, "Would you like to share a meeting?"

"What would you like me to share, and which meeting?"

"It's the Quality Indicators meeting. I need a share."

"But what do you want me to share?"

"The quality indicators."

"What about them?"

"That is what we have to determine. Which indicators to use."

"You want me to share the indicators?"

"No"—her exasperation was noticeable—"just the meeting."

Back and forth, back and forth, until it finally struck me.

"Oh! You want me to *chair* the meeting."

"Yes. That is what I said. Share."

Another time I was in a meeting. I was not sharing this meeting. Sorry, I didn't mean to make light of it. God only knows what an utter disaster I would be if *I* tried to converse in Arabic. My *"hah"* and *"ain"* pronunciations are hopeless. Anyhow, the meeting. It had to do with medical errors. A wrong reading of an X-ray film leading to a missed diagnosis but caught on time. And now we were trying to find out what went wrong and how to prevent it from recurring. Saudi doctors and technicians sat around the table along with IT men and women.

A radiologist was presenting the issue. "You see, every time I put the film in the fewer . . ." and he went on to make his point.

"Excuse me." I leaned forward, cupping my hand behind my ear. "Could you please repeat that?"

He turned toward me, "When I put the film in the fewer—"

"I am sorry. Where do you put the film?"

"In the fewer." He raised his hands up to his eye level and made a square. "To few the film."

I should have kept my mouth shut instead of exclaiming: "Oh! You mean the VIEWER!"

Now I have embarrassed him.

"Yes. The fewer," he said, not missing a beat, and continued.

Now, I can conjure up many jokes as in vocal or focal, vast or fast, veal or feel; but that wouldn't be nice. We all know the quirks of the English language, particularly the spellings that make no sense as in *no* and *know*; *too, two,* and *to*; *snuff* and *enough* . . . But I can't resist this one last one.

My father would tell this story of a long time ago when he lived in England. It was the 1950s. One day, he and his friends were driving through town, and on reaching their destination, started looking for a place to park. Finding an empty spot, they pulled over. Not sure if this was a legal parking spot, one of his friends—an Arab—rolled down the window (the days when you *could* roll down the window). Anyhow, he leaned out and asked the policeman standing by, "Officer, can we bark here?"

"Sir, you can bark here. But you cannot park here."

I didn't make this up. Scout's honor.

A Game of Numbers

Subject: Calendars

Dear All,

I have been here over four months now, and I am still having adjustment problems with—of all the things—the numerical systems, be it the calendar, numerical order of dates, military time, or the metric system.

As I told you earlier, Saudi Arabia follows the Muslim Hijra calendar but also uses the corresponding Gregorian calendar, in a top and bottom format. It is visually confusing. The calendar is published with Hijra dates as primary and Gregorian dates as secondary. Here is an example: The first month on the Hijra calendar is Muharram. Next to the word Muharram is stated March/April. It lists the Muharram dates of one to thirty, and the corresponding March/April dates are listed in small print below each of the Muharram dates. As an example, Muharram 1 has the number twenty-six below it, which means Muharram 1 is March 26. On the sixth of Muharram, the Gregorian month of March ends, after which the numerical sequence changes. You go from six above and thirty-one below to seven above and one below, the seventh of Muharram being April 1. Got it?

Muharram 1422
March 2001 – April 2001

Sunday	Monday	Tuesday	Wednesday	Thursday	Friday	Saturday
	1 26	2 27	3 28	4 29	5 30	6 31
7 1st April	8 2	9 3	10 4	11 5	12 6	13 7
14 8	15 9	16 10	17 11	18 12	19 13	20 14
21 15	22 16	23 17	24 18	25 19	26 20	27 21
28 22	29 23	30 24				

Just when I thought I had it figured out, I was at the travel agent making vacation plans for November, and he placed a calendar in front of me and asked me to identify the Hijra dates. Now, if I am leaving for New York on Wednesday, November 7 (which I am, by the way, *In sha Allah*), try figuring this out: I have to put in my leave request in Hijra, inform my family of my arrival dates in Gregorian, take a flight in Hijra at the military time of 1020 hours, and land in New York on Gregorian date and nonmilitary time. So, with a sixteen-hour flight going west, minus the eight-hour time difference with no daylight saving time in effect, figure this out for me please: On what date and at what time do I arrive in NY? I have to let my children know when to receive us. Can't ask the airlines, they always make mistakes.

The last time I relied on the airline's itinerary, we arrived in Malaysia a day early. We had flown from New York to Los Angeles, and then on to Malaysia. Imagine our surprise when the hotel in Kuala Lumpur informed us that we did not have reservations for that day.

"But we do, here is the confirmation receipt. It says Friday," I said.

"Madam, today is Thursday."

There is another adjustment problem: the order of the dates. In Saudi Arabia they use the British system (i.e., dd/mm/yy). In the US we use mm/dd/yy. I went from using dd/mm/yy in Pakistan, to mm/dd/yy in the US, and now back to dd/mm/yy in Saudi Arabia. I have been on the job for fourteen weeks, and I still make mistakes. Sometimes I can rectify it if it is something as obvious as 6/26/01. But if it is 6/5/01, who knows if it was June 5 or May 6.

Then there is the British system vs. the metric system.* All my recipes from the States have the ingredients in pounds and ounces. Here, everything is in liters and grams. I am just not getting the hang of it.

---

* Infamously, NASA lost a $125 million Mars Climate Orbiter in 1999 because engineers plotting its course failed to translate English measurements to metric units, causing the spacecraft to miss its intended orbit and fall into the Martian atmosphere, where it disintegrated. (*Wall Street Journal*, August 7–8, 2021, "U.S. Keeps Inching toward Metric System.")

All my dishes taste different. Last week I had to bake my carrot cake twice. I had doubled the baking powder and baking soda and added 2/3 instead of 1/3 cup of oil. Picture that! An exploding cake floating in oil.

Then there is Fahrenheit vs. centigrade. Forty degrees in the US means bundle up or stay indoors; here it means stay indoors and unbundle. I have figured out the conversion formula, but it's irrelevant. It is either very hot or very, very hot or very, very, very hot. Either way, you stay indoors.

Then there is military time vs. whatever the nonmilitary time is called. Anyone? I am constantly calculating on my fingers.

Getting back to the calendar issue. The other day I was in meeting with one of the medical directors from Australia. He was complaining bitterly. "Last year," he began, "there was a mix-up in the calendars."

"What does that mean?" I asked.

"Well, you see, last year there was an error in the official calendars."

"I don't understand. What kind of error?"

"Every year the government publishes the calendar with the Hijra dates and the corresponding Gregorian dates."

This is what he meant: As I've mentioned, the Gregorian calendar has 365 days, but the Hijra calendar, which is based on the lunar cycle, has 354 days. Some Hijra months have twenty-nine days, some have thirty days, depending on the lunar cycle. The government determines in advance—based on the expected cycle of the moon—which months will have twenty-nine days and which will have thirty days, and the corresponding Gregorian dates are inserted into it. Got it? Let's continue with the story.

"I got it," I said to him.

"Well, last year the government, as it always does, sent us an advance calendar stating that this is the final calendar, which will soon be published, so you can use this to make patient appointments. So, we went ahead and started issuing appointments accordingly. When the official calendar was published, it was a day off from the calendar that had been issued to us. One of the months had twenty-nine days in the first version and thirty days in the second version. Now it was too late for us to do anything. Hundreds of appointments had been issued. We were able to adjust the system going forward, but there was nothing we could do for appointments that had already been made. We see five hundred thousand outpatients a year, and most of them are out-of-towners who are difficult to reach. Imagine the hell that broke loose."

"I can certainly picture that." I said, chuckling. "Let me guess what happened next." I was laughing as I proceeded to finish the story for him. "You gave them an appointment for Muharram 2nd, and they showed up on Muharram 1st by your calendar. When you told them that they had the wrong date and showed them *your* calendar, they insisted that they had the right date and showed you *their* calendar. 'No, your appointment is tomorrow, on Tuesday, Muharram 2nd.' 'No my appointment is today. Today, Monday, is Muharram 2nd.' 'Today is not Muharram 2nd, it is Muharram 1st.' 'It is.' 'It is not.'" I went on and on, rocking with laughter.

He sat watching me with a straight face. He didn't think it was funny!

All the best,
Sabeeha

CHAPTER 4

Life after Work

We had just moved into the DQ when my next-door neighbor, an American of Iranian descent, asked me, "How long do you plan to stay in Saudi?" Without missing a beat, I said, "Ten years, maybe?" I wondered about my spontaneous response. Our contract was for two years. What prompted me to think that I was going to be here for the long haul?

My stress level had dropped to zero. No driving an hour each way to work—the shuttle bus stopped at our door—no shoveling, lawn mowing, cleaning . . . Did I tell you about the culture of houseboys? I guess not. These are cleaning men. They don't have cleaning ladies. Either you sponsor a live-in maid from the Philippines or Sri Lanka or you retain a houseboy on an hourly basis. A houseboy coming once a week was enough for our needs. A Bangladeshi with a quiet demeanor, this was his evening job. I even stopped cooking. We would have a big lunch at work and then have a salad at home for dinner. Even though the workdays were long, I wasn't tired at the end of the day. But it was more than that. There was a feeling of peace, calm, contentment, quiet, and all that good stuff. I was relaxed. I wasn't hurried.

As I compared notes with an American friend on how peaceful this place felt, I asked her, "What is it about this place?"

"It's the positive energy emanating from the Grand Mosque in Mecca," she said.

Now, she is not a Muslim—I am the Muslim—yet she had caught on to it. I believe that was it. Some inexplicable force that permeates the air instilling quiet and peace.

◆◆◆

Subject: On Leave

Dear All,

Riyadh is practically empty, and it feels like half the hospital is away on "leave." That is the local term used for "vacation." It is usual and customary for people to take three to six weeks off when on leave. It is understood that since a major component of the workforce are expatriates, they will be going home for leave; home is usually a long flight away, so it is appropriate to be gone for an extended period. In the summer, everyone takes off; it is too hot here, and children are off from school. They leave town and country; no one stays in Riyadh. Since Saudi Arabia is centrally located, people go just about anywhere. The Gulf States, if they want to stay close. Dubai and Lebanon are favorites. Some go to Europe and many to the Far East. Some take safaris in Africa, and now, trips to Iran are becoming popular.*

Going on leave involves thirteen steps. (1) Apply for leave. Obtain your "leave" status from the central database, which lists how much leave you have earned and how much you have already taken. (2) Fill out the leave form and list what type of leave you are taking (i.e., annual, hajj, Ramadan, etc.). (3) Get approval. (4) Send the form to Personnel. (5) Personnel verifies. (6) They sign and return the approved form. (7) Show the approved leave to the travel agent for your airline tickets. If it is an annual leave, you and your entire family are entitled to a free business-class round-trip ticket to the country of your origin. (8) You must apply for that allowance. (9) The riyal amount is deposited with the travel agent located in the hospital. (10) You then exercise your choice in how you want to use your airline

---

* No longer the case due to regional conflict.

credit with the travel agent. Many people get the economy ticket and use the balance for other trips, which is permissible. (11) Obtain exit visa and re-entry visa. (12) Get your passport from the Passport Office and turn in your *iqama*. All these offices are on the same floor, but you have to stand in line for each transaction. (13) Inform Public Relations that you need a ride to the airport and a pick-up when you return. By law, the sponsor must be at the airport to receive you or you may not be allowed re-entry.

The process seems cumbersome, but after a while, it becomes routine. Normally, the department secretary handles that for you. In the event of an emergency, the passport office is staffed twenty-four hours a day, and you can get your papers approved immediately.

I understand that the authorities have eliminated the requirement for getting a travel letter for each time you leave the city and that very soon the need to turn in your passports in lieu of the *iqama* will also be eliminated.*

Of course, we are both here for the summer since new employees cannot take leave for six months. The American Community Services (ACS) has minimal activities except for summer camp and a few weekend trips out of town. We are taking a trip with them to Taif, a summer resort near the west coast. We were supposed to have gone last weekend but got bumped by a prince who needed the hotel rooms for his entourage.

Speaking of princes, last week a prince died in our emergency room. He was the son of the governor, who is a brother of the king, and was brought to the hospital's emergency room with cardiac arrest. He was in his forties. In Saudi Arabia, the dead are buried in unmarked graves. The royal family members are buried outside Riyadh in the desert and the shifting sands claim them, leaving no sign behind.

All the best,
Sabeeha

---

* Labor laws have been revised since this time, and employers no longer hold onto employees' passports.

In the Desert You Are Free

Friday, June 8
Subject: Caravan & Camels

Dear All,

We are back from a caravan trip in the desert with the hospital's social club. Before the trip, I asked Ahmed, the Sudanese trip coordinator, about dress code.

"Pants and sneakers," he said.

"What about the abaya?"

"Don't leave home without it. But once you are in the desert, everyone removes the abaya."

The most amazing part was that here we were out in the open desert at 4 p.m., and we didn't feel the heat. Mind you, it was 110 degrees in Riyadh.

Alighting the tour bus, we realized that Khalid was the only man. There were Australian, Canadian, and American ladies sitting in the bus, their abayas neatly tucked away inside their bags. And then of course there was Ahmed and the bus driver, an old, old, old man.

This desert is an hour's drive northeast of Riyadh. As we left buildings far behind, the landscape turned barren, dry, and so flat that you could see fifty miles ahead of you. The highway had camel-crossing signs. Neat! At one point, Ahmed told the driver something in Arabic, and the driver started driving onto the open field. What is this! Everyone gasped. We had never just driven off a road. Everyone just looked at each other and, in a minute, laughter broke out. We were going off into the desert—did we expect paved roads? This little bus was driving onto the barren flat field that stretched as far as the eye could see. The soil was firm, hard, and level—not a sandy terrain.

"Watch out for the traffic," I joked. And then suddenly, far away, I spotted something white rising above the ground.

"Is that a tent? Is that where we are going?"

"That is it," said Ahmed.

Our excitement was building up as we disembarked. A young Saudi man in Saudi garb greeted us in English and escorted us inside the huge tent, where an Australian couple was already sitting on the carpets, leaning against the cushions. Outside, a Sudanese man was making coffee over a small campfire. A warm breeze was blowing, and the tent, despite no A/C or fans, felt nice and comfortable. Where did the heat go? I sank down onto the padded floor of the tent and leaned against the cushion. Saif (pronounced "safe"), the young Saudi, and the Sudanese man served us Arabian coffee: unroasted green coffee beans in an ounce of hot water sweetened and flavored with cardamon. How can something so hot be soothing out in the desert?! Well, it was. I was still trying to get over the absence of heat when Saif sat down in front of us—there were twelve of us—introduced himself as a Bedouin and started chatting in perfect English with an American sense of humor.

"What's a Harvard graduate like you doing in the desert?" Khalid asked. Well, he represents the tour company the hospital had contracted with. He was a Bedouin, but life changed for him, and he has gone along with that change. He still comes back to desert because that is where he belongs. He walked around barefoot on the rocky terrain, conversing with his friends in Arabic and would then come and take a seat with us and put on his tour guide hat. He served us dates, fresh, sweet, and luscious, and tea served in tiny cylindrical glass cups. So good! Before taking us on a five-kilometer camel ride, he gave us a loadful of camel talk.

Camels in a caravan move in single-file formation. When you see the footprints of a camel trail, it is not one camel as the single footprint would suggest, but dozens or even hundreds of camels in one line.

The Bedouins own land but are always on the move. They use the camels as a shield against sand blowing on the surface of the desert. When camels sit in a file, they form a wall. At night, this camel wall protects the Bedouins from scorpions, snakes, spiders, etc. The camels also serve as a source of food, milk, and water. Camel meat and camel milk one can figure out; but how can a camel be used as a source of water? Well, in times gone by, when water was scarce, they would select the weakest camel from the herd, give it no food for two days to cleanse its stomach, and feed it water for two days until his stomach was full with water. Then they would put a muzzle over its face to prevent it from eating. That being done, they would depart for the journey. When they ran out of water, they would kill the camel and use the water from its stomach for drinking purposes, for men and camels. Other than having an odor—which they would minimize by using flavorings such as cardamon—the water was OK to drink.

"So, what was the cardamon drink you just served us?" joked one of us.

"Could you tell the difference?"

The camel's gestational period is thirteen months. Normally, they can only carry so much weight, depending on age. If you tax them, they won't protest but they will soon die. Camels are vengeful. If you mistreat them, they will first bite you, then throw you on the ground, then kill you by rubbing their "fifth leg," a protruding chest-bone, against your skull. The trade caravans of early times included men only; women stayed back to tend to family. It was led by a guide, with the team leader who made sure the caravan moved at a realistic pace. Upon arriving at a village, they would be greeted heartily by the village folk, because caravans brought news, messages, and items. They were housed and fed, and if the team leader was a man of repute, many would join his caravan. Some joined a caravan to learn about survival, about people, and other lands. They were illiterate, but when they spoke, their knowledge and understanding of human behavior was beyond that of the average person. One such person is in an advisory capacity to the king, and he is reputed to be an extremely learned man with much to offer. *Must be very old.* Caravans took a long time to return, because if some items are seasonal, they waited to procure the goods and then returned.

Camels tend to wander off from the flock, unlike sheep, which stay together. If a Bedouin loses a camel, he can identify it by the footprints. With one look at the footprints, he can tell the camel's sex, if it is mated, or if pregnant. A camel today costs as much as a car, with racing camels costing hundreds and thousands of dollars.

While Saif lives in Riyadh, his cousins live in an outlying village. They are Bedouins who once lived the traditional life. Then came the decree from the government that if Bedouins wanted to keep their land, they had to build on it, and the government would pay for it. They still go out in the desert several times during the year. It is part of their existence, and they yearn for it.

"Why?" someone asked.

"Because in the desert you are free," Saif said. "People say there is freedom in America. No, there is freedom in the desert. In the desert you can do anything you want, as long as you don't hurt anyone. You have no buildings obstructing you, no interference. Bedouin women drive in the desert—"

"Women can drive!" That was me.

"Oh yes," chimed several women in the group, surprised that I didn't know that.

"Yes, a woman can drive in the desert. You don't have the same threats in the desert that you have in the city," Saif said.

"Do you live in the desert?" someone asked Saif.

"Yes. I keep coming back. It is part of my existence, even though life has changed for me."

Khalid then shared the story of a patient of his, a Bedouin. He was an old man, lived in the desert, while his family lived in the village in a house. He was dying of cancer. To take care of him, the family convinced him to move into their house. He agreed but missed his desert. So, they removed all the furniture from the room, brought in sand, spread it on the floor and made a bed for him on the sand. He would lay on the sand and lived that way until he died. They had brought the desert into the house.

Saif took us on our camel ride. A camel is like an airplane: riding it is the easy part, it is landing and take-off that is a challenge. You have to mount a camel while it is sitting, that's easy; then you have to coax the camel into standing up. The camel, who is kneeling while it sits, first gets up on its forelegs, so you lurch backward, then on its hind legs, so you lurch forward. No one fell. The camel-man's little son (a Sudanese and absolutely adorable) sat on the front of one of the camels along with the passenger. Our three camels were tied together. And then the bumpy ride began, which was so much fun. All we saw around us was the flat land stretching infinitely across the horizon. When you disembark, you are so sore that you stagger. It was quite a sight, seeing us all stagger away.

If you haven't ever been falcon hunting, here is a glimpse: falcons, with patches covering their eyes, were brought into the tent along with a flock of pigeons. First, the pigeons were released and flew out of the tent. Then the eye patches were removed from the falcons, and they flew out, hunting and killing the pigeons. A sport. Within minutes, the desert patch was strewn with pigeon feathers. Not pretty.

By now it was 6:30, and the sun was setting. We all stood there petting the camels, taking pictures, and watching the sunset. The men laid out prayer rugs at a distance. They had arrangements for ablution, and toilet tents were in the back at a distance. We all just lingered out in the open, watching the sun set, taking in the fresh air, open space, and just relishing the solitude.

We noticed the Bedouins cooking dinner for us outside the next tent. And nearby, a generator went on to light up the tents. We were served tea as we unwound, and Saif joined us for an after-ride talk. We couldn't get enough of him. In the Bedouin-style, dinner is first served to men and then to women.

"So women get leftovers?" a women asked.

"If there are any leftovers." Saif played along.

Dinner was served Bedouin-style: laid out on a low table, twelve inches above the ground and looked oh-so-sumptuous. The main dish was placed in a large round metal platter in the center. It had meat, cheese, and spaghetti. Around it were side dishes—yogurt, salad, humus, and bread. And for dessert, bread pudding and fruit. We all sat around on the rug enjoying the meal. Then we were asked to come back to the next tent and have camel milk. That didn't sound very appealing.

As we stepped out of the tent, we found ourselves in a gigantic planetarium. While we were eating, it had gotten dark outside, and the stars were out. We all stood there, recalling our astronomy lessons and trying to identify the stars we once knew for sure; and just lingered, savoring the night.

In the next tent, they were heating camel milk over the campfire and started serving it in tiny cylindrical glass cups. Well, why not, it's an adventure, isn't it! So I took a sip of the camel's milk. It was hot, flavored with ginger, which left a tangy aftertaste. I encouraged Khalid, who also helped himself. Not bad. We all sat back against the cushions, gently sipping the drink. And then Saif put on Arabic dance music (CD player and all). Someone asked him to dance, and in a minute, the tent had become a dancefloor as some of the ladies joined him. He was carrying a stick across his shoulders, and holding onto it as he danced, going back and forth, his companions lined up on either side.

And then, before we knew it, the bus engine started, and now no one wanted to leave. A rush of photographs, thank-yous, goodbyes, and we were back in the bus. Amazingly, the driver made it effortlessly off the desert onto the road.

All the best,
Sabeeha

Red Sand Dunes

Saturday, June 16
Subject: Red Sand Dunes

Dear All,

This weekend we took a trip to the Red Sand Dunes, and that is exactly what they are—a rust RED, an hour northwest of Riyadh. As you drive through barren countryside with perpendicular cliffs towering over plateaus of sand, you suddenly come across red sand dunes from out of nowhere. They are like red rolling hills, each one rising successively higher.

Ahmed, our trip coordinator, told us that we were to climb the dunes for an hour and a half. Riyadh was 100 degrees when we left. I took a big drink of water, put on my cap and shades, and started out to brave the gorgeous, awesome dunes.

We made it to the very top. It wasn't nearly as hot as Riyadh.

The sand is smooth on one side of the dune—as if a giant iron had smoothed it over—with ripples on the other side. The ripples are so symmetrical even a computer couldn't do better. They are like small waves in an ocean that seemed to have paused momentarily. The sand is red, but glistening through the fine layer is a teal-colored sand below. How can you have two different colors, layered one on top of the other? A fine film of sand was gently blowing over the ripples, leaving the waves intact. As the sand culminated at the peak of the dune, it would leave a sharply defined edge, so fine and fragile yet so perfectly chiseled. We were reluctant to tread on the smooth surface, knowing that it would mar its perfection.

Climbing the dune was not easy. Picture this: Your foot digs in before you have had a chance to balance yourself, and now both feet are stuck, both feet are close together, and your upper torso is waving back and forth as you swing your arms to balance. You can't hold onto anything either—remember, sand is not about to be gripped. If I wasn't laughing so hard, I would have been more stable. And each time I laughed, I had to stop myself from breathing in—there was sand blowing around. As soon as you get to the top, there is another wave of dunes looming ahead. Now you walk down, and then up again, and again, and again.

From atop dunes, we spotted an oasis. Ahmed took us there. It's a farm owned by a hospital employee. We were his guests, all thirty-seven of us. Some people went right for the swimming pool by the thatched-roof cabana. They had come prepared with their bathing suits. By the way, most of the people were wearing shorts on this trip, and the farm workers didn't blink an eye. In fact, some of the people asked the elderly bus driver to pose with them. He was obliging, looking very distinguished as he folded his hand and posed in his robes, flanked by men and women in shorts. Khalid and I chuckled, wondering how his wife would react to the photos—if she got to see them.

There are no birds or insects in Riyadh. Here they had it all: birds, bumblebees, butterflies, and as night fell, the crickets. Isn't it amazing that, even in the middle of a desert, if there is an oasis, there will be birds and there will be bees. It was cool, lush vegetation, grapes, watermelons, lemons, you name it, all kinds of fruit and vegetables were growing in this same soil with this modern irrigation system. What amazed me were the date trees. These were not your usual two-hundred-foot-high palm trees—they were no more than six feet high, and ready-to-pick ripe dates hung in enormous bunches by threadlike stems. I just gawked at the low-hanging fruit, so, so heavy, yet hung by such thin twigs strong as rope. The owner explained to ignorant me, when I asked him if these mini-date trees were hybrids, that these were regular trees in their young stage that will eventually reach their full height and will continue to bear fruit each season. The only date trees I had ever seen before were full-grown, and I'd assumed they bear fruit only when they achieve their maximum height.

After the sun went down, the caterers drove in, and as the lampposts went bright and the BBQ coals started burning, a feast was laid out. Picture the setting, the red imposing dunes in the back, the cool breeze, the crickets, the laughter, the aroma of grilled kabobs.

I Love the Desert!

All the best,
Sabeeha

* * *

Cows with an American Passport

July 27
Subject: Al-Marai Farm

Dear All,

The Social Club took us on a half-day trip to the Al-Marai Farms. We had no idea what to expect but seeing how enjoyable all our trips with the Social Club had been, we decided to go.

When we got onto the bus, a totally different group awaited us. Unlike previous trips when most of the people were single females from the West, this time we were greeted by families—Arab families. We were the only couple without our children. Women in the veil, women without the veil, and many gorgeous children. After all, this was a farm trip. Did the parents know that their children would end up watching an assisted delivery of a calf?

Whereas Saudi Arabia imports most of its products, this farm is a unique example of Saudi production from seeds to cheese—a jewel in the Saudi crown. The farm grows the food for the livestock and is irrigated with desalinated water. It houses the second-largest dairy farm in the world—the US having the largest—with 5,400 milking cows and 4,000 calves, and produces milk, yogurt, and every milk product, all on the same grounds. The Holstein cows are imported from the US. After our bus was given a disinfectant spray, we drove through the cow houses where the cows lounged in "prepared" mud under cooling mist sprays. The cows wore bright yellow tags in their ears, like earrings; the tags link their biodata and medical history into a database. We watched them go off to take their showers under the sprinklers and file out, walking to the milking area. The hospital shed had all the medical equipment, and every day all 9,000 cows get a medical checkup. We watched pregnant cows lounging in Vacation Land, where they are brought in the last two months of their gestational period to hang out with their fellow expectant mothers. We were treated to the Labor Room, with a cow in labor, an assisted delivery by Filipino mid-husbands; the Nursery with cuddly day-old calves enjoying their private rooms; and Teen-land with play-grounds and all the accompanying teen stuff. Lucky cows. Well, just the females; male cows are sold away.

I wondered how the veiled women would handle lunch. At the end of the tour, we were taken to the conference room which was not segregated. As I looked around and saw the veiled ladies take their seat, I recalled an experience I had in the hospital cafeteria just a few days ago. A veiled lady came up with her tray and sat down next to me, a little to the left, at the 11 o'clock angle. I went back to eating. After a few minutes when I looked up, a different woman was sitting in her seat. For a minute I was taken by surprise, because I had not felt her leave her seat. Then it struck me. It was the same woman but without the veil. She had removed her veil to eat—you cannot eat with a veil over your face. I looked around then, and none of the ladies in the cafeteria had veils on, and when I looked closer, I saw black pieces of fabric hanging over the arms of the chairs. And all this time I just assumed that these girls were veilless. This lady had a regular face, nothing exotic; she could have been anybody. The mystique of the veil was gone. And when these girls got ready to leave, I watched them don the veils, and all of a sudden, you didn't know who was who.

Now, as I saw the veiled women take their seats in the farm's dining area, I was wondering how are they going to eat? They are not going to remove their veils in mixed company. I didn't want to stare, but I couldn't help it. One of them pulled a scarf over her head, lowered it down to her chin, removed the veil covering the nose, and then lifted the scarf just a little each time she took a spoonful—then let it drop. It looked dainty and delicate but not a comfortable way to eat. No one got a glimpse of her face. These ladies were creative and must be used to it because they seemed to be very well-practiced at the art of keeping their looks private.

I am still in awe of the cows. What a life!

All the best,
Sabeeha

A Midsummer Snowfall

August 1
Subject: Abha

Dear All,

Abha is forty degrees cooler than Riyadh. Centigrade. Forty degrees!
That is seventy-two degrees in Fahrenheit. Which means that in the
middle of summer, it snows in Abha. No kidding! Not hailstorms but
the snow-flake type snowfall, and just last week, no less. When we
stepped out of the plane on what seemed to be the tarmac, we saw a
white ceiling looming over us. And then the cool misty air hit our faces;
we realized that we were outdoors and this was no ceiling—it was the
clouds that had descended upon us. I hadn't tasted cool air since April.
And this was not cool—it was cold. And it felt good, so refreshing. The
change in temperature and the shock at being cold in Saudi Arabia
was wondrous.

Now, let me start at the beginning.

Once you leave the hospital compound, the world around you
becomes dysfunctional. Riyadh was 117 degrees when we left for the
airport. When we arrived, we heard that there was an earlier flight to
Abha. We asked if we could take the earlier flight and were told that it
was full. Oh well! As we settled in the lounge, I started feeling hot. The
air-conditioning wasn't effective. Until then the abaya was a non-is-
sue for me, but now it felt like a nuisance. So I just loosened it, let my
headscarf fall loose, and started fanning myself, groaning in the heat.
I then noticed that all the Arab women sitting in the lounge in their
abayas were completely motionless. They were fully covered, even their
faces were veiled, and yet they did not look uncomfortable—like me;
or groaning—like me; or fanning themselves—like me; or loosening
the abaya—like me. I don't understand! What is it? A higher tolerance?
I felt embarrassed at making such a scene. If *they* are not hot, what's
my problem?

When the earlier flight started boarding, Khalid remarked that for a 747, this did not look like a full flight. After all the passengers had boarded, we saw a family of ten running toward the gate; then another family of five came running; then another family of who knows how many came running; and this went on and on for a good ten minutes, with the officials shouting, "Hurry, hurry, plane is leaving." It still didn't seem like a full flight.

"Do you think it's worth it to check and see if we can get on?" I asked Khalid. So, Khalid walked up to the gate and inquired.

"Do you have baggage to check in?"

"No."

"Then come on in and hurry."

Khalid motioned to me, the officials took our boarding cards, did their computer thing, assigned seats, literally in a minute. "Run, the plane is leaving." We dashed into the plane. Now for some cool air. Wrong! People in the plane were fanning themselves in their seats, even the abaya ladies. There was no A/C. *Well, it won't be long, the plane is leaving and as soon as it turns on its engines, we will be nice and cool.* Wrong! The engines turned on, and it remained hot. The plane took off, and it remained hot. It reached cruising altitude, and remained hot. So, I called the flight attendant and asked her to turn on the A/C. "It will get cool in a little while," she said.

"I guess by the time we land?" Khalid showed some humor. I didn't find it funny. I made a trip to the ladies' room, and the door lock was broken. I came back to my seat and decided to read. The reading light was broken. I leaned against the armrest, and it broke and fell off, almost tripping the flight attendant.

What about our hotel! We never got a chance to inform them of our change in plans. So, whatever time we saved, we will lose in waiting for our ride. This vacation had not gotten off to a good start at all.

Suddenly, it got cool. We landed, and stepped out into the refreshingly cool night, and it felt wonderful. It had to be 60 degrees. As we made our way through the exit, looking for a phone to call the hotel, we spotted a man holding a sign: REHMAN. How did that happen?

We waved excitedly and ran toward him; he waved excitedly and ran toward us, whisking our bags away, "Welcome, welcome, this way please," and in a few moments we were in the car, on our way.

"You were supposed to come on the next flight," the driver said.

"Yes, yes, but we took an earlier flight at the last minute, and there was no time to call. How did you know that we took an earlier flight?"

"I was here to drop off a passenger, and seeing that a flight was coming in from Riyadh, I decided to stay in case you took an earlier flight. Otherwise, it takes me twenty minutes to go back and another twenty minutes to come again."

Good thinking. Impressed. Grateful.

As soon as we pulled into the hotel, young suited men surrounded us. "Welcome, welcome, Dr. Rehman, Mrs. Rehman, welcome . . . I am the manager, here is my card." A waiter walked up to us and served us freshly squeezed orange juice right at the reception counter. Another came up and gave us garlands, like the lei in Hawaii. Wow! And this was not one of your glitzy five-star hotels. It was quite nice but not the Plaza by a long shot, yet what a reception and what customer service.

Dinner! Well, in addition to the very elaborate spread of all the courses, for all palates, the chef came and gave us the whole run-down on the city and the hotel, served us his specialties, making us feel really welcome. No abaya requirement in the hotel. We were chatting out on the porch when suddenly the sky broke loose, thunder and pouring rain. Rain in Saudi? The lush trees were swaying, and it all seemed so unreal.

Next morning as we sat down to breakfast—again a very elaborate buffet with all the customary trimmings—a young man walked into the dining room. He was ceremoniously dressed: over his white robe he wore an A-line-shaped white tunic with side slits, a bright red striped sash across his chest and flowing down from each side with tassels, and a silver engraved belt around his waist with a small, encased dagger. And then of course, a white headdress with leaves sticking out of it. Who was he? A prince? Someone accompanying the royalty?

When we stepped out of the dining room, he walked up to us.

Why is he coming to us?

"Dr. Rehman?" he said.

He even knows us.

"Yes." That was Khalid, as I stood wondering what was coming next.

"I am Ibrahim, your tour guide."

Wow! I just gaped!

Ibrahim turned out to be as colorful a tour guide as the traditional outfit of Asir he wore.

Now, this was a trip arranged for us by the hospital's Social Club. By chance, we were the only two people who had registered. So we were able to customize it to our liking, and Ibrahim obliged.

Abha is in the southwest of Saudi Arabia, close to the coast. Ibrahim drove us into the Al Souda Mountains, the highest point in Saudi Arabia. The winding roads hugging the cliffs reminded me of Murree in Pakistan. Ibrahim stopped at the scenic lookouts for photo-ops and made a point of telling us, "If you want to take my picture, it is OK." Saudis don't like to be photographed—generally. The hills all had terraced slopes, carefully laid out all the way down into the valley. Ibrahim drove with one hand and held a *tasbeeh* (similar to rosary beads) in the other. Occasionally, he would pull out his *miswak* (a twig) and start polishing his teeth. He kept alternating between the *tasbeeh* and the *miswak*. Driving in Saudi is very bad, and Abha was no exception. Ibrahim was relatively careful, but fasten your seatbelts and pray. We watched the landscape: drop-down-steep cliffs, canyons, narrow valleys and gorges, the clouds descending on the valley, the mist, and the cool air. Ibrahim took us on a trail down to a lookout point. The trail had been asphalted and bridged with boardwalks. There was a cable car going down.

When I had stepped out, Ibrahim said, "This is not Riyadh. You don't need the abaya." But I kept it on for warmth. This is all volcanic rock, unlike Riyadh's surroundings, which are sedimentary. After our workout up and down the mountains, Ibrahim announced that it was time for a tea break. He drove us to a camping ground and set up a picnic table. The white linen was whipped out, and a table was set up for us with music and all, and Khalid and I sat down for a cup-a-tea in the park. The cool air was blowing, the tea was nice and hot, the trees were fragrant. . . . Take a deep breath and just savor it. Khalid finally picked up the courage to ask Ibrahim why he had these leaves sticking into his turban. "These are herbs for fragrance." Cost-free, fresh, no-artificial-anything cologne.

Small little tents on the roadside were loaded with merchandise, and all run by women, with male employees. The women quickly dressed me up in a traditional Asir dress, jewelry, and all. One woman was shouting out orders to her male employees: "Bring the silver necklace, bring the yellow scarf." I was surprised, because in Riyadh you don't see female saleswomen, and this woman was the owner. I bought a few small bread baskets and fresh Sidra honey.

As we walked through the Basket *souk* (market), the vendors were calling out to Ibrahim, asking him to bring his guests to *their* shop. Ibrahim insisted on doing the bargaining for us, which really wasn't necessary; everything is so inexpensive. *Let these folks make a living.* But Ibrahim wanted to impress us. Noticing many of the shops manned by women, we finally asked Ibrahim.

"This is not Riyadh. Women can work in the stores."

At a hundred-year-old traditional village we made a quick stop. The village appeared desolate, with no sign of life. Just then, a bunch of boys looked over the balcony of the house beyond.

"Hi," a little boy called out.

"Hi," I replied and waved.

"Bye," he called out again.

Now this is a remote village in the boondocks, and this little boy knows that to the lady walking around in a *shalwar kameez* he has to say "Hi" and "Bye."

At Al Habala Hanging Village, Ibrahim decided to impress us with his connections. He walked up to a door marked closed and tapped on it with his sword. He had picked up a sword in a gilded case at the market and was now clinging to it like a child who gets his long-awaited toy. He would sway it as he walked, his robes swaying too, and now he put on the air of a VIP. Someone came running and opened the door for him. He looked back, bowed, swung his arms, and beckoned to us to enter. This royal treatment was getting to be a bit much. We'd rather go through the regular door, like everyone else. But then we didn't want to deprive him of the joy of showing off. So, we proceeded on to a plaza and a covered promenade overlooking the steep slopes and canyons. We got tickets for the cable car, and Ibrahim got in for free. *Show off!* He kept telling people that we were VIPs. He could have passed for one with his colorful regalia, but Khalid and I looked beat, worn out, and so very ordinary in our wrinkled clothes. Sometimes this made us uncomfortable, sometimes Khalid and I would quietly exchange a knowing smile.

On the way back, we noticed that all along the roadside, people had set up tents.

"Who are these people"? I asked.

"Saudi vacationers from out of town. They bring their own tents and a generator and set up home here in the open fields for a month or so. They don't like to live in hotels."

All around, tents were scattered, with four-wheelers parked by and fires going. It costs SR1,000 ($225) a month to rent a tent. I guess it must be the desert in them that brings them out here to live in the open fields. Problem is, they leave a mess behind. They don't clean up after themselves.

The package for this trip had cost us $350 per person, which included airfare, two nights hotel stay, three meals a day, and guided tour for a day and a half. And we could keep the room until midnight on checkout day. Not bad at all. I must let the Social Club know how well we were treated.

Then we came full circle. Things started going wrong just the way the weekend had started. Flight delays, more delays, an all-nighter at the airport. I was told that this happens a lot during summer. We got home at 4 a.m., just as the *adhan* for *Fajr* prayer was called. And then back to work at 8:00 a.m.

All the best,
Sabeeha

Bumped by the Prince

August 24
Subject: Taif

Dear All,

Taif is the summer capital of the Kingdom of Saudi Arabia. It is situated 1,700 meters (5,600 feet) above sea level and is in the western province. It is a favorite summer spot for people seeking a respite from the scorching heat. Its pomegranates, grapes, and honey are said to be the best in the world.

Let's start from the beginning.

Remember how we got bumped by the prince the first time we tried to go? Well, we got bumped again—almost. On the Sunday before our rescheduled trip, we heard a news report that the crown prince was again in Taif, this time for the opening of a new hospital. How long was he going to stay? We held our breath. On Tuesday, the news reported, he would preside over the opening of some power project. Well, we thought, maybe he will leave right after that. He didn't. On Wednesday I called the ACS.

"Are we still on?" I asked Karen.

"Yes, we are all set. We will meet you at the airport in Riyadh."

"Who will be meeting us?" I asked.

"Sandy," Karen said

"How will I know who Sandy is?"

"I will call you back and let you know what she will be wearing. I guess [pause] she will be wearing [pause] an abaya."

"And let me guess." I laughed. "It will be a black abaya. Right?"

Embarrassed laughter from Karen.

"And all I have to do," I wasn't letting go, "is look for the woman in the black abaya. As soon as I spot her, I will know that it's got to be Sandy. Right? No problem. I'll find her. Just look out for the black abaya." I was laughing hard.

Poor Karen was so embarrassed, she couldn't even appreciate the humor. Anyhow, she called back and told me that Sandy would be carrying an ACS sign and is blonde. As soon as we entered the airport, there she was: a blonde in a black abaya with the ACS sign. And that is when she broke the news.

"I hate to tell you this, but yesterday we got a call from the hotel informing us that we would have to cancel our trip because the prince is still in town and his entourage has taken over the hotel. We had to negotiate long and hard and explained that this is the second time, etc., etc., and so they finally agreed to put us up in a villa on the hotel grounds, with an extra charge per person. It's supposed to be a very nice villa, just for VIPs."

No problem, as long as we don't have to cancel our trip.

At the hotel reception we were given our room numbers.

"But we are staying in the villa," Khalid said.

"The prince left this morning, so the hotel is now available."

Everyone sighed in disappointment. Deep down we all were kind of looking forward to the villa experience. Oh well! This is nice too. Actually, the lobby was very, very nice. This was your classic glitzy, grand style, made-to-impress five-star hotel.

Now how come the hotel didn't know the prince was leaving? For security reasons, his travel plans are secret. The prince stays in one of his palaces across the highway; it's only his entourage in the hotel. In fact, the prince has two palaces across the highway, and which palace he stays in is not publicized. The hotel has a windfall profit when the royal entourage comes. The prince, known for his generosity, tips the hotel staff $15,000. They all look forward to his visits.

The hotel was a showpiece designed more to impress than to serve, with emphasis on glitz, glamour, grandiosity, and little attention to functionality. The room had modern décor and was furnished with all the necessary amenities, but the layout was so badly planned that if you were not careful, you could end up at the chiropractor. Let me take you to the bathroom.

I stepped into the bathtub for a shower. Whoops, the bathtub has a window—not frosted! I crouched. I reached to turn on the water. No controls. It did have a shower head. *How do I turn on the shower?* I stepped out of the bathtub, looked around, and there they were: below the sink. I turned on the water, stepped back into the bathtub. *Ouch!* Too hot. Stepped back out, adjusted the controls, back in. *Oooh!* Freezing. Back and forth until I got it right, all the while trying not to slip or trip or fall. Shower done, I looked around for a hair dryer, but I didn't see one by the mirror. I looked here, I looked there. Found it: it was hooked up on the wall opposite the wall with the mirror, at an eight-foot distance. If you were facing the mirror, the hair dryer was behind you. I tried stretching the cord so that I could look in the mirror, but I was still seven feet away. Good thing I had kept my travel hair dryer. I retrieved it, and now I couldn't find an outlet close to the mirror. And the toilets? Well, they were on the far end, behind a glass wall with a fancy opening, perched on a raised platform—like a throne.

Breakfast chatter next morning was all about the bathroom experience.

The highlight of our trip: camel races. These are organized and sponsored by the royal family twice a month during the summer. The royal family gives away four-wheelers and big cash prizes. Racing camels are slender, have even longer than usual legs, and a taut stomach. (I was called a "camel" when I was a teenager during my awkward years.) But the part that gets to you is the jockeys. They are petite little boys no more than seven years old. These are Sudanese boys brought here to race camels, and they get 10 percent of the prize if they win. One of the boys fell off the camel when the race started and had to be rushed to the ambulance standing by. They all wore helmets.

The races are held in a large open desert field. A large reception tent is set up at the finish line with seating for VIPs. Lined up next to the tent are the prize cars. Guards stand by wearing khaki uniforms, breeches, and the red-and-white-checkered headdress.

The track is ten kilometers, or a little under six miles, long. There are three ways of watching a race. You can drive up to the start line, which is far away; you can stand by the finish line; or you can stay in your vehicle and chase the camels as they race. The last item needs explaining. There is a wide dirt road that runs parallel to the racetrack. On this dirt road, cars line up and wait for the race to start. As soon as the race starts, the cars start riding parallel to the racing camels. Among these cars is the sports announcer. The car ride can be treacherous, since there are no marked lanes; everyone is trying to get as far ahead and as close to the racetrack as possible, and there is dust flying all over.

We took the conservative route and told our driver to stay as far behind as possible, and let every car pass us, and so what if we are left chasing the losers. It was more fun, because we rode alongside the camels last in line and kept giving morale-booster cheers to the poor jockeys. The little boys got all excited and started putting on a show for us. The jockeys were carrying walkie-talkies, and their coaches were coaching them from the cars.

A prince was sitting at the finish line with his bodyguards, and we were not sure where to stand, since we didn't want to block his field of vision. Our guide said to us, "It's OK for you to stand here. They won't say anything to foreigners." We declined. Just then one of the prince's bodyguards walked up to us and invited us to stand at the best spot, exactly where we thought we shouldn't stand. "Please, please, come and stand here. Watch the race." So we took up our places just by the fence and got a close-up view of the finish. "Please stay, we have many more races," the guards insisted. They were very hospitable, but we had to take our leave.

Ever been to a rose factory? The Al Gadhi Rose Factory: this is where they make rose oil used as a perfume. Imagine the fragrance inside. When the roses are in season—in May—they are brought in by the truckloads and cooked in these urns, and through a condensation process, the oil is extracted. To make one hundred grams of oil about twenty-five thousand roses are used. The price for this one hundred grams of oil is over $6,000. According to the factory staff, only the Royal

Family and VIPs can afford to purchase it. We savored a sample. The oil is also diluted to make rose water, which is affordable and used as flavorings in foods.

We found the same phenomenon on the mountains as in Abha. Weekend vacationers had pulled up their four-wheelers onto the plateau, spread out a tent, and were camping away. And again, people don't clean after themselves. Mom and Dad were sleeping in the tent while the children just went off mountain climbing. Safe. It is virgin territory, and I saw no signs of camping facilities such as bathrooms, electrical outlets, telephones. Of course, cellular phones are ubiquitous (we don't own one). The mountaintops are not paved, but it won't stop the campers. They will drive up to a favorite spot, park, and camp. Even in Riyadh, when driving down the highways on weekend evenings, we see people picnicking on the grassy knolls by the highway. I find it too hot to be anywhere that is not air-conditioned, but the locals not only do OK, they seem to prefer the warm outdoor nights to the air-conditioned interiors.

Our Sudanese driver put in very long hours, and we gave him a tip. Poor man was so happy he couldn't stop thanking us. Most of these drivers work two jobs and get no break. They come here from third-world countries and send all their savings back home to support their families. Often their other job is something like bricklaying, which has them out in the sun all day. Same is true for the traffic cops, who are locals. They are out there standing in the heat.

We are just plain spoiled.

All the best,
Sabeeha

Socializing in the Diplomatic Quarter

Our villa was across from the Singapore ambassador's villa. Almost all the villas housed western expats, mostly from Canada and the US. I felt at home. If we weren't traveling out of town on weekends, we were socializing. And when we socialized, we didn't just invite those we were close to, we invited everyone. If I was taking a walk and noticed an expat, we'd say hello, exchange phone numbers, and invite them over. Some were doctors, some were nurses, and some were in research. One of the doctors had a pool, so we had poolside parties. Alcohol consumption is forbidden in Saudi Arabia, yet some parties were not so dry. Some expats obtained it from their embassies, and one gentleman we knew made moonshine at home, in his bathtub. I suppose many more did the same. Then there were karaoke parties, BBQs; if anyone had a birthday, you had to have a party. Anniversary? Have a party. Just returned from a trip? A "come see our photos" party. Family visiting from back home? A meet-my-family party. We exchanged books, traded recipes, went bicycle riding, watched movies on video, even had ladies foot-massage spa evenings. Our social life meant the world to us.

Each time one of us left for vacation back home, we would put the word out: "Anything I can get you?" Often it was either an electronic gadget or "I am out of Clinique face moisturizer." Sure, no problem. We were one multinational happy family.

Expats got creative and resourceful when it came to entertainment. I'd get a call: "There is an opera this weekend at the _____ compound," or "They are showing *Runaway Bride* at the _____ compound," and we would all flock to the entertainment. We didn't own a car, so we would just call the hospital's Haala Cab. By now we had taken a liking to one of the Haala Cab drivers—Tariq, a Bangladeshi—so he became our cabbie.

My American friends—the ladies—would often joke about what life would be like when we returned to the States.

"I can wait to pump gas in my car," or "Oh, the pleasures of looking for parking."

We were seduced big time.

Five months into our stay, the towers fell.

CHAPTER 5

September 11, 2001

My parents were visiting from Pakistan. Ever since Mummy and Daddy had performed the hajj almost two decades ago, they had yearned to return and perform *umrah*, the lesser pilgrimage.* Now that we were in Saudi Arabia, it made the pilgrimage so much easier.

"It feels as if you both are newlyweds," Mummy said. "A new home in a new place, all new stuff, and no children."

We did our usual thing (i.e., have a "meet my parents" party), inviting all our Pakistani friends, who kept calling Mummy and Daddy "uncle" and "auntie." We took them around town, had them spend a day at the hospital, meet Samir. Daddy was truly impressed with him: "What an enlightened man."

We booked hotels in Mecca and Medina and made the flight arrangements. On the afternoon of September 11, we boarded a flight to Jeddah. We were on the flight when the telephone in Khalid's office rang; a friend had heard the news of an attack in New York and was calling to ask if our family was OK. A missed call.

---

* *Umrah* is the pilgrimage to Mecca that can be performed any time of the year and completed in a couple of hours, versus the hajj, which is performed only during the Hijra month of Dhul Hijjah, lasts five days, and includes travel to multiple holy sites.

At Jeddah airport, we hailed a cab to take us to Mecca, a forty-five-minute drive. We were all in a state of *ihram*—a sanctified condition of dedicated abstinence, symbolized by wearing the special clothing for *umrah*.* The cab driver turned on the radio as the cab hurtled through the darkening night.

"What was that?" Khalid cried. "Did you hear that? Turn up the volume."

The cabbie nodded. "Yes. New York has been attacked. The World Trade Center. And the White House. The Pentagon," he said.

WHAT? When? How? Who? Oh my God, my children!

The newscaster, speaking in English, wasn't making sense. A scratchy signal, disbelief, shock. . . It can't be. All four of us talking over one another, and the cabbie drove on. I couldn't comprehend it. As soon as we got to the hotel, we rushed to our rooms and Khalid turned on the TV. CNN. "The second tower has fallen." And then the TV switched to local news.

"The towers of the World Trade Center have fallen," Khalid said.

I thought he meant the antennas had fallen.

"Bia, not the antenna, the Twin Towers have fallen."

"It can't be! How can the towers fall! Switch the channel."

The TV had only one channel, and it was showing Arabic local news.

The children. Our younger son, Asim, was working at City Hall and often had morning meetings at the WTC. Oh my God! I went rushing down to reception and asked if I could make a long-distance call to New York.

"We are sorry, but we cannot make overseas calls. You can try the call center."

I started shaking. "I need to call Asim. I need to call Asim."

Daddy was standing by. "Bia, go do your *umrah* first. You are at the

---

* Men wear two pieces of unstitched white fabric; women can wear any attire as long as it is loose fitting and covers her body from head to feet, with her face uncovered.

house of God. Go to His house and pray to Him. After that, we will go to the telephone exchange."

I listened. We walked across the courtyard to the Grand Mosque and began our *umrah*, circumambulating the Kaaba. This is the house that Prophet Abraham and his son Ishmael built and dedicated to God, the large cubic structure draped in black with Qur'anic verses embroidered in gold thread, and is the *qibla* (direction of prayer) for Muslims around the world when performing the five daily prayers. It is the center of our universe. I prayed hard. God, please, please, please let my children be all right. I cried, I pleaded, I circled around and around the Kaaba, holding up my hands and praying. We walked between the Safa and Marwa hills, paying homage to Hagar's struggle for *her* baby, and prayed for *my* babies. In an hour, our *umrah* was complete.

The hotel receptionist gave us directions to the telephone exchange, and we hurried over, only to find them pulling the shutters down. "Can you please keep it open for just a few minutes. New York has been attacked, and we want to call our children. We don't know if they are OK."

He raised the shutters.

I called Asim.

No answer.

I called Saqib.

No answer.

I called Khalid's sister-in-law in Long Island. She is not a phone person and seldom answers the phone. Always, I have to leave a message. This was a last resort call. She answered on the first ring.

"It's Bia."

"Everyone is fine," was the first thing she said. "I have spoken to Asim. Both your children are fine. I had been calling them for the last four hours, repeatedly pushing redial, getting no response, and I finally got through in the last ten minutes. They are OK."

And then I cried.

When we walked back into the hotel, the receptionist handed us a message. It was from Asim. "Saqib and I are OK."

It's a family habit that before any of us leaves town, we share our itinerary with the family. What they must have gone through thinking about how worried we would be. And so many who didn't get that call.

Daddy was right. Had I tried to make the call before doing *umrah*, I wouldn't have gotten through and the stress would have shattered me.

We spent the next day at the Kaaba immersed in prayer. Prayers for our children, for the families of those who perished, for home and country, for humanity. We were cut off from the world and from the news. There were no newspaper stands, TV was mostly Arabic, and all we could do and did was seek strength in communion with God. In Medina, at the Prophet's Mosque, we ran into an acquaintance from New York. *Is your family OK? Are our friends in Staten Island OK? How about Sherri? Doesn't he work at WTC? Don't know. Oh my God!*

It was when we boarded the flight back to Riyadh and the flight attendant handed us the newspaper that we had our first contact with the news. Seated in the cabin, I couldn't tell if Saudis were talking about the attack, language being a barrier. Besides, I was absorbed in my own problems, worrying about my family in New York.

Returning home, I rushed to the computer. There were emails from Asim and Saqib. I touched my children through the screen. I wanted to get on a plane and hold my children in a hug, just feel them. All flights had been canceled.

Emails from our sons.

From: Asim Rehman
Subject: World Trade Center
Date: September 11, 12:05

I'm OK. The courthouse was evacuated after both World Trade Center towers were hit, and I saw the first tower fall after I left my building.

Asim

♦♦♦

Date: Tuesday, 11 September 2001 12:40
Dear Family,

I'm OK. Thanks for your calls. I was at the downtown courthouse when
the planes hit the World Trade Center. I saw the first tower fall after
I was evacuated from the building. Things are pretty devastating here,
but all my friends are OK.

Asim

◆ ◆ ◆

From: Saqib Rehman
Subject: WTC attack
Date: Tuesday, 11 September 2001 22:28

Assalam Alaikum everyone,

Just to let everyone know, Asim, Saadia (and the almost-baby), and
myself are all OK. Some of you have called or are trying to call us and
we appreciate your concern. We were all at work today when this
happened. Asim was evacuated from his building, which was nearby, and
he saw the buildings collapse nearby but got away all right. Saadia was at
the hospital today where she put in a full day of work. They were told to
try and discharge as many patients as possible to make room for casualties. But not too many casualties came to her ER. I was at Kings County
Hospital in Brooklyn, which is a trauma receiving center. I saw the first
building burning just before I went into the OR. Then we had to cancel
our case since the hospital and OR were on emergency standby. By the
time I came out, both buildings had already fallen. The attached picture
is what I saw from our hospital in Brooklyn. We had a disaster triage
setup, but not too many patients showed up. This was the same situation in most area hospitals except for a few near the disaster, which are
actually quite overwhelmed. Apparently, they have not been able to start

going through the rubble yet due to the fires and gas leaks. I think in the next forty-eight hours they might be pulling people out and sending them to the hospitals (so as an orthopedic surgeon, I might be pretty busy on call tomorrow). The city is in a state of emergency, and the streets have mostly police and emergency vehicles. Bridges and tunnels are mostly closed except for emergency vehicles and some pedestrians trying to get out of Manhattan. Let's pray that the worst is over.

Saqib Rehman

◆ ◆ ◆

We tried calling home. Couldn't get through. I turned on the TV. The attack dominated the news. That is when we learned that the White House had not been attacked, and the plane had crashed in Pennsylvania. I didn't see the video of the towers falling; CNN and BBC news had moved on to breaking news in the aftermath. Seeing is believing, and I was unable to comprehend that the towers had fallen. The internet was not as robust in 2001.

The next morning at work I was in a daze. All our department staff were expats, and that is all we could talk about. It felt like a support group. People were angry and would break into tears: "I hope they catch them." Thousands dead, four hundred firefighters perished in trying to save lives. And then they identified the perpetrators: Muslims, most of them Saudis. They talked about a group called Al-Qaeda. I had never heard of it. Samir called me into the office, asked if my family was OK, how I was holding up, if there was anything he could do to help, did I want to take time off.

As I walked the hallways and crossed paths with anyone I knew, Saudi or expat, they would stop and ask: "Is your family OK?" One of the women in my Arabic class said: "I am leaving. My family wants me to come back. I had wanted to stay for many years, I had just started learning Arabic, I liked my job and my life here, and now I have to leave. I am angry."

I ran into another American employee.

"Is your family OK?" I asked.

"Barely. My sister was in a cab on her way to the World Trade Center for a meeting when they closed the street. I am getting out of here."

Back at my desk, I could not focus on work. I opened my computer and in my inbox was an announcement from the hospital addressed to all expats. Starting with a message of sympathy, the administration offered its support: take time off if you want to; restrictions on using the internet off hours for personal use is being lifted, making it available around the clock; if employees want to break the contract and return home, there will be no penalties; and psychological counselors have been appointed.

Putting work aside, I went into my Hotmail, and scores of emails from family, friends, and colleagues, in shock, devastated. I took it all in. Khalid's former secretary wrote that there isn't any family she knows on Staten Island that hasn't lost a family member, most of them fire-fighters. What struck me was an email from my former boss: "I worry about retaliation against Muslims in America." I was taken aback. Call it my naivete, but I couldn't fathom why anyone would retaliate against Muslims. They didn't have anything to do with it, so why hold an act of terrorism against all Muslims? And then there were more. My friend Robin promising to push back on Islamophobia, Bob offering to house my children until the anti-Muslim sentiment subsided, and more. I appreciated their support, but I knew it wouldn't come to that. And then it did.

At lunchtime, I joined a group of American nurses at their table. We were seeking out "our own" in these moments of shock. As one of them spoke of the terrorists, she glared at me. I was stunned by her silent accusation, where the hatred in her eyes spoke louder than words. In measured tones, I told her about my son being so close to ground zero, my fears when I first heard the news, and how it made me feel, hoping that she would see that we were all in this together. Later, Asim's email confirmed the fears of my friends.

◆ ◆ ◆

From: Asim Rehman
Date: September 16, 2001

Dear Family,

You're obviously well aware of what happened in New York, and no doubt have heard scores of personal stories recounted on the news. Here is my story (or at least part of what I've been writing this week). It probably won't shed any additional light on the facts as you know them, but at least writing it down will help me deal with what I saw.

September 11, 2001 – The Day

I work in the federal courthouse, which is located in downtown Manhattan, right by City Hall and a half mile from the World Trade Center. The World Trade Center towers over all the other buildings in downtown Manhattan, so I would often see them when I looked out the window while waiting for an elevator in the courthouse. Yesterday morning, I went to the cafeteria after readying the courtroom for what would be closing arguments in a week-long trial. As I approached the cafeteria, a number of people were looking out the same window that I referred to above. A plane flew into one of the Twin Towers, I was told. Assuming that it was a small aircraft—something like the plane that attempted to fly into the Oval Office some years back—I looked out the window. No small plane could have caused such damage. The pictures tell it all. Smoke. Fire. A broken building. It was as if a giant with a fiery hand had punched a hole through a straw fence. The damage was devastating. We all stood in awe, disbelief, and curiosity. An accident, perhaps? Yes, it must be an accident. I rushed back down to the courtroom to see if the judge had come down from chambers with news. A few minutes later, the defense attorneys walked in with blank stares. A second plane had flown into the other tower, they said. This was no accident. I can't even describe the emotion that we all felt. It wasn't panic. It wasn't shock.

It was more like confusion. What is happening? What are we supposed to do? What? Who? How? Why?

The courthouse was evacuated, and the surrounding streets closed off. I walked some of my office colleagues to a busier street where they could catch a bus home. Then, out of curiosity, I went back to get a better look. I walked to City Hall where some people were scurrying out of the downtown area, many in fear. However, most people were just gathered in the open space around City Hall, looking up at the two smoky towers. Again, this is less than a mile from the World Trade Center. Suddenly, the south tower started to collapse. There was a collective gasp, followed by screams. The upper third of the building started to tilt eastward and broke away. It did not seem real. In our lives we have seen so many images of buildings being demolished that my brain simply couldn't incorporate the fact that there were people trapped in that building. Then came the thundering crash. The upper portion of the tower fell into the remainder of the building, bringing the entire structure to the ground with a fierce roar. I was overcome by shock. The building was gone. Completely. Most New Yorkers couldn't imagine this city without the Twin Towers. It was the highlight of our skyline and never ceased to catch my eye as I rode the ferry from Staten Island. Now only one tower stood. People began to run. Many people just stood and stared, dumbfounded. Within a minute, a cloud of soot and smoke began to creep up the street corridors and in our direction. That's when people really began to panic and started to run uptown. It was hard to walk without being pushed, so I had to pick up my pace.

I cut through Chinatown to get a better look at the remaining tower, and stood watching it with a large crowd of people just south of Canal Street. Presuming that the worst was behind us, I began to walk uptown. Another thunderous roar, as if a large cargo truck had just driven behind me. I ran back down to where I was standing and couldn't see the remaining tower. Maybe I didn't have the right angle of view? Was I standing in the wrong place? No. The second tower had just fallen. Unreal. Simply unreal. Just a month ago, I was having lunch at Windows on the World, the restaurant atop the north tower. The view was marvelous, and I looked forward to bringing my out-of-town guests there for a meal or just a drink. Now it had just been wiped off the face of the earth.

The streets were full of people heading uptown as emergency vehicles zoomed downtown. I was just a few blocks from my place when I saw another cloud of soot. What? How could the dust-clouds have crept this far uptown? It was a line of ambulances racing to the hospital. A thick sheet of soot covered the vehicles like a fresh snow.

The rest of the morning was spent watching the news and trying to get in touch with people. Thankfully, all of my friends who work downtown were safe.

That afternoon, my friend and I went around town seeing what type of service we could volunteer. The hospitals in lower Manhattan had been desperate for blood donors, but at that time their facilities were full. We also went to Chelsea Piers, which was the staging area for all the relief equipment. They had their fill of volunteers as well. It was comforting to know that everyone was coming to help in full force, but it also left us feeling helpless. Here was this disaster, and there was nothing we could do about it. And from almost every angle I could see the smoke and dust rising from downtown.

In lower Manhattan, some streets were full of people and emergency vehicles while other streets looked no different than usual. We walked back to my friend's place and caught up with the news. By the evening, one could still see the smoke, and the neighborhood was pretty active. People were gathering on the sidewalks to talk about what happened, peering into the bar windows to watch the TV coverage, and crowding around cars that had radios broadcasting the news.

The streets in my neighborhood* were closed. Barring the occasional siren, things were pretty quiet by nightfall. Still, that didn't make it easier to fall asleep. Every time I closed my eyes, I saw the image of that first tower tumbling down. It was hard to believe that just fifteen

---

* He lived in the East Village in Manhattan.

hours earlier I was walking down those same streets on my way to work, and it was no different from any other day.

September 14, 2001 – Prayer

Friday. No work. Lots of rain. After spending the morning at Saqib's watching the "National Day of Prayer" Service on television (at which there was an imam representing the Islamic Society of North America), I took the bus to the Tenth St. Mosque for Friday prayers. Outside the mosque, a police officer was on post. Quite appropriate, given the numerous anti-Muslim / anti-Arab statements and attacks made since Tuesday. As I walked home from the mosque, about ten yards behind a group of Muslims with long beards and heads covered, I heard some-one shouting in our direction. Across the street, a man on the fifth floor of a construction site stood near the edge. "Go the f*#k back to your country!"

Asim

♦ ♦ ♦

I stopped writing. My almost daily emails to family and friends came to a halt. I couldn't focus on work. When I came home to the villa, I didn't know what to do with myself. I needed help. Taking up the hospital's offer, I made an appointment with a psychologist. An American, he under-stood, and counseled me. My neighbor Cathy in Staten Island advised me to do something with my hands, like knitting, crochet, or cooking. But all I did was absorb all the internet had to offer: images, more imag-es, stories of terror and despair. On weekends we would huddle with the western expats, feeding off one another's pain, each of us coping in our own way. The Pakistani expats for the most part did not believe that the Taliban had anything to do with it (none of us had heard of Al-Qaeda). "Muslims would never do such a thing" is what I heard the women say. They believed that the Muslims had been framed.

A member of the healthcare association I belonged to in New Jersey emailed me: "I will no longer receive emails from you." My friends in the US were asking: what is the Saudi response; are the rumors true that Saudis were happy about it? A resounding *No*. I didn't hear anything even close to it; not at work, not in the print news, not on TV. Saudis at the workplace refrain from engaging in dialogue other than work-related. Saudis were angry and believed that Al-Qaeda, an organization committed to dislodging the Saudi royal family, was conducting "holy war" against the House of Saud,* and had targeted and framed Saudi Arabia by using Saudi men to carry out the attack, putting a Saudi face on the terrorists; that Osama bin Laden, who had been exiled from Saudi Arabia, could have recruited perpetrators from any country given his vast network, but he chose his terrorists from Saudi Arabia to weaken the country.

(Years later, one Saudi employee shared her thoughts with the group at a camping trip. Her take: bin Laden has always been a threat to the well-being of Saudi Arabia; we wish he *was* the leader behind this attack, so that he can be brought to justice, but he doesn't have the capability to have masterminded such a sophisticated attack and with such secrecy. If you listen to him talk, you will see how limited he is. So who did she think carried out the attack, I asked her. That she couldn't answer.)

As soon as our six-month probation was over, we flew back home in November. Going back sooner would have meant breaking our employment contract. We got to hug our children and hold our grandson, Omar, now a month old. Our neighbors came rushing out to hug us, saying, "Thank God you are back." The phone started ringing that evening; everyone, as in friends and colleagues, wanted to talk about how we were faring in Saudi Arabia post–September 11 (the term 9/11 had not yet entered our lexicon); they wanted to come over to visit, and my calendar filled up. The next morning, we made our pilgrimage to Ground Zero. We drove down Victory Boulevard to catch the

---

* Ruling royal family of the Kingdom of Saudi Arabia.

Staten Island ferry. As soon as the Manhattan skyline came into view, I burst into tears. The Twin Towers, always looming above the skyline, gone. We walked to Ground Zero, the charred framework still smoking, papers with burnt edges stuck in the road signs. That's when it finally hit me.

Friends and colleagues—almost all of them—came to visit. We had come from the homeland of the terrorists, and everyone wanted to know what it was like to be there. One of my friends asked me, "What are Saudi people like?"

"They are people just like us."

She completed the sentence for me, "They have the same aspirations for their children, the same dreams for a good life, the same worries about their health, the same needs."

They asked if we going back after our vacation was over. Yes. My friends hadn't disowned me because we were Muslim; I wasn't foregoing my Saudi acquaintances because some misguided people in their country had committed acts of terrorism. They understood, but there were exceptions. Let me put it this way: those living in the metropolitan areas understood; some in far-off places couldn't. I sensed a distance, and I let it go. Over time, it passed.

Yet, America had changed. Muslims were afraid and were not taking any chances. My Pakistani friend shed her *shalwar kameez*; others put up American flags outside their homes, and "we love America" stickers on their car. One of them who came to visit said, "I didn't feel safe, so I removed my hijab." When I walked into the shopping mall—no abaya this time, and it didn't even feel odd—the thought suddenly struck me: *Should I be afraid?* I found myself being extra courteous, and it felt unsettling. I went to see my orthodontist, and while doing the procedure, he looked down at me and said, "I lost many patients. It was a day we will never forget." Neither will I, except that he was glaring down at me. How does one respond to micro-aggression? Not to mention with a suction tube in one's mouth.

One of our family friends on Staten Island, Sherri, had a near-miss. He was in his office on the ninety-first floor of the South Tower of the World Trade Center South when the North Tower was hit. Told to evacuate immediately, he and his colleagues took the elevator to the lobby and walked out of the building, just minutes before the South Tower was hit.

One evening, the doorbell rang. It was Terry Troia. A minister, she ran Project Hospitality, a food kitchen for the homeless. Khalid had worked with her on the board. She heard we were in town and dropped in. Sitting in our living room, overlooking the Richmond Valley as the sun descended, she spoke about her role in identifying victims of 9/11. She worked at the landfill where the debris was being processed on conveyor belts, and her job was to identify remains of bodies among the concrete and steel; hands, limbs, a finger. . . . I shuddered as she spoke. And then I opened up, sharing my distress. She listened. And then she spoke to me. I don't recall what she said, but by the time she got up to leave, I felt that the ship had turned. As we walked her to her car, waved goodbye, walked back in, shutting the door behind us, I felt that I had finally begun to heal. Terry had been ministering to me.

We said goodbye to our children and our dear little grandson, just two months old, and flew back to Riyadh in December. But not before our encounter with TSA at JFK.

♦♦♦

December
Subject: JFK

Dear All,

We are back in Riyadh and jetlagged to no end.

Things got rocky as soon as we arrived at JFK airport. We had learned that no guests were being allowed inside the terminal, so we said our goodbyes at home and took a cab. We had been advised to come four hours prior to departure for security checks. Inside the terminal our luggage was put through the X-ray machine. As I stood aside, waiting to be processed, the security person watching the screen stopped the conveyor belt and beckoned to me: "Please come over." I wondered what the problem is. So, I walked over.

"Are you carrying silverware?" she asked.

"Yes."

"It is not allowed."

"But it is in my check-in luggage. I am not carrying it in my carry-on bags."

"I understand. But you cannot carry it in any of the bags." She was polite. "Please open the carton."

Now I had the flatware in one of the two cartons, and I didn't know which one, since the conveyor belt had moved and now all my luggage was stacked at the end.

"Then you have to open both cartons to find the silverware," she said.

If you know how much trouble it is to tape a carton and then tie it with rope, you will understand my reluctance to have to unnecessarily open both cartons.

"OK. Let's just put it through the X-ray machine again and find the right carton." She was being understanding. So the porter put the boxes through the machine again, and the carton was identified. Now began the task of carefully peeling off the tape, and then looking through the carton to find the box with flatware, without disturbing the carefully packed items. We found the box, and the security person pulled out the forks and knives that I had carefully bound into stacks.

"These are sharp objects, and you cannot take them," she said, waving them.

"But they are in the check-in bags."

"I know. But that is the rule. Please turn them over to your family outside."

"But we don't have any family outside. We took a cab. We were told that no family was allowed inside the terminal. Besides, if that is the rule, I wish we had been told about it."

"Can I speak to your manager?" This was Khalid. Grateful, she beckoned to the guard who escorted Khalid inside, carrying the forks and knives. She winked at me in sympathy as I waited.

Now, here is the story. I didn't care much for the flatware the hospital had provided, and besides, it was incomplete. It had no salad forks, no pierced spoon, serving fork, cake spatula, etc. Why buy another set in Riyadh when I had all that flatware at home in NY?

After a while Khalid walked back. "They say it is the absolute rule. No forks, period. It doesn't matter what bags they are in. They are going to mail it to Saqib in New York. Let me re-pack the carton. Can you give them Saqib's mailing address?"

Now Khalid, in anticipation of the cartons being opened, always keeps masking tape and string in his carry-on. It came in handy, the tape that is. He should have been a boy scout.

I walked toward the manager's office. "Excuse me, can I see the manager?"

"Why do you wish to see him?"

"I have to give him my son's mailing address."

"I'll be right back," the guard said. He went in. In a few minutes, the manager came out. An Irish-looking fellow.

"Are you the lady with the forks?"

It could have been worse. I could have been called "the lady with the knives."

"Yes, I am."

Anyhow, I gave them Saqib's mailing address; they immediately prepared the FedEx package and gave me the tracking number as well as the manager's name and telephone number.

It didn't end there.

At the boarding area, the tables were lined up and all carry-on bags were being opened for inspection. I put up my bag, and a pleasant man started going through my belongings.

"Why are you carrying masking tape?"

Oh no! Not again.

"Because when the cartons are opened, I have to retape them."

"These are not allowed in carry-on bags. Next time just pack them inside the cartons." He was polite.

"OK."

"Why are you carrying this rope?" he held up the bag with the string in it.

"For the same reason. Last time at Customs they had cut the rope with scissors, and so I need extra rope to retie the cartons."

"You cannot carry these," he said, taking out the bag with the string in it. "I am sorry."

"No problem."

"Khalid," I yelled across the table where Khalid's bags were being opened. "We cannot carry the rope." Khalid shook his head, and the poor guard started apologizing to Khalid for taking away his rope. I can understand why a rope and masking tape inside a plane could be problematic. But no forks in the check-in luggage! I suppose I should be more understanding of the circumstance.

It didn't end there! We got to Riyadh after thirteen hours. As the porter walked us to Customs, he advised us that if we were carrying CDs, our bags were bound to be opened. Sure enough, as the luggage started going through the X-ray machines, our carry-on bag with the CD was pulled over.

"You are carrying CDs?" the Custom's officer inquired.

"Yes."

He went through the bag, looked at the contents, and then waved us through. The authorities are looking to prevent objectionable material from entering the country, as in pornography. The CD has baby Omar's photographs on it.

Yesterday, friends came to visit us. I served them tea and fruit, and as they dipped into the fruit salad with oversized forks, I related the story of the "lady with the forks."

Stay safe,
Sabeeha

♦♦♦

Riyadh, in the few weeks we had been away, had become a changed city. The American Cultural Center: shut down. Private movie showings in compounds: shut down. Arabic classes: shut down. Western expats: under pressure from their families, with many recent recruits gone. We were recent recruits, but the thought of leaving never entered our minds. We didn't feel threatened or unsafe. Hearing about the anti-Muslim and anti-Saudi sentiment in the States, Saudis were switching vacation spots from USA/Europe to the Far East. They were pulling their children out of college in the States and looking to the Gulf states and Malaysia. Over time, NYU and other prestigious colleges would open campuses in Dubai. Years later, when I asked a Saudi executive if he was going to the US to attend the annual medical conference, he said, "I will not go to the US. I will not be humiliated by the immigration officials. They are directing their anger against all Saudis for acts committed by a few."

CHAPTER 6

Ramadan Like Nowhere Else

Friday, December 14
Subject: Ramadan in Riyadh

Dear All,

The month of fasting is coming to an end. Today may be the last day of Ramadan if the crescent is sighted this evening. The entire focus of the nation is on Ramadan. You live and breathe it. Every activity revolves around Ramadan. For one thing, day turns into night and night into day.

Store hours are 1:00 p.m. to 4:00 p.m., and 8:30 p.m. to 2:00 a.m. That's right! Here is why: *suhur* is at 4:30 a.m. (i.e., the time when you wake up to have breakfast and begin your fast). Iftar is at 5:00 p.m. (i.e., the time you break your fast and start eating again). So, after *suhur*, people go back to bed and sleep late into the day. Then they open for business in the afternoon for a few hours, closing at 4 p.m., an hour before iftar. After they break their fast, they offer evening *Maghrib* prayers, have dinner, and then businesses open again at night. That is the time when the crowds flock the streets, restaurants, shops, and picnic areas. The crowds grow as the night grows, and it is all festive with a lot of feasting. At 2:00 a.m., businesses shut down, people go home, have *suhur*, start the fast, and go to sleep. Having stayed up all night, they sleep late. And that is how it goes.

When I first read about the store hours in the newspaper, I could not comprehend it. I decided to experience it for myself. So Khalid and I went to glittering, newly opened Kingdom Mall at 8:30 p.m., which is normally my "wind-down time." This is on the ground floor of Kingdom Center, a towering building recently built by Prince Talal (whose donation to the WTC victims was returned by Rudy Giuliani). As our cab pulled up, I noticed police activity outside. With Ramadan bringing more crowds to the malls, they had been stationed to ensure compliance with "family rules."

Inside was quiet, too early to be crowded, and the mall sported a classy look. Open, uncluttered, and stylish. On the first floor of Saks, the cosmetics' section is "ladies only." This was a first for me: women working in a store in Riyadh. A suited gentleman sits at a shiny desk by the grand entrance just to let you know he is watching for trespassers. Inside, the chic salesgirls—all of Arab descent—are ready to make you up if you let them. The third floor is for ladies only. Guards are stationed at the ladies elevator to the third floor to keep men out. Here, the entire staff is female. I left Khalid downstairs and went to explore.

Women were checking in their abayas and emerging in jeans and colorful tops. This floor, with a 100 percent female staff and fitting rooms, the first of its kind, has been created to allow women to shop in privacy. I gather that having no men on the floor gives them a sense of security. Good for business because most expats I know buy their clothes when they go back home on leave. The salesgirls were assertive. The moment I would enter a store, they would flock over and start their sales pitch. I hung around to give them encouragement. Ramadan Sale signs decked the windows. As I came downstairs to join Khalid, someone said something that seemed to be directed at me. I kept going. The voice boomed out again, "Cover your head." It was the *mutawwa*. My scarf had slipped. I instantly pulled the scarf over my head and kept walking.

"Khalid, I had a run-in with the *mutawwa*."

"Where? On the ladies floor?"

"No. Right here. There." I pointed out to the two gentlemen who had just walked right past us, one in a thobe, the other a young skinny cop.

As we stepped out of the mall at 10 p.m., cars were lined up at the entrance to drop off the shoppers—the crowd was just beginning to swell—and we encountered lines of men sitting on the ledge right across the entrance and driveway, facing in our direction. At first we couldn't understand why they were just sitting there, their legs dangling. It was intimidating. We later realized that these were the chauffeurs of the ladies who were inside shopping. There is a parking lot in the basement, but they need a place to hang out while they wait. They are not allowed inside the mall, so they sit on the ledge. Traffic was bustling, the town was alive, and we hailed a cab and got home. I am told that the town truly comes alive after 11 p.m. That is too late for me.

Remember I mentioned that we get five days Ramadan leave. Well, it's more like a floating holiday: you can take off five days anytime in the year. Traditionally, people like to take time off during the last few days of Ramadan, go to Mecca, and then come home for Eid. We used up our Ramadan quota plus earned annual leave to spend time with family in New York.

One morning when we got on to the bus to go to work, a Saudi woman said to me, "Now that Ramadan has started, I am going to put on weight." The irony was not lost on me. For some, Ramadan, the month of fasting, becomes a month of feasting. Another phenomenon: special TV programs and soap operas come alive during Ramadan, all through the night, beamed from Egypt and other Arab countries.

At the hospital, working hours are cut back from ten hours to six hours for Muslims. Non-Muslims have the routine ten-hour day. Some offices send out memos on the Ramadan hours; our office, which has only two Muslims other than the department head, gave us flex hours: we can pick and choose our schedule. I picked 8 a.m. to 2 p.m. It is wonderful to be able to come home when it is sunny and bright. We have iftar on the patio; imagine, outdoors on December evenings. In the US, the work-life balance during Ramadan took some doing. During winters when iftar was any time between 5:00 and 6:00 p.m.,

I would have to break my fast either at my desk or while driving home. Sometimes I had to break my fast while attending a board meeting. I never asked for special consideration. Here, it's a breeze.

  Very little work gets done during Ramadan. It is a given that little will get done. Even at 8 a.m., normally rush hour, the roads are deserted. There is only one couple other than us on the shuttle bus, the driveway of the hospital is empty, the hallways are quiet. Standing meetings are canceled. Take the summer schedule in the US to the tenth degree. And this is the case where the majority of the workforce is expatriates and most non-Muslim, adhering to the ten-hour day. Think of what it would be like when the Saudization of the workforce is completed. Coffee-kitchens in the offices are shut down. I decided to check out the cafeteria, so one day I went there during lunch hour. It was open, because all those not fasting have to eat. I expected it to be quiet and half-empty. The men's side was quiet, but the ladies' side was bustling. Then I realized that most of the expatriate employees are female, nurses being the largest bloc. Next week, the week of Eid, the hospital will become very quiet. When at work, every now and then I get a signal on my PC: "You have Mail." When I open it, it is an Eid greeting card from my colleagues. They keep coming.

  Last Friday I accompanied Khalid for *Jumma* prayers at a mosque in the DQ. The ladies' section is on the third floor. The sermon was in Arabic, of course, but later, the imam translated it into English. This is unique to this mosque. *Thank you.* The same night, I accompanied Khalid for the *Taraweeh* prayers in the mosque. These are special prayers offered in Ramadan during the night prayers and last for over an hour. The imam recited the Qur'anic verses slowly in melodious *qirat*. The sound has such an appeal to the senses, producing a very serene effect, and you just want it to go on and on as the *qirat* resonates through the mosque.

  In Muslim countries, the Eid day is subject to sighting of the moon.* But here is how it gets confusing in Saudi Arabia: each year, the government publishes the official calendar, which has the Hijra dates

* In the US, some Muslim communities observe moonsighting; others set the date based on the naval observatory's determination of the date of the new moon. Public schools in New York City set the date in advance.

and the corresponding Gregorian dates. But then, Eid is celebrated in accordance with moon sighting. I don't know how they reconcile the discrepancy if the dates do not coincide. For example, according to the official calendar, Eid is on the sixteenth, but depending on the moon sighting, it could be either on the fifteenth or the sixteenth. The Supreme Judiciary appoints a body to oversee the moon sighting and makes the announcement in the evening, in this case, on December 14. Government offices are officially closed for twelve days (December 10–21), so there is no issue with taking a day off on the right day or the wrong day. Banks and semi-official establishments get only one week off, and private sector employees just four days. Schools are off from December 6 to 29. Only essential services will operate, on a partial, emergency basis.

What is striking is that Eid is not an official holiday at the hospital. How about that! Actually, the hospital has no official holidays—no long weekends, no national day, no anything. The two-day weekends are all the fixed holidays you get. Other than that, if you want to take time off, you have to take it from your allotted leave days (vacation, Ramadan days, hajj days, post-leave). One can take these days anytime during the year. In other words, if hajj is in February, I can take my ten days of hajj leave in July. In medical departments, they prefer that doctors take the time off during Eid and hajj, since all clinics are closed at that time, but it's not a requirement. So, for the first time in my career, we are not taking Eid day off. Our rationale: What are we going to do on Eid? There is no family here. Friends are at work. So why lose a day's vacation and sit at home? So, Khalid and I will go for Eid prayers, which are at 6:30 a.m. after *Fajr* prayers, come home, and then go to work at 8:00 a.m. Feels strange. Our Pakistani friends have arranged for an Eid gathering on Tuesday evening, which should be nice.

According to *Arab News*, "Civil servants are facing a pay cut for unauthorized absence during Ramadan. . . . Twelve thousand prisoners are to be released in Royal Pardon on Eid Al-Fitr. . . . The general pardon is to mark the twentieth anniversary of the King's accession to the throne. The pardon will benefit more than 40 percent of about thirty thousand prisoners in the Kingdom's jails." Executions do not take place during Ramadan.

Ramadan is the month of giving charity. Although charity is required to be a way of life, it takes on a heightened importance during Ramadan. It is very visible on the Saudi scene, particularly in Mecca and Medina. One of the workers in my house was relating what he encountered the last time he was in Mecca during Ramadan. A woman walked up to the plaza of the Grand Mosque and sat down hauling a large plastic bag full of Saudi riyals. The needy immediately lined up. She kept digging into her bag, pulling out currency bills, and handing them out to each person. The currency was in all denominations: one, five, ten, twenty, fifty, one hundred, two hundred riyals—you name it. It was the recipient's luck as to what fell into his hand. And she kept doling out until her bag was empty. That, I hear, is a common occurrence.

Arab News, December 12, 2001, described the scene in Mecca: "Hundreds of thousands of Muslims poured into the holy city of Mecca yesterday seeking the blessings of the Night of Power, the most blessed night in the fasting month of Ramadan. Thousands had to attend the congregational prayers outside in the streets leading to the Grand Mosque because of the huge crowd. Many have specifically come to the *haram* to spend the night in prayers and supplication, hoping to be blessed during the mystic Night of Power. A number of Muslim heads of state have also arrived in the Kingdom to perform *umrah*. An equally large crowd converged on the Prophet's Mosque in Medina to offer special prayers and take part in *Taraweeh* and *qiyam-al-lail* prayers."

Each year, Muslims all over the world eagerly await the twenty-seventh night of Ramadan, believed to be the *Laylat al-Qadr*, or the Night of Power, when the Holy Qur'an was first revealed to the Prophet Muhammad. According to the Qur'an, the angels and the angel Gabriel come down by God's permission carrying His orders that determine the fate of humans and other creatures. Muslims believe that Allah forgives the sins of all those who seek His pardon on this blessed night, "which is better than a thousand months."

Scholars differ on the exact date of *Laylat al-Qadr*. According to the Hadith—the sayings of the Prophet Muhammad—he asked his followers to *seek Laylat al-Qadr* on the odd nights in the last ten days of Ramadan (i.e., the twenty-third, twenty-fifth, twenty-seventh, and twenty-ninth night). Many believe that the twenty-seventh night is the most probable.

The authorities are prepared for the heavy rush expected during the last ten days of Ramadan. They have mobilized thousands of policemen, firefighters, religious guides, scouts, cleaners, and others as emergency staff. Thousands of workers have been working around the clock to keep the holy mosque and surroundings clean. All ninety-five gates leading into the Grand Mosque have been opened to facilitate the pilgrim's flow, which is monitored by 118 officers through 670 television and close-circuit cameras.

King Fahd, Crown Prince Abdullah, deputy premier and commander of the National Guard, and senior members of the Cabinet are stationed in Mecca to oversee the services. Zamzam water* is being supplied through fifteen thousand water coolers kept in various parts of the mosque. Wheelchairs are available, free of charge.

Six health clinics inside the Grand Mosque are providing emergency services. Parking lots in the entrances of the city have been reserved for pilgrims' cars. The police have set up special rooms with recreational facilities for lost children and opened lost-and-found counters.

According to *Arab News,* the policemen at the Grand Mosque in Mecca arrested ten pickpockets. During hajj and Ramadan, the number of pickpockets always increases.

During Ramadan next year, I too hope to be in Mecca and perform *umrah, In sha Allah.*

EID MUBARAK

All the best,
Sabeeha

---

* Water from the Zamzam well, the spring that miraculously erupted in the desert when Hagar was running back and forth between two hills looking for water for baby Ishmael. Details in chapter 8.

CHAPTER 7

Countdown to Hajj

February 8, 2002
Subject: Hajj Preparations

Dear All,

Hajj begins on February 20. It's the largest gathering on earth, and this year Khalid and I intend to be there.

Let me share my observations with you as we begin our preparations and as the Kingdom gears up to host the pilgrims.

More than two million pilgrims from different parts of the world are expected to perform hajj this year. Another half a million are expected to come from within the Kingdom.

It was in late December when Khalid and I had made our intention to perform hajj. Hajj is incumbent upon all adult Muslims who can afford the journey and is to be performed once in a lifetime. Fortunately, Khalid and I were able to perform the hajj in the summer of 1986. We are now ready for a second hajj, not a requirement but a spiritual journey we would like to experience once again—a recharge.

Hajj is a journey in which we walk in the footsteps of Prophet Abraham, the patriarch of monotheistic faiths. All the rituals commemorate Prophet Abraham and his wife Hagar. We walk around the Kaaba, the House that Abraham and Ishmael built. We walk seven times between the hillocks of Safa and Marwa, in the footsteps of Hagar when she ran back and forth in the desert looking for water for baby Ishmael. We travel from Mecca to Mina, Arafat, Muzdalifa, and back to Mina.* We sacrifice a lamb to commemorate Abraham's willingness to sacrifice his son and his sacrifice of a lamb. And we defy the devil, as he did when the devil tried to dissuade him from obeying God's instructions. The procedure of performing the hajj was laid out by Prophet Muhammad when he performed the hajj.

The first step was to look for a hajj agent. You cannot just go on your own. A certified agent who puts together a group of pilgrims must serve as your custodian. The agent is responsible for obtaining the necessary approvals, transporting you from place to place as the rituals require, and providing board and lodging (in tents). During this period, the agent holds on to your passport or *iqama*. After performing hajj, foreign pilgrims must go back to their country of origin, and it is the responsibility of the agent to ensure that. The agent also escorts the locals back to their destinations. Foreign pilgrims stay anywhere from a week to three months or so. We had stayed here for ten days when we arrived from New York for hajj in 1986. Those staying longer spend all their time in Mecca and Medina. The visit to Medina, where the Prophet is buried, is not part of hajj but is a *ziyarah*, or visit to a holy place. It is a city rich in Muslim history.

Whereas pilgrims arriving from outside the Kingdom must submit their paperwork months in advance, local pilgrims like us do so just a few weeks prior to hajj. This is because once the "foreign" pilgrim count is received, the Ministry of hajj then allocates the quota of pilgrims to the local agents. We had some difficulty finding an agent. There was no advertising and no telephone listings. We spoke to people here who had performed hajj last year, and their agents were either out of town or would not answer the phone. Finally, I went to the hospital's Social Club and got a reference. Many of our friends were also in the market

---

* Mecca to Mina: 8.8 kilometers; Mina to Arafat: 13 kilometers; Arafat to Muzdalifa: 12 kilometers; Muzdalifa to Mina: 8 kilometers; Mina to Mecca: 8 kilometers.

for hajj agents, and every day we would compare notes. In the end, our friends Nadia and Nadeem selected an agent, Al-Eteqan. So, in the name of God, the Beneficent, the Merciful, we signed up. The group will leave early the morning of February 20, the first day of hajj (eighth day of the Hijra month of Dhul Hijjah), for the five-day pilgrimage.

As we began our preparations, which involve putting your mind and heart into the spiritual mode, reading and studying about the hajj, and some minor shopping, I began to follow the Kingdom's preparations as the country geared up to receive, house, feed, and transport 2.5 million pilgrims.

Here is what I am learning from reading *Arab News*:

Sixteen days to hajj (Feb 4): As I read the news, I can't help but think about the difficulty pilgrims have to undergo to perform the hajj. Afghanistan is just one example. I had no idea there is no Saudi embassy in Kabul to grant the visas. So Afghanistan is requesting from Saudi authorities that visas for the fifteen thousand pilgrims be provided by the Saudi embassy in Pakistan or be presented to them when they arrive in Saudi Arabia. I do hope it works out for them.

Then there are the three hundred Bangladeshi pilgrims who were abandoned by their travel agents at a camp close to Dhaka airport, leaving them without airline tickets. If they don't arrive in Jeddah before February 17, they will miss the hajj. When I think of how much emotion these pilgrims have expended in planning for hajj, let alone the expense, and then to be left out in the cold, literally, it breaks my heart.

On a positive note, it is interesting that despite the tension between Saudi Arabia and Iran, Saudi Arabian Airlines is transporting Iranian pilgrims. That is the spirit of hajj.

Fifteen days to hajj: I was always aware that the hajj drew pilgrims from all over the world. But in reading the details, the scope of it is striking, not to mention the various modes of transportation involved. There is China, with about 2,100 pilgrims expected. I hope I run into them. I have never met a Chinese Muslim. Then there are the 750 Iraqi pilgrims who are making a twenty-four-hour journey by bus enroute from Baghdad. Let's not forget sea travel. The lucky Egyptian and Sudanese pilgrims were greeted upon arrival by ship by Prince Abdul Majeed, the Mecca governor, with gifts and warm words of welcome.

Are you familiar with the problem of squatting? Every year during hajj, thousands of pilgrims who cannot afford the accommodations set up camp sites in the vicinity of the Grand Mosque in Mecca. In addition to obstructing pedestrian traffic and contributing to unhygienic conditions, this practice has led in the past to fires resulting from cooking. To address the issue, Prince Abdul Majeed has announced stringent new policies aimed at ensuring the safety of all participants. I am not familiar with what the policies entail, so let's see how this pans out.

It is heartwarming to see high-level officials of the Saudi government, like Crown Prince Abdullah, involved in welcoming the pilgrims and ensuring their welfare.

Fourteen days to hajj: A two-hundred-bed hospital in Mecca has been equipped with sunstroke and heat exhaustion units.

One Thousand Roads to Mecca

I started reading this book by Michael Wolfe. Wolfe is an American, who converted to Islam years ago and in 1990 performed the hajj. CNN did a hajj documentary on his experience. His book is a compilation of travelogues by people who performed the hajj over the last thousand years. I learned that it used to take people over a year to get to Mecca. They would come from all parts of the world—Spain, Persia, Morocco, India—and travel along the pilgrim routes, on camelback, in caravans. Many never made it. They traded along the way, took up jobs, made some money, and then resumed their travel. Those without means survived on the charity and hospitality of their host countries. Men of learning—lawyers, scholars, writers, scientists, explorers—were engaged by the courts of ruling sultans and by institutions of learning, where they shared their knowledge, and brought back their experiences. They were raided by bandits, taken sick, and continued with the journey until they reached Mecca. They would live in Mecca for several months, sometimes for a year, before beginning the journey back home. They were welcome wherever they went, such was the thirst for learning. Travel lodges were set up along the pilgrim routes where centers of learning were established, and each learned from the other. When the pilgrims left after each brief stay, they were provided provisions, guides, and guards.

When I read about the challenges people faced and the charity of those who came to their aid, I am embarrassed at the trivia we indulge in. In deciding which agent to engage for the hajj, we were getting picky over the quality of washroom facilities, air-travel versus the ten-hour bus travel, et cetera. In preparing for travel, we are getting anxious over, "Am I going to be hot in the day? Am I going to be cold at night? Do I need a blanket? Should I keep my pillow? What about an extra pair of shades, just in case?" True, one must be sensible, but we should not lose focus on the intent of our pilgrimage, which is to immerse ourselves in communion with God while adopting a simple and basic, no-frills state of *ihram*, humbling ourselves before our Creator.

By the way, in Mecca, the temperature is in the nineties on the Fahrenheit scale.

Thirteen days to hajj: *Arab News* reports: "Posters and banners now decorating the city's streets and newspapers all carry the same slogan: *If you intend to perform the hajj this season, we offer the kind of service that best suits you.* They all promise a comfortable journey, including air-conditioned housing and transport, hot meals, and religious lectures. The cost ranges anywhere from a few thousand Saudi riyals to seventeen thousand Saudi riyals.* Local agents serving local pilgrims rent space in Mina and Arafat from the Ministry of Hajj and furnish the tents according to the service category they offer. . . . Pilgrims share tents with fellow pilgrims, the number of people per tent varying according to the price. The ministry has cautioned local hajj establishments from

---

* $1.00 = 3.75 Saudi riyals.

making promises they cannot keep. Many businesses have shifted to Mecca for the hajj, where the largest human gathering is expected to peak over the coming two weeks with a turnover of between ten and twelve billion Saudi riyals.

"Today the Mecca governor inspected preparations being made at the holy sites; visited the hospitals and clinics, warehouses storing charity foodstuffs, and power plants as well as the police headquarters and control rooms."

We were told by our agent that men and women will live in separate tents. When we performed hajj in 1986, that was not the case. Saudi Arabia has become more conservative since then. Couples were together in their tents along with other couples. So, we have decided to split our mobile phones (i.e., Nadia and I will keep one phone in our tent, and Khalid and Nadeem the other phone).

I didn't have quite the right attire for hajj. Whereas men must wear the *ihram* (i.e., two unstitched pieces of white terry cloth), the *ihram* for women is modest attire covering all parts of the body except the face, hands, and feet, with hair well-covered. Since it is very hot in Mecca and one has to do some rigorous walking, you have to dress sensibly. We made a trip to one of the malls and sought out a tailor, who promised to have my clothing ready within a week.

Non-Muslims are not permitted to enter the city of Mecca or Medina. According to Michael Wolf's book, many attempted and performed the hajj. These included people like Sir Richard Burton and John Lewis Buckhardt (who discovered Petra) in the nineteenth century. They were fluent in Arabic, had studied Islam, practiced the rituals, and had spent significant time living in Muslim countries. They took on a Muslim identity, deceived the authorities and their travel companions, and gained access to Mecca and Medina. They then came back and wrote about it.

Twelve days to hajj: Reading *Arab News,* I am in awe of the massive undertaking and the ambitious timeline.

"The authorities approved the construction of a new four-hundred-bed hospital in Mecca, and a new hospital in Mina to handle emergency cases. The ministry has recruited eighty consultant doctors from Europe and America and eighty Malaysian female nurses to serve at the health centers and hospitals in Mecca. More than ninety-six hundred doctors and nurses will serve in various hospitals in Arafat, Muzdalifa, and Mina over the hajj period. Eighty-five new ambulances have been added.

"Today marks the departure of the official British Hajj delegation. Lord Adam Patel, member of the House of Lords, is leading the British delegation. More than twenty thousand British pilgrims are expected to perform hajj this year."

All the best,
Sabeeha

♦♦♦

For a woman performing hajj, Saudi authorities require that she be accompanied by a *mahram*. However, she can perform hajj without her *mahram* if she is traveling with a group and if her *mahram* gives written, notarized permission for her to travel with said group.

♦♦♦

February 18
Subject: Hajj Preparations Part 2

Dear All,

Ten days to hajj: Many of you may know that often stampedes occur at the *Jamaraat*, resulting in deaths. This is the stoning ritual—stoning of the pillar signifying the devil. To address the issue of stampeding, a crowd-control mechanism has been established. The Hajj Ministry has developed a timetable, allotting time slots on a country-specific basis for performing the ritual. It appears that the countries that have been issued time frames may be those that have the largest delegations (i.e., Indonesia, India, Pakistan, and Turkey).

I don't expect there to be any issue with availability of food. *Arab News* reports, "The Commerce Ministry will supply ten million meals, three million cartons of fruit juice, ten million kilograms of fresh fruit, and forty million loaves of bread in the holy sites. Fifty-five refrigerated trucks will be stationed there, from which the various foodstuffs will be sold. One thousand five hundred small trucks will be driving around selling food. In Mecca, the municipality has set up 565 fast food outlets."

The British foreign secretary, Jack Straw, was quoted as saying that the UK was the first Christian state to enable its Muslim citizens to perform the hajj. How about that!

The Mecca governor affirmed that the country would not allow the hajj to be used as a forum for criticizing the US. I wondered if the concern was that foreign pilgrims may politicize the hajj. Governor, I appreciate that. I was also moved by the message of the interior minister, Prince Naif, when he referred to the pilgrims as guests of God, to whom the country owes a duty to serve.

Nine days to hajj: Our paperwork is ready and our leave has been approved. The hospital had to certify our meningitis vaccinations.

Arab News reports: "Gabon's biggest party of pilgrims heading to Mecca was grounded in Central Africa by an outbreak of the feared Ebola fever. Use of cooking gas in the holy sites will be banned for two weeks."

Eight days to hajj: A treat for the pilgrims. They were welcomed by no other than King Fahd.

Help is on its way for the Afghans. Saudi Arabia has sent a delegation to Kabul to expedite the visas for the fifteen thousand pilgrims. More Afghani women than men applied for hajj at a cost of $1,500 each. Now that is interesting!

And the pilgrims keep arriving, this time from Yemen. About ten thousand Palestinian pilgrims are on their way from the West Bank and Gaza.

Often people who do not have a hajj permit try to get into the city of Mecca. Checkpoints are now in place in the outskirts of Mecca. Likewise, fake hajj agents defraud unsuspecting pilgrims, taking their money and issuing false papers. The Hajj Ministry has gone into high gear and is keeping an eye out for these agents. *Hmmm! I wonder how they do that.*

<u>Seven days to hajj</u>: I read in *Arab News* today that eighty-one Egyptians with forged hajj visas were deported. I feel badly for them. I am sure they didn't know that their visas were forged. They probably got cheated by one of those bogus agents.

On an optimistic note, it appears that the Afghan pilgrims will make it after all. The generosity and compassion of the Saudi authorities is off the charts. They have charter flights on standby to fly the Afghanis in as soon as the paperwork is processed. My prayers are with them.

<u>Six days to hajj</u>: *Arab News* reports, "The Supreme Judiciary Council announced: 'It has been confirmed by witnesses that the new moon was sighted on Tuesday evening, which means that Wednesday is the first day of the month of Dhul Hijjah.' Therefore, the hajj will start on February 20; the main day of hajj will be on February 21, with the ritual standing in prayer by pilgrims on Mount Arafat, and Eid ul-Adha will be on Friday, February 22."

More pilgrims on their way, this time from—are you ready for this?—Taiwan. I didn't know that Taiwan had a Muslim population. Did you?

What is amazing at this time of the year is the spirit of philanthropy. Free meals will be distributed by the International Islamic Relief Organization. And how about this: The Hajj Ministry is poised to make house calls—actually, tent calls—using small ambulances, fully equipped, to drive through narrow streets to bring medical care to patients in the tents.

I paid a visit to my tailor today. I have just the right attire for the pilgrimage: long cotton gowns in neutral colors of beige and gray, with full sleeves.

Five days to hajj: See, I was right! Remember those poor Egyptians who were deported? Well, the Madinah governor, Prince Muqrin, gave the order that visas be issued to twenty-eight pilgrims. The pilgrims affirmed that they did not know that they had invalid visas. But then what about the remaining fifty-three pilgrims? There is still time, and I pray that they make it too.

Now this is interesting: A Ladies-Only telephone booth with its own extension, 333. The ladies can thank the National Guard for this service. The idea is that women will use these private booths to reach out to religious scholars if they have questions or concerns regarding the rituals of hajj. Neat!

Four days to hajj: *Arab News* reports, "The hajj security forces have installed fifteen hundred cameras in Mecca, Mina, and other holy sites to monitor traffic.

"A total of 510 pilgrims have arrived in Mecca as personal guests of King Fahd. They include pilgrims from Nigeria, Chad, Cameroon, Indonesia, Nepal, Thailand, Malaysia and Cuba. About 280 more guest pilgrims will arrive today from Sri Lanka, South Africa, and Senegal.

"More than 1.26 million copies of the Holy Qur'an will be distributed among pilgrims as a gift from the king. The ministry of Islamic Affairs will also distribute translations of the Qur'an in the Indonesian, English, Malayalam, French, Tagalog, Urdu, Thai, Spanish, Hausa, Eruba, Tamil, Somali, and Bosnian languages.

"The Presidency for the Two Holy Mosques Affairs has signed a contract with a Saudi company to manage 420 lockers of varying size installed at four places around the Grand Mosque to keep valuables of pilgrims."

<u>Three days to hajj</u>: More good news on the Afghanistan front: The chartered planes that were on standby? They just arrived, carrying eight hundred ninety Afghan pilgrims. *Alhamdulillah.*

As more pilgrims arrive and the risk to safety increases, so does the security presence in Mecca and surrounding areas. Some sixty thousand employees—boy scouts and volunteers—and twenty thousand soldiers and security men have been commissioned. I didn't know that Saudi Arabia had boy scouts. Why *did* I doubt that? Stereotyping?

In anticipation of the thousands of pilgrims requiring emergency healthcare, the Health Ministry has readied twenty-one hospitals and three hundred medical centers, with a capacity of seven thousand beds. Isn't that staggering!

Dehydration is commonplace during hajj, given exposure to intense heat in outdoor settings. Large water tanks have been built in Mina and Arafat. The availability of water will not be an issue.

Imagine the potential for unsanitary conditions with two million people in one location. Yet, I recall that during my first hajj many years ago, it was the cleanliness of the place that struck me. So I am not surprised to learn that the authorities have employed thirteen thousand cleaners with sanitation vehicles.

Sadly, even in the holiest of holy months, bad elements prevail. This time the victims of a scam are the Moroccans, 134 of them. A travel agent took off with their money—just like that. Fortunately, the owner of the agency took responsibility, and made them whole. Hopefully, the pilgrims will make it to Mecca on time.

Prince Turki ibn Muhammad ibn Abdul Aziz has inaugurated the hajj website, with information on all you want to know about the hajj.*

<u>Two days to hajj</u>: *Arab News* reports, "More than 1.5 million faithful from fifty countries have arrived in the Kingdom for hajj. Chinese Muslims flock to Thailand seeking hajj visas. Each year only a very

---

* A major technological advancement considering it was the year 2002.

limited number of hajj visas are issued in China.* This means that thousands more Chinese set out to find ways to get to the hajj indirectly. Bangkok is seen as an easier point to apply for a hajj visa.

"Around eight thousand pilgrims have been camped out in freezing temperatures at Kabul airport for days. Frustrated Afghans waiting to fly to the Kingdom won new hope yesterday as King Fahd ordered Saudi planes to airlift them to Jeddah. Pakistan also sent a plane to collect 270 pilgrims. Britain and the United Arab Emirates are also arranging for transport of five hundred and one thousand Afghans respectively."

Switching gears now. In reading *One Thousand Roads to Mecca,* I realized what an impact colonial powers had on the hajj. In the last half of the nineteenth century, as Europe colonized Muslim countries, they began to introduce controls on pilgrims as they issued passports, etc. European vessels transported them along the sea routes controlled by the Europeans. Trains started becoming a popular mode of transportation. As a result, caravan traffic along camel routes shrank and the bandits went out of business. Prior to this, pilgrims went along routes within Muslim control. Now they had to go through non-Muslim countries and societies outside the fold of Islamic law. They were not sure if the food was halal and were intimidated by the absence of segregation among the sexes, and other practices. But the convenience of modern transport was too attractive to pass up on. Europeans also started charging money and, consequently, only people of means were able to travel, leading to resentment among the hajjis. But, the Europeans, respecting the law of the land, did not enter Mecca.

We picked up our packages today. We have our boarding passes, ID, permits, instructions, tent assignments (as requested), maps, etc. *Alhamdulillah!* I can almost figure out the instructions in Arabic, but I am not taking chances. One of my colleagues will translate it for me. We are packed; scheduled to fly out on February 20 and fly back on the morning of the twenty-fifth, *In sha Allah.* Weather in Mecca on February 20 is expected to be hot—ninety-plus Fahrenheit.

---

* China has further restricted the issuance of hajj visas for the Uyghurs.

One day to hajj: There is seldom a moment at the Kaaba when the *tawaaf* is not being performed, except for a brief period during the second day of hajj, when the pilgrims leave for the plains of Arafat. That day, the Kaaba's cover—the *kiswah*—is replaced with a brand-new cover. So on February 21, in a traditional ceremony, the 658 meters (7,080 feet) of black silk cloth weighing 670 kilograms (1,480 pounds) will be replaced. The *kiswah* is fourteen meters (forty-two feet) high and forty-seven meters (141 feet) wide. The upper half is adorned with a ninety-five-centimeter-wide strip inscribed with Qur'anic verses, embroidered in gold-plated silver thread. It takes ten months and the work of more than two hundred Saudis to prepare and embroider the cloth. In the past, the *kiswah* was prepared by different Muslim countries. I remember the time when it was sent from Pakistan. Thousands thronged the streets to catch a glimpse of the *kiswah*.

Update on Afghanistan: Almost a thousand Afghans have arrived in Mecca.

Pilgrims from over one hundred sixty countries are here. One hundred sixty! Offhand, I cannot even name more than one hundred countries. You can visualize the traffic jams, particularly as one gets closer to the Grand Mosque. But the Saudi authorities are prepared.

Arab News reports, "A hi-tech control room is connected to more than two thousand cameras installed in Mecca and the holy sites. Nine helicopters are also at work. Such is the crush of numbers crowding the holy sites that the slightest problem can result in disaster. Last year, thirty-five people died in a stampede during the stoning of devil ritual in Mina.

"The Kingdom has prevented an Arab doctor recruited for the pilgrimage from entering the country after he was found to have links with Osama Bin Laden's al-Qaeda network."

I understand that CNN is doing a story on hajj this evening.

We are all packed, with bare necessities only, and as required, all fragrance-free. We each have a very small carry-on bag and a pouch with reading material (i.e., a pocket-size Qur'an in paperback with English translation and a magnifying glass for us bi-focalers, a pocket-size book on hajj, and a pocket-size book of prayers). The only thing we are carrying plenty of is medicines. At the urging of my Saudi colleagues, I have started taking vitamin C as a preventive measure. It's countdown time now. We leave early tomorrow morning.

I have arranged to settle all my debts, as is customary for pilgrims. I should explain. In days gone by, when pilgrims went for hajj, they were gone for many, many months, undertook an arduous journey, and some never made it back, victims of disease or accidents. Therefore, it became customary to settle one's debts and one's affairs—children's education and marriage—before going for the hajj. Consequently, people performed hajj in old age. Now that travel has become easier, one can fly over and be back home within a week. Therefore, in my humble opinion, I don't have to pay off my mortgage, but I do want to make sure that I have put a mechanism in place for my debts to be settled in the event I do not return.

It is also customary for pilgrims proceeding for hajj to ask for forgiveness, to ask God for forgiveness, and to ask one's family, friends, and acquaintances for forgiveness. I am doing the same and asking you that if in the past I have wronged you, please forgive me. I will be praying for you and ask that you pray that we have a safe hajj.

God Bless!

All the best,
Sabeeha

CHAPTER 8

The Hajj: Journey of a Lifetime

Emails written after returning from hajj

Subject: Day 1 of Hajj

Dear All,

Wednesday, February 20 (Dhul Hijjah 8)

We were up at dawn for *Fajr* prayers. To prepare for hajj, the first three steps are to take a shower, put on the *ihram*, and make a personal intention for performing hajj. We were instructed by Al-Itteqan, our group, to take the shower at home but put on the *ihram* and make the intention once we get to the *meeqaat*.* So, that is how we left home at 6:30 a.m., praying for a safe journey and a fulfilling experience.

Our flight was to depart for Taif at 10:30 a.m., and we were told to be at the airport at 7:30 a.m. Since both Khalid and I tend to take instructions seriously, we were at the airport at 7:30 sharp. An empty terminal greeted us. Not a soul in sight. *Were we at the right terminal?*

---

* The principal boundary at which pilgrims enter into a state of *ihram* and make the intention for pilgrimage. A state of *ihram* is a sacred state which involves ritual cleansing and abstaining from certain acts such as sexual activity, shaving, clipping one's nails, and picking a fight.

There were no pilgrims walking around, no officials, nothing. We went around searching and finally found someone at the information desk.

"We are going for hajj. Are we in the right place?"

He looked at our boarding cards. "Just go past security and then proceed to gate 34. Hajj *Maqbool* (May God accept your hajj)."

"*Shukran, Shukran,*" we said, beginning to feel the excitement of *hajj*. As we glanced at the monitor, our flight time said: "Delayed. Departure time: 11:30 a.m." Oh well! Nowhere could we spot any representative from Al-Itteqan. We made ourselves comfortable and started reading the Qur'an. Gradually, the pilgrims started coming, wearing the ID badges of Al-Itteqan. Some men were wearing the *ihram*, some were not. It was cold in Riyadh that morning. God in his infinite wisdom chose a year-round hot place like Mecca for hajj where a pilgrim's *ihram* keeps you cool any time of the year. *Alhamdulillah*—All praise to God. Within an hour our waiting area was filled with pilgrims, and it began to feel like hajj. There were as many men as there were women, mostly couples, and some elderly women escorted by their sons.

As we started to board, we ran into an official from Al-Itteqan. I guess they had made it somewhere along the line, but they should have been more visible. No problem, just an observation. But Khalid will be sending them a feedback letter on how to improve their services. As we landed after an hour's flight, the airline played its usual recorded message: "Welcome to . . . Thank you for traveling . . . For those of you who are traveling to another destination, we wish you . . . . " At this time of the year, when the plane is visibly carrying pilgrims, they should customize their message to acknowledge the pilgrims proceeding for hajj and wish them accordingly. Knowing Khalid, he will be sending Saudi Airlines a letter.

As we stepped out of the airport, six buses with large Al-Itteqan signs were lined up at the curb. At our seat drop-down trays, they had placed boxed snacks, and within minutes they were serving cold drinks. A young man got onto the bus and called out a question to the passengers. Everyone laughed. Khalid and I looked at each other. What did he say? He had spoken in Arabic. Most of the people in our group were young

Arab families (one couple with a child). Then the young man asked another question, or the same question, who knows, and everyone laughed again. We didn't know any of our fellow passengers and were too shy to ask. Now, we had been assured by Al-Itteqan that we would be provided with English guides, particularly on the bus. Since one is not supposed to engage in conflict or whine while on hajj, we made a mental note of bringing it to the attention of the authorities. Khalid's letter to the agency is getting longer.

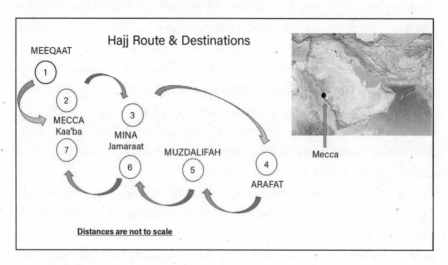

Meeqaat

We got to the *meeqaat* in an hour. The place was bustling with buses, cars, and people; vendors crowded the parking lot and beyond. Vendors were selling *ihrams* by the roadside. Now, why would someone come all the way to the *meeqaat* and not have an *ihram*? By the way, the *ihrams* were made in Pakistan. As we got off the bus, the young man whose question had made everyone laugh called out his instructions in English: "Three hours—come back." Three hours! Why do we want to linger here for three hours?

"Three hours—come back," he continued to call out.

Then someone asked him, "You mean three o'clock?" It was 2:30 then.

"Yes yes, three hours—come back."

Well, my Arabic is not as good as his English, and I am sure I will make enough people laugh if I tried to say, "Come back at three o'clock" in Arabic. I hooked up with two Lebanese ladies, and we found our way to the women's wash area, did our *wudu* (ablution), made the intention for *umrah*, went into the mosque, said our *nafl* prayers to begin *umrah*, and made our way back to the bus. Khalid, of course, had gone into the men's area. Even in the women's area of the mosque, I noticed that the veiled ladies hesitated to remove their veils. I guess it is so much a habit that they cannot bring themselves to uncover their faces in public. Know that when performing hajj, one must *not* cover one's face. Not men, not women.

We were back in the bus in three hours, sorry, at three o'clock, and so was everyone else. But the bus didn't leave until 3:45 p.m. I don't know what the problem was. But pilgrims should not complain. The men who had boarded the bus in their day-to-day attire were all trans-formed. They all had on two pieces of white unstitched cloth, a terry fabric. They all looked uniform, with all distinctions removed. I wore a long dress, like one that the Arab women wear, and a white cape that covered me from head to wrists. Not a single hair on my head was visi-ble, as is the requirement.

As soon as the bus started toward Mecca, men started chanting the *talbiah* or the traditional chant of pilgrims in the most melodious voice:

"*Labek, Allahumma Labek* . . . Here I am at your service, O God, here I am. Here I am at Thy service and Thou hast no partners. Thine alone is All Praise and All Bounty, and Thine alone is the Sovereignty. Thou hast no partners."

They chanted in perfect unison, placing emphasis at specific inter-vals, stretching the word *Allahumma*, pausing at the right places, and with the perfect Arabic sound. And as they chanted *Labek*, it seemed as if every being was uttering *Labek*, as if the wind was swaying to *Labek*, the leaves, the twigs, every movement in the air seemed to be saying *Labek*. Your heart, your mind, your soul, your body, calls out *Labek*. *Labek* is on the lips of all the people in our bus, the buses behind us, the buses ahead of us, the people walking up to the Grand Mosque, all around you, one is surrounded by the sound of *Labek*. What a glorious, uplifting, and humbling feeling! There wasn't anyone who was not moved by the sound of *Labek*. You are visiting the House of God, and you announce that you are coming to His house and are at His service.

We passed by Mina on our way to Mecca and saw thousands and thousands of white tents spread out all over the valley. Most of the pilgrims had already arrived in Mina. By the end of the day, all two million pilgrims will have arrived in Mina.

We were on our way to Mecca when Khalid's phone rang. It was Tariq, Khalid's brother. He and his wife, Meena, came from Pakistan for hajj. We were planning to meet each other in Mina. In days gone by, such a meeting was impossible. Now, with cell phones, it can be arranged. Tariq was already in Mina, and we told them that we still had a long way to go, so he decided to call us after *Isha* prayers.

Mecca

The road to Mecca was lined with pilgrims. Families with loads of luggage atop their cars and trucks, and pickup trucks loaded with goats and sheep, being transported to Mina for sacrifice. As soon as we reached Mecca, traffic slowed down and we did not get to the Grand Mosque or Masjid al-Haram until 6:00 p.m. *Haram* means sanctuary, a place of refuge. That part of the house where women would live was also called the *haram,* for the same reason: it was a sanctuary for women. Over the centuries, its meaning got distorted, but that's another discussion. The plaza outside the mosque was dotted with pilgrims, a haze of white, distinguished only by bare shoulders.

We were told—in Arabic—to be back to the bus in four hours, by 10 p.m., after which the bus would take us to Mina. This was my sixth visit to Mecca, but no matter how many times I have been to the Grand Mosque, I always experience that feeling of anticipation and quicken my pace as I get close.

Men and women have separate entrances. At the door, we removed our shoes and put them in a bag. I did not want to leave my shoes in the shoe rack, lest they get mixed up. I surged ahead and felt a tug. A female guard—veiled—pointed at my pocketbook, and in seconds, removed my nail-clipper. I rushed through the aisle. Pilgrims sat on either side, some reading the Qur'an, some praying, others chatting in whispers, some stretched out taking a nap. And then the Kaaba came into view. Speak to anyone and everyone who has been to the Kaaba, and they will tell you that whenever you lay eyes on the Kaaba, it moves you to tears, and you feel the presence of God. *Thank you, God, for bringing me here.* I stood rooted, relishing the moment, praying for all I could wish for.

God says in the Qur'an that this is His house, His symbol on earth. This is the place toward which every Muslim, from every corner of the world, turns in prayer. This is the structure that Abraham built at Allah's instructions, and people have been circumambulating it for some five thousand years. God says in the Qur'an that people will walk and ride on lean camels to come here. And I had just witnessed that (without the camels).

We found a place in the courtyard surrounding the Kaaba and sat down on the cool white marble floor to wait for *Maghrib* prayers. I am told that cold water pipes run beneath the surface. In front of me was a group from Indonesia, beside me a group from Iran. Each of them had their nationality written on their capes to identify the group. Many from Malaysia, Africa, and Arab countries. What I didn't see were pilgrims from Pakistan or India. Pakistan sends the largest contingent, followed by Indonesia, and then India. I figured they had already moved to Mina.

Allahu Akbar! The muezzin's voice resounded, calling the Muslims to prayer. The *adhan* in Masjid al-Haram is the most beautiful sound to experience. There is nothing comparable, and especially at this time of the day. When you are sitting under the open sky, with the Kaaba in front of you, draped in black and gold, the sky has changed color, the day is cooler, the minarets have lighted up against the sky, and all of a sudden you are struck by the muezzin's call, *Allahu Akbar.* Everyone stops moving. It permeates through the mosque and through your entire being. People line up evenly in straight rows, shoulder to shoulder, circling the Kaaba. Within seconds, hundreds and thousands of people demonstrate order and uniformity. There is no sergeant general calling out orders, people individually fall into line, and it is perfect. People from 160 nations, of varying socioeconomic ranks, of every language, fall into line, say the same prayer, in the same language, perform it exactly the same way and in perfect unison. What an extraordinary demonstration of unity of purpose—they stand in submission to God. *Alhamdulillah!*

After *Maghrib* prayer we performed *umrah*, doing the *tawaaf* around the Kaaba seven times, saying *nafl* prayers, drinking Zamzam water, and then doing the *saee*—walking seven times between Safa and Marwa. It took less than two hours. During this time, one concentrates on prayer, asking God for forgiveness, for blessings in this life and a place in heaven in the hereafter, praying for family, friends, and country, praying for anything and everything. People around me were crying, overcome with emotion; people kissing the black cloth draping the Kaaba and imploring God for forgiveness. A man held his elderly mother's arm; a woman carried her infant; two men carried an infirm person on a palanquin; someone pushed a disabled woman on a wheelchair, all moving in a circular motion, keeping pace with the crowd. It was not too crowded since most of the pilgrims had moved to Mina.

While we were doing the *saee*, the *adhan* was called for *Isha* prayers. We stopped where we were, found a place to say our prayers, and then picked up where we had left off. After *saee*, we performed the obligatory ritual of cutting a lock of our hair (and discarding it) and with that, our *umrah* was complete. Now we were officially out of the *ihram*. To begin the hajj, we would have to re-enter the state of *ihram* in Mina. I noticed the Malaysian women sitting on the Safa and Marwa mounts, absorbed in prayer, looking like white fluffy dolls.

Have you heard the story of Zamzam water? The oldest running spring in one of the most arid areas on earth. Abraham had left Hagar alone in the desert with baby Ishmael. When the baby started crying of thirst, she went looking for water, running between the hills of Safa and Marwa, back and forth, back and forth, seven times, and then,

Allah's miracle: at the place where the baby was kicking in the sand, suddenly a spring of water gushed. So much water that she had to cry out, "*Zam zam,*" stop, stop. Soon a town grew around the spring, with Hagar controlling the water rights. We honor Hagar by running in her footsteps, seven times between the hills, just as she had done, commemorating a mother's struggle. Think of it, two million people honoring a woman, year after year, century after century. I wondered if I ever had a Hagar moment in my mothering. The sleepless nights perhaps. "Hagar walked barefoot on hot sand in the scorching sun; and I am exhausted walking in an air-conditioned hall," I said to Khalid as we drank from the spring of Zamzam, now from taps.

The 105-foot-deep spring is located inside the Grand Mosque complex, just a few feet away from the Kaaba. Geological surveys indicate it is being fed by three underground canals that meet under the Grand Mosque. Worshippers in the mosque drink Zamzam from hundreds of taps scattered all over the place. Zamzam water is regularly examined by the Ministry of Health and is sterilized three times, the last by ultraviolet rays. The holy water is considered to have healing power, making it a favorite carry-home item. People at the receiving end back home eagerly partake of it, especially the sick and the infirm. A common sight at the airports is pilgrims carrying large plastic containers of water.

Exploring the rooftop of the mosque, what struck us was the view of the Kaaba below. It seems as if people are standing on a moving platform circling the Kaaba. It is quiet, distant, open, and an entirely different experience compared to sitting close to the Kaaba in the courtyard.

We stayed in the mosque until 9:30 p.m. and then headed out to the bus stop. Vendors dressed in long robes lined up the streets selling prayer rugs, prayer beads, scarfs, dates, prayer books, doing brisk business. Buying souvenirs during the hajj is a tradition keenly observed by pilgrims, who spend millions of dollars in this holy city every year. In between performing prayers and religious rituals, the pilgrims become shoppers, to the delight of Mecca's merchants. Some pilgrims, mainly from Africa and the former Soviet Republics, even manage to combine their religious duty with trade, displaying handicrafts and prayer rugs on the roads leading to the mosque. While some shops were feeling the pinch of the global economic slowdown, the US fast-food chains in the holy city buzzed with pilgrims queuing in their white robes for a quick fix of McDonald's, Kentucky Fried Chicken (all halal, same menu as in New York minus the bacon), and Baskin-Robbins.

Our bus was late. Meanwhile another bus came. The driver, who spoke some English, told Khalid that he is welcome to go in this bus.

"What about our baggage?"

"Don't worry about the baggage, it will get there," he assured Khalid.

"No, I don't think so. I have items in my baggage that I need right away, and I don't want to risk it," I said.

A few minutes later our bus arrived. It was parked at the other side of the street. We had missed out on that part of the instructions, which were in Arabic. The traffic was so congested that it is a marvel that anyone got through. Cops were busy directing and moving the traffic, but they must absolutely disallow single-passenger cars in this area. One of the sights new to me was cops and workers wearing face masks. Many pilgrims were wearing face masks to protect themselves from catching an unwanted virus. Our group had made the masks available to us, but I chose not to use it. For one thing, I have difficulty breathing, and then I feel that I am being disrespectful and rude.

We were waiting by the roadside when Tariq called again on the cellular phone.

"We are still in Mecca," Khalid said. Tomorrow being the Arafat day, we asked him to call us the day after tomorrow.

An old Pathan man came up to us. He was lost. He kept saying in Pushto that he wanted to go to Arafat. He tried to get onto our bus, but the bus driver wouldn't let him. He had no ID on him and no bracelet. I wonder what became of him. He was old and frail.

We arrived in Mina within half an hour. Authorities had laid out forty-four thousand air-conditioned tents. After a fire broke out in Mina a few years ago, the government installed fire-retardant tents. The hi-tech fiberglass Teflon-coated shelters are equipped with sprinklers, air coolers, and fire extinguishers. All two million pilgrims will spend the night in Mina as they prepare for the next day's standing in prayer on Mount Arafat. King Fahd and Crown Prince Abdullah have instructed government officials to exert maximum efforts to help the pilgrims perform their religious duties in ease and comfort. Two million people on the move means: congested highways, fatigue, sunstroke, lost pilgrims, and the responsibility to feed them and house them. Hajj transport companies readied 13,500 buses to carry the faithful to Mina and other holy sites. The Civil Defense Department deployed a fleet of nine helicopters for rescue missions and monitoring pilgrim movement. It also deployed 250 fire-fighting units.

Mina

It was dark, and the place was illuminated by the glow of white tents lined up row after row as far as the eye could see. The conical tops of the tents had openings for ventilation. The symmetrical rows gave an orderly look to the place. But what moved you was the sight of those who were camped out in the open. People who cannot afford a tent just camp out wherever they can find a nook or corner. Rows and rows of people sleeping on mats on the ground, sitting in groups and chatting, eating dinner by the roadside, some sleeping under the bridge, pilgrims everywhere, in white. Remember, in the movie *Gone with the Wind*, the scene at the railway station where the camera zooms out and the screen is filled with the wounded lying on the platform? That is how expansive it was, except that these were not the wounded but pilgrims catching up on their sleep. How powerful that feeling, how strong the pull, that people with little means will spend their last penny and be willing to sleep on the sidewalks, completely exposed, using their baggage for a pillow, just to be here at God's service.

While we were taking in the sights, our bus driver was busy getting lost. By now we were tired and wanted to get to our tents. *Patience does it!* We spotted the sign of Al-Itteqan outside a cluster of tents. Everyone yelled out to him. Now he didn't know how to get there. So at the first clearing he found, he just stopped. That was it. Khalid took it upon himself to open the luggage compartment of the bus, and everyone helped themselves to their bags. *Now, how do we get to the tent?*

It was dark. We had to lug our bags and make our way through the pilgrims sleeping on the streets, being careful not to disturb them. We kept reminding ourselves to be grateful that eventually we would have a roof over our head unlike these pilgrims sleeping in the open with no protection.

Khalid was not a happy camper. As soon as we reached Al-Itteqan, a porter in uniform leaped toward us to greet us and handle our baggage. It didn't do much for Khalid. His looks said it all: Where were you when we needed you? The place was all lit up and welcoming. Banners, signs, lights, all the regalia that goes along with a welcome. The gentleman that we had met at the Al-Itteqan office was standing by the doorway. Khalid immediately let him know just how disappointed he was in their service. "*Astaghfaar,*" he kept saying (forgive me). "We will talk later," Khalid said as we moved on. You can bet on that.

I went past a curtain and entered the ladies' courtyard. Tents surrounded a clearing, which had the *wudu* area and bathrooms. Looked pleasing. I wondered if Nadia was still up. I was in tent number five. As I walked in the tent, I found most of the women sleeping. Nadia had stayed up for me. Oh, what a joy to see a familiar face. And then another. A woman in the corner spoke up. "Are you Sabeeha? I know you. I work at King Faisal and I see you in the prayer room every day."

My first order of business was to take a shower, re-enter the state of *ihram*, and make the intention for hajj.

"OK. So where is my kit?"

"What kit?" asked a sleepy-eyed girl.

"My toiletries, towel, and sheets."

"Well, no one gave us any toiletries, but there are your sheets."

"I had to fight for towels, and I saved one for you," that was Nadia, as she handed me my towel.

Since the agent had told us not to bring toiletries, I hadn't. I could have, it wasn't a big deal. So, I walked out to the men's area or common area and sought out a familiar official.

"I need my toiletries kit." My tone was demanding.

"Excuse me," and he went running to get an English-speaking person.

"Can I help you?"

"Yes. May I have the toiletries kit?"

Blank look!

I wasn't giving up. "Toothpaste, toothbrush . . ."

"Of course. One minute please." He actually ran and came back running with the most beautifully gift-wrapped package. No one had ever given me toothpaste with such a fancy wrapping. Now I was embarrassed. I was only trying to . . . well . . . never mind. When I walked back into the tent, all the women, who were up by now, thanks to my late arrival, squealed. Funny how ladies, no matter how old, still squeal.

"How did you get that?"

"I asked."

"Wait till you see the bathrooms. They are an experience."

They were indeed. Very clean, well-maintained, well-stocked with all the toiletries (except toothpaste), clever use of space, quite a novel design, but an experience nevertheless. They were topless. Get the idea? Hint: picture stars.

Nadia told me of their experiences the previous day. They had selected this agent because they were the only agents who guaranteed a wheelchair and an escort for her husband. Nadeem is unable to walk long distances. They had charged a big sum for that service. Well, when they arrived at the Grand Mosque, the escort was not there. No one knew what they were talking about. Nadeem showed the agent the contract and they then assigned an escort. When they arrived at the entrance of the mosque, that person refused to go farther, saying that he did not have an *iqama* and couldn't risk going past security. An undocumented! He took off with the wheelchair and left them stranded. Then they had to scramble. The mosque also provides wheelchair service, but you have to go through a multitiered process. They were running out of time to catch the bus to Mina. They eventually made it but were completely stressed out, exhausted, and distressed. The agent later apologized and promised not to let it happen again.

I entered into the state of *ihram* and made my intention for hajj. I offered thanks to God for our safe arrival and prayed for our safety for the remaining period. I felt guilty getting upset over the minor inconveniences along the way, which now seemed trivial. As I lay down on my comfortable mattress and pillow, and new linen, my thoughts again went to the people on the streets who lay on concrete ground with a straw matting for a mattress, their bags for a pillow, and no privacy. How do I cope with that? Guilt? Charity? Gratitude? A woman sleeping next to me was not on a floor mattress. She had a regular bed. *Hmmm!* The last thought before I fell into grateful sleep, was the sight of a wheelchair in the corner of my tent.

Tomorrow we leave for Arafat after *Fajr* prayers, at 6 a.m. We must be in Arafat for *Zuhr* noon prayers for our hajj to be valid. I was now spiritually ready for the hajj, and we all turned in for the night.

Sweet dreams!

All the best,
Sabeeha

Arafat Day

Subject: Day 2 of Hajj

Dear All,

Thursday, February 21 (Dhul Hijjah 9)

Mina
In the morning, the courtyard was teeming with women, all lined up to take a shower, towels in hand. Yesterday they had on the veil and were anonymous. Today, they all had an identity. Most of them were blonde or light brunettes and were light skinned. They look European, but not quite. They chatted with me in English with an American accent

using American lingo; their style was western and sophisticated in their mannerisms and conduct. I continued to grapple with picturing these girls behind the veil. It didn't seem to fit with my stereotype. Back inside our tent, I got a glimpse of the woman next to me in the regular bed. She was handicapped. Before I could get to say much to her, the maids came in and whisked her off in her wheelchair to the bathroom.

At 6:30 an announcement was made over the PA system, in Arabic. Then the phone rang. These tents had house phones. It was Khalid. The announcement was that the buses were ready to leave and won't wait for us. We all darted outside. We ladies could venture into the men's area, but they cannot come into ours. Someone in charge was gesturing, hurry, come on, the buses won't wait. Out on the street, people were marching ceremoniously as they began their march to Arafat, walking briskly with a strong sense of anticipation. Someone led us out of the compound, and asked us to stand by a double-decker bus, which was running, emitting its exhaust on us. We stood there and waited and waited.

"Where is the bus that was leaving without us?"

"It is coming."

"Whose bus is this?"

"The princess's."

We had a princess among us. I had noticed a tent in our compound with the sign: VIP. Speaking of princesses, the king and crown prince had arrived in Mina to supervise the hajj operation.

We waited and waited. We could not move from where we were standing because the street had become extremely congested. Imagine two million people leaving Mina. Trucks, buses, pedestrians, everyone was out on the streets making their way to Arafat. Every inch of street space was taken up. No wonder our bus was late, but then they should keep track of its location and bring us out accordingly. Another item to add to Khalid's letter. We also noticed that not many people from our group had lined up. They probably know better than to hurry up and wait. Eventually, our bus arrived and we took our seats and headed to Arafat.

Arafat is seventeen kilometers (a little under ten miles) east of Mecca. It is usually a fifteen-to-twenty-minute drive. It took us an hour, and for those who came later it took several hours. Thousands just walked. The white sea of faithful was surging to Mount Arafat. Waves of men in seamless white robes and women in long dresses joined voices in a crescendo chanting, *Labek Allahumma Labek*. Although many in the crowds were wearing white, it was a colorful scene due to the proliferation of umbrellas and flags. The flags were either banners adorned with religious verses or standards of national identity. Group leaders carried the flags to keep the pilgrims together. Some group leaders were holding aloft makeshift identifiers, such as a shoe nailed to a stick. In another attempt, people were walking hand in hand, loudly chanting the *talbiah*. Every pilgrim was wearing an identifying bracelet. Most also had an identification card tucked into or pinned to their *ihram*. We all did. The bracelets and cards contained all their identifying details including blood type, written in both English and Arabic.

Arafat

This is where Prophet Muhammad delivered his last sermon when he performed his first and the only hajj. On the *Jabal-e-Rahmat*, mountain of mercy, is where it is believed that Adam and Eve were finally reunited after having been expelled from the *Jannah* and separated from one another, and where we will all congregate on the Day of Judgment. Here in Masjid Nimra, pilgrims will offer combined *Zuhr* and *Asr* prayers. Here pilgrims will stand in prayer from dawn to dusk. This day is the climax of hajj.

Simple tents served as resting areas. One could see pilgrims resting or eating in these tents. The camp managers keep tight control over which pilgrims are allowed to use the shelters.

The bus dropped us in front Al-Itteqan's tents. By some fluke, they ran out of space in the women's area and had to assign us to a VIP tent in the men's VIP tent area. Pretty fancy, with sliding doors, settees arranged around the walls, air cooler running, and a picnic box stocked with ice-cold drinks.

As soon as Nadia and I settled down, they brought us boxed breakfast and hot beverages. Wondering whatever happened to the lady in the wheelchair and two others from our tent in Mina, Nadia and I settled down to read the Qur'an. In a short while, the two Saudi ladies from our tent in Mina came in. They were upset at being put in the men's area. One of the women was very young, petite, with a light complexion and dark hair. Her sister-in-law was tall, big, and blond. They shut the sliding door, removed their veils, and sat down to read the Qur'an. (They weren't supposed to be wearing the veil.) They kind of kept to themselves but by the time we parted, they had thawed, and we actually got to know each other. Nice girls. The younger one is a student of art and plans to go into teaching.

At 11:30 Khalid knocked on our tent. He and two of his companions were going to walk over to the Masjid Nimra for *Zuhr* prayers. Did we want to come? Or would we rather pray in the tents. Both Nadia and I leapt at the offer.

We had to make our way through the alley—a dirt road. On the roadside, pilgrims had taken their place, suspended a mat for cover from the sun, and were immersed in prayer. We walked past a large outdoor kitchen where lunch was being cooked, free of cost, courtesy of Saudi government. One of Khalid's companions, Shahid, would turn out to be everyone's guardian angel. We eventually found ourselves at the edge of Arafat in the plaza outside the mosque. The place was teeming with pilgrims. The sun was very strong and even though we carried umbrellas, it felt very hot. Beggars were all around, vendors selling their wares, trucks handing out free boxed lunches, water trucks handing out ice packs that one can drink when thawed, trucks and vans of corporate sponsors giving out juice, food, ice cream, you name it. Often, it lacked organization. A group of workers tossing ice cream bars from the back of a truck nearly caused a stampede. The pilgrims would hold the plastic-wrapped ice against their foreheads until it started to melt and then would drink the delicious cool water. There was no shortage of food. Prepared meals had been brought in from as far away as Jeddah. No one went hungry that day.

As we got closer to the mosque, we realized that we would not be able to get inside. People were already camped outside.

"I don't think I can sit outside in the heat. Why don't the two of you stay, and we ladies will head back."

"You will get lost," Khalid cautioned.

We relented and took our place in the plaza. Later, I was glad we stayed. Shahid had a floor mat and we opened our umbrellas, took a sip of water, and sat down. Fortunately, they have installed sprinklers that spray a fine mist of water that is soothing. We watched the personification of the glory of Islam. Old men, hobbling on their sticks, finding their way; hunched-back little old ladies, looking around for a place to sit, young men carrying toddlers on their shoulders, mothers sitting and nursing their babies, the blind, the lame, the infirm, the young, everyone was congregating here to glorify God. Some pilgrims had come in family groups where three generations of relatives were performing the pilgrimage together, sharing guidebooks for the rituals, immersed in prayer. People of all nations, of all colors, all races, had come together to stand in service of the one God. The sun was blinding, the heat intense, and the faithful, especially the elderly, had to struggle to perform their acts of worship. Pilgrims were clustered around water mist sprayers, taking what relief they could.

When I did my first hajj in 1986, there was no electricity in Arafat; there was no misting system. Hajj that year was in August. Pilgrims could be seen collapsing throughout the day, overcome by heat stroke. Dramatic improvements have been made since then. The water misters not only cool the pilgrims, they help keep down the dust, a known vector for disease transmission. You could see people wearing protective masks. And then the imam's voice was heard over the loudspeaker and a quiet descended on the congregation as he began his sermon.

Prophet Muhammad had delivered his last sermon here on the Jabal Rahmat mountain, fourteen hundred years ago. Some excerpts from his sermon that are widely quoted:

"Oh people, lend me an attentive ear, for I know not whether after this year, I shall ever be among you again [he passed away soon after]. *Just as you regard this month, this day, this city as sacred, so regard the life and property of every Muslim as a sacred trust. Return the goods entrusted to you to their rightful owners. Hurt no one so that no one may hurt you. Remember that you will indeed meet your Lord, and that He will indeed reckon your deeds. . . . It is true that you have certain rights in regard to your women, but they also have rights over you. Remember that you have taken them as your wives only under Allah's trust and with His permission. . . . Do treat your women well and be kind to them, for they are your partners and committed helpers. . . . All mankind is from Adam and Eve, an Arab has no superiority over a non-Arab, no non-Arab has any superiority over an Arab; also a white has no superiority over a black, nor a black any superiority over a white, except by piety and good action. . . . All those who listen to me shall pass on my words to others and those to others again; and may the last ones understand my words better than those who listened to me directly. Be my witness, O Allah, that I have conveyed your message to your people."*

The imam's sermon was in Arabic. I read the English translation in *Arab News* the next day. Here is an excerpt of what was reported:

"Delivering the Arafat sermon, the Kingdom's Grand Mufti, Sheikh Abdul Aziz al-Sheikh, strongly defended Islam against terrorism charges made in the wake of the September 11 attacks. 'It is unfair to associate Islam with terrorism,' he said. 'Terrorism equals tyranny and injustice, and these are alien to Islam. How can terrorism be linked to a religion that orders respect for human life . . . a religion that advocates justice and promotes peace rather than war? Islam strictly forbids the killing of women, children, and innocent people.' He also urged Muslims not to pin the blame for all their woes on others. 'What is happening to us was (partly) caused by our sins. It is unwise and irrational to blame our enemies for everything that harms us. Weak faith, disputes, and differences among us are other causes,' he said."

We stood in prayer as the imam lead the *qasr* prayer (shortened prayer for travelers) for *Zuhr*, and then the prayer for *Asr*. As soon as the prayer was over, people rose and started walking back and chanting, "*Labek Allahumma Labek*." The sound and sight brought tears to my eyes. Nadia and I looked at each other, grateful that we had stayed. We filed out with the million others and started walking back. It was a slow walk, an orderly walk, people keeping pace with those ahead of them—amazing that, with so many people, in such intense heat, there was no expression of impatience or a hurry to find shelter. It was the most exemplary display of discipline and devotion. Slowly people walked back, chanting *Labek Allahumma Labek*. Soon, it seemed as if the whole valley was echoing with the sound of *Labek*.

On the walk back, I got separated from the other three. I raised my Al-Itteqan umbrella way up and Khalid was able to find me. Back in the tent, they had our lunch ready for us, and the cool air in the tent was a Godsend. Bathroom facilities in the ladies' section were very adequate, and I was able to take a shower. At 2:00, the three missing women from our tents showed up, huffing and puffing. The lady who is paraplegic had opted to leave on the last bus, assuming that the crush of crowds wanting to leave first will have ebbed. It didn't work. The traffic was worse as the day wore on, and it took them five hours to get here. They were stressed out at the thought of getting in late and missing the hajj. Fortunately, it was still Zuhr time. Another two-hour delay, and they would have missed the hajj. In that case, one has to do the hajj again another year.

I stepped outside and raised my hands in prayer. I prayed for my parents, my children, my husband, my family, friends, colleagues, our nation, for Muslims, for humankind; for peace, for forgiveness, for a place in heaven, for a virtuous life. . . . I had requests for prayers from people who had asked that I pray for them: for his son's health, for her daughter to find a good husband, for ease from financial hardship. . . . I pulled out the list and went through it, line by line, to make sure I don't miss anyone. After all, at my age, one has gotten to know a lot of people, and it's a nice long list of people to pray for.

I would later read that tears rolled down the cheeks of pilgrims as they climbed *Jabal-e-Rahmat*. The mountain was dotted with pilgrims in white who sat or stood there for hours contemplating and praying. Standing at Mount Arafat in prayer before sunset on this day is the high point of the hajj. It is a sublime moment, perhaps the most sublime in a Muslim's life. Oblivious to all that is going on around them and in utmost tranquility, the pilgrims, black and white, rich and poor, women and men, young and old, extend their arms to Almighty God and pray for His mercy. It is this genuine call for deliverance that is the very essence of the hajj.

At a clinic on the outskirts of Arafat, the medical staff was busy but not overwhelmed. Most of the pilgrims receiving treatment were elderly. Despite numerous advisories, pilgrims often underestimate the stamina that will be required to complete the acts of worship. They do not prepare their bodies in the months before hajj with proper nutrition and exercise to cope with the strain.

The Anti-Begging Department rounded up fifty female beggars on Tuesday in Arafat.

Muzdalifa

At 5 p.m., we were told to board our bus. We knew full well that it wouldn't leave before 6:30. Pilgrims must leave Arafat after sunset. However, we preferred to sit in the bus and read the Qur'an than have to wait on the clogged street for a later bus. Glad we did that. The bus left at 7 p.m., and at 7:30 we were in Muzdalifa. For many, it took longer. Even for those on motor bikes and scooters, the journey to Muzdalifa, which normally takes just a few minutes, lasted two hours. As the evening wore on, some pilgrims in Arafat got agitated as they realized they could not find their transport. Many gave up and simply walked. In the twilight, all one could see was waves of pilgrims in white. Men and women, men with children on their shoulders, men and women with walking canes, old and young, walked to Muzdalifa, as we watched from our comfortable air-conditioned buses. Such a display of devotion and purpose.

Our bus stopped at a clearing fenced by a row of trees. Floor rugs were spread out, and we all sat down for a night under the stars. Bathroom facilities were nearby. The first order of the evening was to say combined *Maghrib* and *Isha* prayers. We said our prayers on the rug out in the open, as did everyone else. Boxed dinner was served, after which we collected our pebbles. The agent had given us pouches. You must collect at least forty-nine tiny pebbles to stone the pillars signifying the devil over the next three days. A serene night under the stars, so dark and quiet that the only sight was the silhouettes of people stooping to gather pebbles and the only sound that of the pebbles, *tick, tick, tick*.

Immersing myself in prayer, I held my lighted magnifying glass to read the pocket-size Qur'an in the dark. The night was cool, you are under the stars, sitting on the earth in the most sublime of nights, when all one does is take in the quiet night and commune with God. Everyone around you is absorbed in the same activity; the air is still and quiet. Isn't it marvelous that with two million people out in the open in one place, there is no noise, no chaos, no rowdiness, no negative energy whatsoever. Just everyone, doing their own thing, in peace and quiet.

All the best,
Sabeeha

♦ ♦ ♦

Here is a bit that I did not include in my email to my family and friends:

"See, they are taking their birth control pills," Nadia pointed out the ladies sitting on the rug not too far from us. I had remembered to take mine. I was not on birth control pills but had asked my doctor to prescribe them for hajj, to stop the menstrual flow. It is believed that a woman cannot perform the *tawaaf* if she is menstruating. In days gone by, women would perform the hajj in their later years, after menopause.

* * *

Eid Mubarak, Stoning, and Sacrifice

Subject: Day 3 of Hajj

Dear All,

Friday, February 22 (Dhul Hijjah 10)

Mina

We arrived in Mina early in the morning, the day of Eid-al-Adha. Today we walk in Prophet Abraham's footsteps. We stone the devil to commemorate his defiance of the devil when the devil tried to dissuade him from obeying God. This ritual, called *Rami*, is carried out by stoning three pillars—the *Jamaraat*—signifying the devil. Three times the devil had tried to prevent Abraham from carrying out God's command, hence the three pillars. And we sacrifice a lamb, as he did. We then cut our hair; women cut just a lock, many men shave their heads entirely, the preferred way. With that, we come out of the *ihram*, partially, until we have performed the *Tawaaf-e-Ziyarah*—the *tawaaf* of hajj (also called *Tawaaf al-Ifadah*).

The three pillars of the *Jamaraat* stand at a distance from one another. *Jamaraat* is the plural of *Jamraah*, which means "pebble." Today we stone only one pillar, the *Jamaraat Al-Aqaba*. Tomorrow and the day after we stone all three. The pillars rise through an opening in an overpass above. The overpass is a pedestrian walkway and serves as a second level for the stoning. This is the most challenging ritual because of crowding around the pillar. The overpass is restricted for that reason, and therefore less crowded. You can give your proxy to someone else to do the *Rami* for you if you are infirm. Many people exercise that option.

As the four of us started walking toward the overpass, bags in hand, the cops stopped us: no bags allowed on the overpass. Nadia's bag was small, and so they let her and Nadeem go, but Khalid and I had to go to the lower level—the crowded one. We were worried about Nadia and Nadeem being on their own. Hundreds of thousands of people were walking to the *Jamaraat*. We pulled out our pebble pouches. As we began to near the *Jamaraat,* the crowd swelled. Something comes over people when they come to the *Jamaraat*—they get aggressive. People who were so serene in Arafat and Muzdalifa, despite the crowds, get out of hand. In their eagerness to stone the devil, they exhibit a negative energy, unnecessarily pushing and shoving. One group held hands in a file, and then ran, charging through the people. Why? Anyhow, we made it to the pillar, which is surrounded by a low circular wall. As long as your pebbles fall within the periphery of the wall, consider the devil stoned. I said *Allahu Akbar* and prayed that God give me the strength to repel the devil, to prevent the devil from tempting me, and hurled my first stone, then second . . . and finally the seventh. I was done and so was Khalid. And people kept pushing. Then they started hurling shoes at the pillar with anger, cursing the devil. I am telling you, something devilish comes over them.

We made our way back to our tent and were greeted with a mini bouquet of flowers on each bed, and a velvet case with a bottle of perfume—a hajj gift. Nice welcome! Nadia and Nadeem made it back without incident. Thank God.

At 10 a.m., we were informed that our sacrifice of the lamb had been carried out at the abattoir. The majority of the pilgrims chose to have the ritual slaughter performed on their behalf by Islamic charities, as we had. But pilgrims have the choice to carry out the sacrifice themselves at the abattoir or allow the butchers to do it for them. The sacrifice ritual can be performed on the tenth, eleventh, or twelfth of Dhul Hijjah. One person can sacrifice a sheep, and seven or more people can sacrifice a camel. Scores of butchers attend to the sacrifices at any one of the nine abattoirs in Mecca and are expected to handle more than nine hundred thousand carcasses of animals. More than 70 percent of the meat is put into the hands of the Islamic Development Bank for distribution to Islamic countries and needy people in Saudi Arabia. The bank plans to distribute the meat of around 620,000 sheep, 40 percent of which will be shipped to twenty-seven countries in Africa and Asia. Six hundred shari'a students were appointed to ensure that the program was carried out in conformity

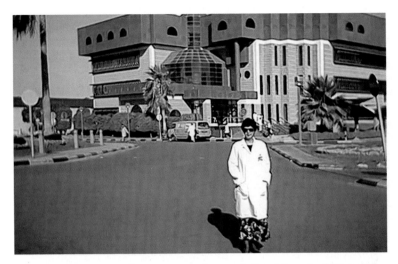

On the campus of King Faisal Specialist Hospital, Riyadh.

Hospital park on campus with Faisaliah Tower in the background.

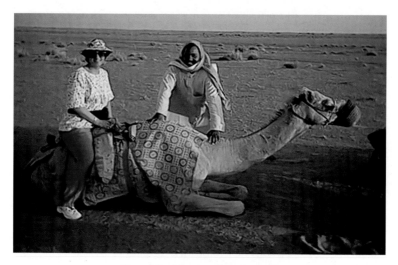

Camel ride in the desert.

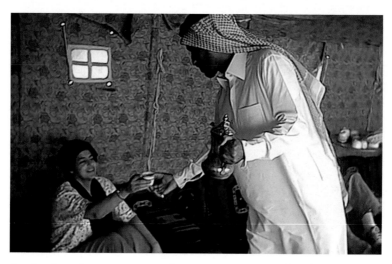

In the hot desert tent, ready to savor a cup of Arabian coffee.

Falcon ready to hunt.

Falcon, after pigeon hunt.

Sliding down the red sand dunes.

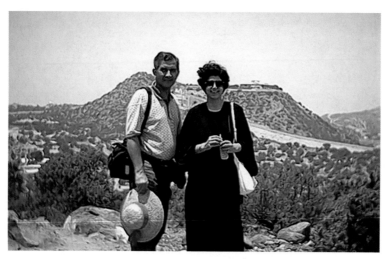

In the mountains of Abha with Khalid.

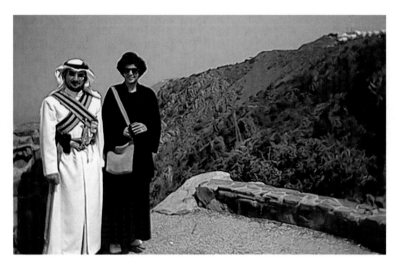

Ibrahim, our Abha tour guide.

Traditional Asir outfit.

Camel race in Taif.

Mama camel and baby camel in Hufuf.   Climbing a date tree in Hufuf.

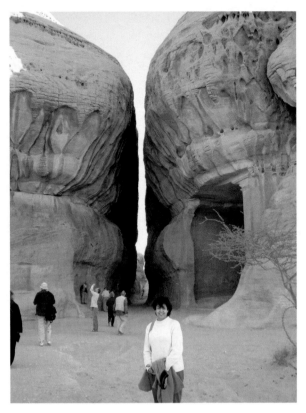

Mada'in Salih, archaeological site in the
Medina Province of the Hijaz.

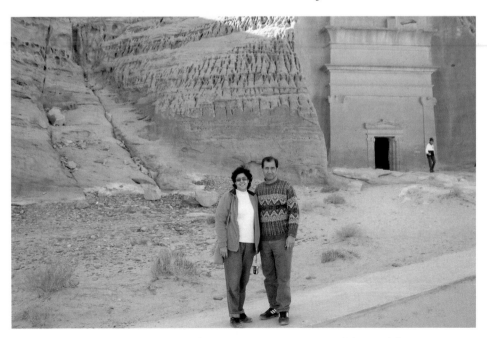

Dwellings carved from mountains in Mada'in Salih.

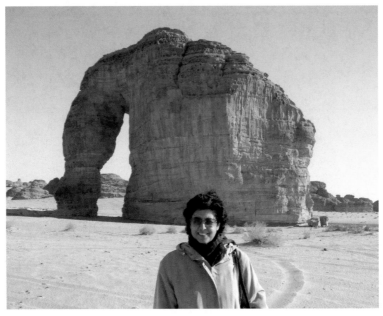

Mada'in Salih dates back to the Nabataean kingdom
(1st century AD).

The sand is their prayer mat. Khalid with the bedouins
and Sudanese tour guide.

with religious specifications. The bank has also appointed 1,100 veterinarians and 45,800 butchers, supervisors, and laborers.

Haircut time. Khalid and I gave each other a haircut. Shaving the head is not obligatory, but a sunna.* Partially out of the *ihram,* the men could now wear day-to-day clothes and shave. I could use perfume, not that I did.

Now it was time to wish everyone EID MUBARAK.

I called Khalid over the phone from the women's tent.

"I am watching the flow of Allah's servants," he said.

"What do you mean?"

"Come take a look."

Wow! A sea of people in white just flowing toward the *Jamaraat* so purposefully with their pebbles in plastic bottles. They walked in silence, millions of them, right in front of us. All walking in one direction, all going to stone the devil. Awesome sight! It was getting hot, so I retired to my tent, and all us ladies settled down to read the Qur'an.

The new tent city in Mina is impressive. All tents are air-conditioned, well-lighted, and carpeted. For journalists, the tents are equipped with telephone lines and a fax machine.

Tents can accommodate four to sixteen people. Mine had seven, others in our compound had fifteen to twenty people, depending on their package. Services are divided into six grades, from VIP down. A standard tent must have electricity, air coolers, and toilets nearby. There are more than sixty thousand toilets and showers in the city. VIP tents are hired out to couples who wish to remain together, at a cost more than SR 40,000 (approx. $10,000) with amenities such as TV and a regular bed. Our tent had floor mattresses, a mini fridge stocked with drinks, and intercom between the tents. There was very little floor space for our baggage, but we managed.

In the lower grades, however, tents accommodate up to fifty pilgrims. This costs SR 2,000 per person from abroad, less for people

---

* Sunna is the traditions and practices of the Prophet Muhammad.

living in the Kingdom. Pilgrims who cannot afford such expense sleep and cook on the streets and use public bathrooms.

Mina, hemmed in by hills, suffers from its limited size and the fact that all pilgrims must be together at the same time in the same place.

Outside the tents are huge numbers of food vendors. Tables were groaning under the weight of incredible amounts of food and beverages. Every imaginable type of edible was available except for western fast food. Shawarma grills were beside platters of biryani, which competed with fried chicken and batter-dipped vegetables. Cookies and fruit were piled in colorful mounds. Soft drinks and water were being hawked on every corner. All foodstuffs were price controlled, with maximum prices set in advance by the municipality. Even though hajj is only to be performed by those who are of means, beggars were everywhere. Some went to great lengths to disguise the fact that they were able-bodied. When offered food or water, they refused. They were only interested in cash.

With the huge crowds milling around, movement was a challenge. Police officers were clearly stressed as they attempted to keep traffic flowing. They did not want to be interrupted with questions and instructed people to just move along. Buses had to keep moving while passengers were trying to get in and out.

Around midday I called Khalid on the inter-tent phone.

"He is standing outside serving humanity," someone told me.

I have got to see this.

I stepped out in the blinding sunlight. Khalid was stationed outside the compound next to a giant board with the map of Mina on it, surrounded by lost pilgrims. They had come back after the stoning and had lost their way. Most were old men, most were Pakistani. Khalid was trying to link the information on their ID cards to the location on the map. He was soliciting the help of a guard from the tent who spoke only Arabic to decipher the Arabic notations on the map, getting someone to translate the guard's Arabic to English, then he would translate English to Urdu or Punjabi. Some he had to redirect to the Hajj Ministry Lost and Found office across the street, and it was heart-wrenching to watch the old men, tired and fatigued, struggling with their canes.

As we women sat in our tents reading the Qur'an, we got to know one another. Someone would pause and ask a question related to a Qur'anic verse, and we would join the discussion. This went on for most of the day. I was amazed at the handicapped lady who had made it to the hajj. Saba contracted polio at the age of two and was left paraplegic. She is a mother of two, and her husband is a doctor, who also contracted polio and has a clubbed foot. In Arafat, as he helped her out of the wheelchair, they both fell on the grass and burst out laughing. They are accompanied by another couple, who made this pilgrimage to enable Saba to complete the hajj. Both couples are from Pakistan but live in Saudi Arabia. The fifth woman, single, also of Pakistani origin, kept to herself, immersed in the Qur'an. Admirable. By the end of the day, the ladies were trying to find a suitable match for her.

In the adjoining larger tent, a female speaker was giving a talk on some religious topic in Arabic. We protested: we were told that the lectures would be in English. The coordinator smiled and said, "In sha Allah next year."

In the adjacent dining hall, breakfast was elaborate, so was lunch and dinner. Well, it was Eid, so they went all out. At first, I had refrained from eating raw vegetables, fearing contamination. But by now it was evident that the emphasis on hygienic food handling was beyond anything I had seen, so I relaxed. Even the plates were wrapped in cellophane in batches of twelve. No one got diarrhea. The dishes were a mix of Saudi and Western (i.e., foul and scrambled eggs for breakfast, lamb chops Saudi style, and fried shrimp for dinner). Hot and cold beverages were available around the clock.

Many people do the *Tawaaf Ziyarah* (hajj *tawaaf*) on this day. Our group's sheikh advised us against it stating that it was Eid and a Friday—which is not usually the case—the Grand Mosque would be too crowded, so we should go the following day. Today, in his Eid al-Adha sermon, Sheikh Saud-Al-Shuraim, the imam of the Grand Mosque of Mecca, highlighted the role of hajj in promoting unity and equality. "While performing hajj, a Muslim learns to respect the right of fellow Muslims. One who has performed hajj will not attack or harm anybody or do any injustice to others." Shuraim criticized international human rights organizations for being indifferent to the killings of Muslims and the violation of their rights. He urged Muslims to follow Islamic teachings and keep away from internal wrangling and bloodshed.

King Fahd and Crown Prince Abdullah reaffirmed the Saudi government's commitment to the hajjis in their Eid-al-Adha message: "We consider it a great honor for being given the opportunity to serve the two holy mosques and receive the guests of God, the pilgrims."

The stoning at the *Jamaraat* continued all day with military precision. Lines of police directed the crowds. Security measures were stepped up and a fleet of ambulances was lined up, but there was little need for their services. Thousands of security men, paramedics, guides, and civil defense personnel stood guard as pilgrims came in and out of the *Jamaraat*. Helicopters constantly hovered overhead to monitor the huge crowds with the help of more than a thousand hi-tech cameras. Too often the pilgrims did not help themselves in the ritual. Many insisted on toting large bundles to the stoning. Women were seen approaching the site carrying children at hip level while balancing bundles on their backs. Actually, women were more aggressive during the ritual than men. Many pilgrims had ignored the Holy Prophet's example of throwing pebbles the size of a pea. Instead they were throwing large rocks, chunks of concrete, sandals, and even cell phones over the other pilgrim's heads. It's amazing that nobody got hit accidentally.

After stoning, those pilgrims who had not deputized the authorities to perform the sacrifice on their behalf proceeded to the abattoirs to personally perform the ritual. They slaughter the animals themselves by first invoking God's name (asking His permission) and then performing the slaughter in the prescribed manner to ensure that the animal feels as little pain as possible. Thousands queued at abattoirs on the outskirts of Mina. Small trucks brought the animals to the abattoirs where they were selected by the pilgrims. The poor of Mecca congregated to take away their share of the meat, and there was a long line of refrigerated trucks standing by to distribute the meat to charities in the city and beyond.

Sunburn was one of the biggest problems the clinics were dealing with. The pilgrims were also harming themselves by smoking. Even at Arafat pilgrims neglected their devotions in order to take a puff. No one appeared to be embarrassed at indulging in such an unhealthy habit in the course of performing rituals of intense spirituality.

After completing the rituals of the day, thousands of pilgrims lined up by the public phones to call home to wish family Eid Mubarak. Telephone cards were sold on the streets near the public phones. Many in the queues were women.

The Planning Ministry put the figure of pilgrims at 1,834,168, with 1,354,184 arriving from abroad. The majority of the domestic pilgrims were expatriates; I presume the locals had either performed the hajj, or, knowing that they can perform it anytime, had postponed it to a later date; whereas expats would like to avail the opportunity while they are still in Saudi Arabia.

Sixty-three pilgrims died. Most of the fatalities were over sixty and had died of a heart attack.

One of the pilgrims in our group was pickpocketed. Someone just ripped the string from around his neck and took off with his ID, *iqama*, cash, etc. He reported it and eventually his ID was recovered.

There are eight Sudanese maids that work round the clock in the ladies' area, supervised by a coordinator. They have been waiting on Saba, cleaning the tents, serving food, keeping the place clean, replenishing the supplies, food, toiletries, etc. A large plastic basin is being used for people to do their laundry. A clothesline is provided and clothes dry instantly. We are impressed by their service, despite the problems that we initially encountered. And we are grateful.

The Italian ambassador, Torquato Cardeilli, is among us (though not in our group) and is performing hajj, just three months after converting to Islam.

All the best,
Sabeeha

◆ ◆ ◆

Repelling the Devil, and *Tawaaf* of Hajj

Subject: Day 4 of Hajj

Dear All,

Saturday, February 23 (Dhul Hijjah 11)

I had gone back to sleep after *Fajr* prayer when the telephone rang. It was Khalid.

"Can you and Nadia come out? We need to do some consultation."

I donned on my cape, and we stepped out.

"We are thinking that we should go right now for the *Tawaaf-e-Ziyarah* to Mecca, so that we can be back in time for the *Jamaraat* in the evening. What do you think?"

"Fine," Nadia said, and I echoed her.

"Can you be ready to leave after breakfast, around 10:30 or so? Al-Itteqan is providing an escort with a wheelchair."

"We will be ready!"

"Go and come back safely; we will be praying for you," said Saba. The two Saudi ladies who by now had warmed up to us were reassuring us, "Don't worry if you are late. It will take you eight hours to get back. Just take it easy."

Muhammad, the escort, led us to the bus stop, which was all the way at the edge of town. It was a long walk, and a hot walk. We had our umbrellas to shield us from the sun, and water to keep us hydrated. We got onto one of the city buses, which took off right away. We got to Mecca at 11:30 a.m. We were still in the bus when Khalid's cell phone rang. It was his brother Tariq. They wanted to come and see us.

"We are in a bus to Mecca and will be back in the evening. See you then."

Mecca

Tawaaf-e-Ziyarah is the most difficult ritual of the hajj, entirely due to overcrowding.

Once we arrived at the Grand Mosque, we laid out our plan: we would split up, then meet on the steps outside Hotel Intercontinental. We had our cell phones. Good luck! *Allah Hafiz.*

Since Khalid, Nadia, and I were planning to do the *tawaaf* on the second level, which was covered, we gave our umbrellas to Nadeem to hold in his wheelchair. Mistake #1.

The three of us headed toward the Grand Mosque, entered through men and women entrances, met up, took the escalators up to the second level, and made our way to the starting point.

The Kaaba is situated in a courtyard of the mosque. People usually make the *tawaaf* here. In one corner of the Kaaba lies the *Hajar-al-Aswad*, the Black Stone. It is lodged in a silver encasing. The stone is believed to have fallen from heaven and has been part of the Kaaba since time immemorial. Recently, the stone was geologically examined and determined to be a meteorite. Prophet Muhammad, when he made the *tawaaf*, had kissed the stone. Since then, all pilgrims attempt to kiss the stone. Only a few succeed. You can see people lined up against the wall of the Kaaba for a chance to get to the *Hajar-al-Aswad* and kiss it. It is at this corner that the *tawaaf* begins.

There is a black line painted on the floor to enable pilgrims to identify the starting point. The same is marked on the upper level, and on the rooftop. You stop at this line, raise your right hand, look at the Kaaba in the direction of the *Hajar-al-Aswad*, say *Allahu Akbar*, lower your hand, make your intention, and begin circling the Kaaba counterclockwise. You go with the flow. You walk on the marble floor, which is cool to the feet even in the hottest of weather. The circle ends at this line. Each time you begin a new circle, you repeat this ritual. This is the point where you end your *tawaaf* after the seventh circle, after which you must walk away and say two *nafl* prayers.

The circumference of the upper levels is very large, since it is set far back. When the courtyard fills up, people perform the *tawaaf* on the upper level, which is less crowded, is covered, but takes longer. Much, much longer. The rooftop is even less crowded but is completely exposed to the sun.

No sooner had we gotten close to the starting point on the second level than it got crowded, and within minutes, we got sandwiched.

Nadia was holding onto my hand, I was holding onto Khalid's shirt, and it seemed like we would lose each other any second. For a few minutes we were just jostled from here to there without making any headway.

"Let's go on the rooftop," Khalid said. "I cannot concentrate on *tawaaf* under the circumstances."

"What do you say?" I asked Nadia.

"Let's go."

There on the rooftop, it was ninety degrees at 12 noon; the sun was at its peak. We realized our mistake in giving our umbrellas to Nadeem to hold. But there were no crowds, the marble floor was cool, and despite the heat and the very long *tawaaf*, we were able to concentrate as we circumambulated the Kaaba seven times. It took an hour and a half, and each time we reached the starting line, we felt a sense of exhilaration, one more round completed, with the grace of God. We stopped at the water coolers; when it was *Zuhr* time, we sat down with our fellow pilgrims and said our prayers and continued again. Here, on the rooftop level, no one attempted to segregate men and women during prayer time. I wondered if they would have separated us on the second level. We could see pilgrims making the circles on the level below us and below in the courtyard. And then, we were done. We said two *nafl* prayers and then decided that we would do the *saee* on the second level. I was afraid that we might get heat stroke up here. Mistake #2.

We took the escalator down to the second level and began our *saee* at the mount of Safa. We were to walk seven times between the hillocks of Safa and Marwa commemorating Hagar's search for water. It was not crowded, and we made our way across with ease until we started getting close to Marwa. Someone in front of us raised his hand, then another, and people stopped. Hands went down. People moved. Pilgrims had taken it upon themselves to caution people behind them when it got crowded. As the people neared the end of the first round, the path makes a U-turn from Marwa back onto the lane to Safa. It is in this U-turn that it gets crowded. As we continued forward toward the

U-turn, the crowd became impatient, and people started pushing. It got dangerous, and we were afraid that one false move and someone would get trampled.

"Let's go back upstairs," Khalid said.

By now the sun had lost its intensity. It took another hour and a half to do the *saee*.

"It's Nadeem!" Nadia exclaimed. There he was with Muhammad pushing the wheelchair, right ahead of us. In a minute, they were lost in the crowd. Now we knew that he too had done the *tawaaf*. We completed our *saee* before *Asr* prayers and made our way outside the mosque.

We passed by the station where the Zamzam water was being dispensed. Pilgrims who want to take back home large quantities of water line up here. We went through the shop-lined streets with pilgrims sleeping, praying, resting, talking, pilgrims everywhere. They were all out of the *ihram* now, in regular attire.

Not only are there 658 cameras installed at almost every corner of the Grand Mosque, but cameras are also mounted on the main streets and tunnels of the city and nearby holy sites. All the cameras are linked to the main control and command room where a 165-strong team of officers and technicians sit in front of seventy large television screens twenty-four hours a day. The cameras help security officials monitor the movement of pilgrims and act immediately in case of any eventuality, notably traffic jams and overcrowding. There was no sense of anxiety over a terrorist attack. A zoom-in on any event at any time will give an instant picture.

We all met up at Hotel Intercontinental, sat on the steps, and had lunch and rested our tired feet as we watched the pilgrims. We said our *Asr* prayers in the plaza outside the mosque and then headed to the bus stop.

Mina

What an adventure!

We couldn't get into a bus. Each time a bus came, and they just kept coming, lined up one against the other, the pilgrims would crowd the door and we would be left watching, while the bus filled up and pulled away. Bus after bus after bus. And we were left standing.

Now what!

So Khalid went and talked to the dispatcher.

No luck.

Finally, when the next bus pulled up, Muhammad stationed himself at the door with us by his side. As soon as the door opened, he partially got in, partially blocking the door, and then didn't move until the four of us had gotten in. Phew! Really, our group should have arranged this for us.

Khalid's cell phone rang. It was Tariq. He was calling from our tent site.

"I am on a bus on my way back to Mina."

"We will wait for you."

Just then we got stuck in traffic for an hour, getting us to Mina at 6 p.m. Then began the walk to our tent site. Officials were making announcements over loudspeakers in six different languages, instructing people to keep moving, not to linger after pelting the stones. I caught the announcements in Arabic, Farsi, Urdu, English of course, Pushto, Malay, and one other, perhaps Turkish. Every now and then a mini ambulance would make its way through the crowds, and everyone had to squeeze to let the vehicle through. We made stops to buy juice and water. Empty water bottles, juice boxes, food wrappers, shoes, plastic bags, anything and everything was thrown on the streets, and a row of sanitation men would descend on the street and scoop up and sweep away, despite the crowds. They just kept cleaning. There were garbage cans situated every few meters, but many pilgrims didn't even pay attention to them and simply discarded their trash anywhere. And there were vendors all over with their wares spread out on the ground on a colorful sheet.

Beggars were active, resorting to using their children to solicit alms.

Khalid's cell phone rang again.

It was Shahid. He was assuring Khalid that he was taking care of Tariq and his wife Meena, that they were comfortable, and take your time.

We continued to walk. It was now 6:30 p.m. We heard the *Maghrib adhan*, and people started making room on the streets to say their prayers. We quickened our pace to make it to the tent on time for prayers. It was a relief to get back, and we were so grateful. Muhammad was given a good send-off. What a nice man!

The tent went up in cheers when we entered.

"We have been entertaining Meena. Welcome back. Mubarak."

Meena had been waiting for me. I gave her a big hug and ran off to say my prayers. We then sat down just savored having made it so far. Meena had made friends with everyone, and there was a party going on inside the tent. We asked Al-Itteqan if it was OK to invite our guests for dinner, and they graciously agreed. Once we had gotten our strength back, it was time for the *Jamaraat*.

Shahid offered to handle Nadeem's wheelchair, and we all took off for the long march to the *Jamaraat*. It was less crowded now. Once we got to the ramp going to the upper level, we were stopped by the cops. "No wheelchairs on the upper level. Go down."

Now what!

We protested, reasoned, but a rule is a rule, whether you agree with it or not.

Saba had no choice. So she and her husband took the route down the ramp and Parveen and her husband accompanied them. Nadeem decided to walk on the upper level. But what do we do with his wheelchair? The cops refused to hold it for us. Then Shahid, our guardian angel, came up with an idea.

"I will hold onto the wheelchair; I did my *Rami* today. You all go ahead on the upper level, and I will meet you below the exit ramp."

Great idea. Nice of him.

So, the six of us proceeded up the ramp. This bridge is 1,600 meters long. Tariq and Meena were with us. We got to the small *Jamaraat* and threw seven stones at the pillar. It was not crowded. We prayed for God's help in giving us the strength to keep the devil away. Then the middle pillar, same ritual, no crowds; then the large pillar, same ritual, no crowds.

We walked down the exit ramp.

No Shahid.

Where was he?

We looked around.

No Shahid.

We waited a little.

No Shahid.

Did we get our signals crossed?

Tariq said that it is possible that he may have meant to meet us at the other end of the highway. So Khalid told us to wait and went to look for him.

We waited and waited and waited.

Half an hour later Khalid came back.

No Shahid.

We decided to head back to the tent. Tariq and Meena said their goodbyes and headed to their tent nearby. We were worried about Shahid, and we also wondered how Saba and Parveen had made out.

It was a while before Parveen came back, without Saba.

"Everything all right?"

"It was very crowded, and we got separated from Saba and her husband. She was worried sick."

"Does anyone know where Shahid went?" I asked.

"Yes. He was with us. He helped Saba and her husband do the first Rami, then he helped them do the second stoning, and all this time he also had the folded wheelchair with him. Then he saw a woman bleeding who was almost passing out, so he put her in the wheelchair and left."

Later we learned that Shahid had seen the wounded lady to her place, then went to meet us. We had gotten our signals crossed on the meeting point. He looked around for us for an hour, panicking and worried, unable to make a cell phone connection, and eventually gave up and came back, empty wheelchair in hand.

Everyone spent the next day thanking Shahid.

Think of the woman whom Shahid helped with the wheelchair. She will have some story to tell when she goes home. I can just imagine her saying, "I was bleeding, I was ready to pass out, I prayed to God to help me and just then a man emerged from out of nowhere with an empty wheelchair and offered it to me. Imagine, who walks around the *Jamaraat* with an empty wheelchair at 10 p.m. God answered my prayers and sent me an angel of mercy. . . . It was a miracle."

The spiritual and positive energy of the hajj brings out the best in people. They become God's vessels for mercy to mankind, and those of us who receive that mercy when we least expect it call it a miracle.

A baby was born in Mina yesterday, to an Egyptian pilgrim.

Tomorrow is our last day in Mina. Hajjis are required to leave Mina before sunset. If you are here after sunset, you must stay the night, do the *Rami* the next day, and only then can you depart. We have been told that tomorrow we have to do the *Rami* after *Zuhr*; board our bus after *Asr* prayer at 4 p.m. for Mecca, where we will do the farewell *tawaaf* and then head back home. We have a four-hour window in which all two million will be doing the *Rami*. That means crowds.

Hajj Farewell

Subject: Day 5 of Hajj

Dear All,

Sunday, February 24 (Dhul Hijjah 12)

This is the fifth and last day of hajj.

We were getting ready when an announcement was made over the PA system—in Arabic.

The phone rang. It was Khalid.

"You were right! There has been a fatwa issued this morning by the Ministry of Hajj. Residents of Saudi Arabia can do the *Rami* this morning. All others will do it after *Zuhr* prayer, after 12 noon."

I had been telling everyone over the last two days that it was quite likely that a fatwa would be issued that morning, extending the *Rami* time to include the morning. No one had taken me seriously.

"We want to go right now, before breakfast. Do you want to come, or would you rather give us your proxy?" asked Khalid.

188 | SABEEHA REHMAN

"We'll come."

I hung up the phone.

"Guess what everyone? We can do our *Rami* right now. That was a fatwa we just heard over the PA system," I informed our tent friends.

Now the ladies started questioning the fatwa.

"Is it really OK to change the rules?"

"Did the Al-Itteqan issue the fatwa for their own convenience?"

I checked into it. Al-Itteqan had nothing to do with it. It was definitely a fatwa from the Ministry of Hajj.

This was Khalid's take:

"Yes, rituals are important. But so is assuring the welfare and safety of people. And if, for the purpose of saving lives, you reduce the crowds by expanding the hours of the ritual, it is OK."

That explanation appealed to the ladies. Saba gave her proxy to her husband, and Nadeem gave it to Khalid.

We did our ritual and then headed on to Mecca and performed our farewell *tawaaf.*

Our hajj was now complete!

Mecca

What a feeling of exhilaration. But it's not the kind of feeling where one throws up one's graduation cap in the air or calls out in jubilation or waves a fist in the air, saying, *Yeah, I did it,* nor is it a sense of relief. Quite the contrary, a feeling of quiet descends on you, and you feel still, calm, and at peace. One feels light, rejuvenated, re-born, and humbled; immensely grateful, after having spent five days in a tent and seeing so many people with so many ailments and disabilities; overwhelmed at seeing the utter devotion of the pilgrims, and in awe of being a guest in the House of God amongst millions of devotees. What a blessing! What an honor! There is no experience like it. No one can appreciate it unless they live through it. The surge of adrenalin, the ease with which one dismisses discomforts, the stamina that one miraculously acquires, the sudden rush of emotion, so much positive energy, is a feeling one has to experience to appreciate.

We made our way out of the mosque and turned back to take one last look at the Kaaba and say our farewell.

Back in Riyadh

<u>Monday, February 25, and onward.</u>

The first day home all I did was sleep. We called Shahid. He was so sick you couldn't hear him. Nadeem called. Nadia had taken ill.

The next day I fell sick and for the next four days remained sick. Everyone, they say, gets sick after hajj. Our tentmates have been calling, and everyone we have talked to is sick. We will get over the bug, In sha Allah. It's only the flu.

Prince Naif has ordered that all security officers who have participated in the hajj operation be given hajj medals. The government declared that the hajj was trouble-free. The *Rami* passed without any incident, and there were no stampedes.

Considering that what we have here is two million people constantly on the move between the holy sites, the safety rate is nothing short of miraculous. The management of hajj by the Saudi government is a classic case of quality improvement. Each year, they learn from their experience and improve their management and services. They are considering building a monorail and streamlining the process to speed up procedures at the Hajj Terminal, which currently takes more than ten hours to process the pilgrims at the airport. We will be giving our feedback to Al-Itteqan to help them improve their services. They took very good care of us, but like all services, they can do better.

Newspapers are filled with personal interviews with pilgrims from every part of the world. The photographs in the papers are precious and worth saving. I have kept the clippings and am bringing them with me to the States.

We leave for the States early tomorrow morning. In sha Allah.

All the best,
Sabeeha

CHAPTER 9

Cultural Snapshots

A Gift from the King

Each time a Saudi person graduates from a university, the king bestows a gift on him or her. It's a parcel of land in the location of his or her choice, for him or her to keep. All land in the Kingdom is the property of the king. He has in turn allocated parcels to members of the royal family. If anyone needs to buy land, they must purchase it from the princes or princesses. Some people merely petition the king and ask for land, and he may bestow it as a gift to them. If one wants to construct a house, loans are available. Loans must be interest-free, but banks do charge an 8 percent fee for handling the loan. How about that!

No Alcohol

We knew that alcohol consumption was forbidden. But here is what we overlooked: Khalid had instituted "Universal Precautions" at the hospital in preparation for the JCIA survey.* In addition to handwashing,

---

* Joint Commission International Accreditation (JCIA) surveys are conducted by the Joint Commission, a US-based organization that accredits healthcare organizations.

he had the hospital order hand sanitizers in bulk from the hospital's procurement office in Maryland. Customs at Riyadh airport refused to release the shipment: it had alcohol. Hospital staff had to convince Customs that this was not for drinking. In case you are wondering, mouthwash containing alcohol is also forbidden.

No Morphine Either

When the Palliative Care program was put in place at the hospital, they ran into a snag. Palliative Care physicians rely on morphine for pain management of terminally ill patients. However, patients were reluctant to have this drug administered, believing that it was contrary to Islamic beliefs. The director of the program had the ulema issue a fatwa, allowing the use of morphine for terminally sick patients.

A Patient Patient

I needed surgery. For years I had been coughing, not constantly, but whenever I caught the flu the cough would kick in and last several months. That's right—months. I couldn't sleep at night; I'd be coughing in meetings, couldn't get in more than a sentence before I'd start coughing, and people around me would get uncomfortable and anxious. It was totally anti-social, not to mention how it made me feel physically. I had gone through all kinds of tests in the US, was told that I had a sensitive airway and would have to live with it. Now I was being put through the tests all over again.

I went to see an otolaryngologist, a young Pakistani doctor.

"I am going to order a CT scan," he said.

I groaned.

"CT is our gold standard," he said. "If we don't find anything, then we will leave it at 'sensitive airway.'"

I yielded.

The results came back.

"You have a fungus in your nasal cavity, the right side. You need surgery."

Finally, a diagnosis.

I made an appointment with Dr. Al-Karim, a very senior Saudi otolaryngologist.

"I have a fungus in my right nasal cavity. Here is the CT report," I said, handing it over to him.

"What is your problem?"

"I have a cough that won't go away. The CT shows I have a fungus."

"Why are you coughing?"

"Because I have a *fungus* in my nasal cavity. It's in the report I handed you. Please take a look."

More questions.

My answer: "I have a *fungus*."

Finally, he turned around, placed the report on the counter, read it along with his assistant, then turned back to me and said:

"It's a fungus."

Whoa!

"You need surgery."

I know.

The two of them huddled over the calendar and gave me the date for surgery.

"Will removal of the fungus cure my cough?"

"It might."

Well, fungus has to go, so let's hope it cures the cough.

Later that day, I told a Saudi male colleague that I was having surgery.

"Who is operating?"

I told him.

"No, no. You can't have him operate on you."

"What do you mean?"

"He will ruin your surgery. Don't let him touch you."

Gee! One of the most senior doctors.

I was pretty shaken up. I started making inquiries, and all reviews pointed away from this doctor. Then who? All references pointed toward a Sudanese doctor. So, I went to him.

Now, how do I explain why I don't want his boss to operate?

"I am scheduled to be operated by Dr. Al-Karim, but I would like *you* to handle my surgery."

"That's fine." No questions asked. *Phew!*

"Do you have a preference for an anesthesiologist?"

I didn't even know I had a choice.

I made contacts with the admissions office, and they arranged for a private room for me. My neighbor, a nursing director, arranged for me to meet the chief nurse of that area so that she could look out for me.

On the day prior to my surgery, Khalid accompanied me to the admissions office to have my paperwork processed. I sat across the table from the admissions officer, in my white lab coat, with my ID prominently displayed, filled out the form, and handed it over. He looked at it, put it aside, and then handed a form to Khalid.

"Please sign the consent form."

What?!

"*He* has to sign my consent form? *I* am the patient."

"Yes, but you are his dependent."

He was polite and was just doing his job.

He doesn't make the rules.

I am an administrator; I influence policy on medical care; and I cannot give consent for my *medical care!*

I yielded. And therein lies the problem. We yield for the sake of expediency, to not make waves in the sand dunes, to not be labeled a troublemaker . . . and guess what!

I had come across enough medical errors to know that there was a slight chance that I might end up being operated on the wrong nasal cavity. As soon as I was wheeled into the operating room, I started telling the OR staff around me: "It's this nasal cavity," putting my hand on the right side of my nose, instead of saying "my right side" and risking them confusing their right side with my right side. When the Swedish anesthesiologist walked in, I waved to him, "It's this side of my nose." He smiled. And then I went under.

The next day I wrote to my parents.

◆◆◆

April 7, 2002

Dear Mummy and Daddy,

Happy Birthday, Mummy!
I came home just a few hours ago after my surgery, and I am fine. Went smoothly. Normally, this is an outpatient procedure, but here they keep you overnight.

Saturday, immediately after surgery, I was groggy and completely knocked out. They had packed the nose so that I had to breathe through my mouth, which would get dry, but I wasn't allowed to drink water, and it brought the Karbala battlefield* to mind. But it passed. Khalid stayed at the hospital in my room that night. Even though the chair converts into a nice sleeper, he chose to sit up all night, because he didn't want to fall asleep in case I needed help. Every time I turned, he would jump up and be by my side. He nursed me all night. Every fifteen minutes, my throat would turn dry, and I needed a sip of water. And you cannot drink more than a sip, or you will throw up, so it had to be very measured. Nursing care at the hospital was very good but nothing like having Khalid by my side. At six in the morning, I insisted that I was much better, and he should go to sleep. He then pulled out the sleeper and took a nap. Today I am fine. The packing has been removed. I still

---

* Battlefield in Iraq where Prophet Muhammad's grandson Hussein and his family suffered from thirst in the scorching heat. The story of that suffering is related every year on his death anniversary.

have oozing and am still stuffy up in the nose, but so much better than yesterday. Khalid took the afternoon off and is home with me.

I will call tomorrow when my voice is better and I can speak clearly. But no need to worry—if I can write this long letter, I must be doing well.

Lots of love
Bia

♦ ♦ ♦

My cough didn't go away.

It was in 2016, when my memoir was published and I was scheduled to do a series of book talks and narrate the audio version, I turned to the ultimate healer: "Dear God, how am I going to give book talks with this cough. Please, do something. Cure me, please."

That is all it took.

Paradox of the Veil

Before we feel sorry for Saudi women, know that they don't feel sorry for themselves. They take pride in their values. From our perspective, we are outraged at what we see: a women oppressed. They don't see it that way. And by "they," I mean the women. So, who are we to judge?

I have observed veiled women who will staunchly defend their right to be veiled. I first encountered this phenomenon when I was taking an Arabic language class where a Saudi female teacher was going over the rituals of hajj with a group of women, Arab, Pakistani, and Indian. When she got to the prescribed attire for women, she said:

"Women are not allowed to cover their face during hajj."

The women erupted into loud objections, waving their hands.

"No way."

"We cannot reveal our faces."

"It's against Islam."

"No man should see my face."

Guess what the teacher did? Just take a guess. She backed off. She gave them an out.

"You have an option. As long as your veil doesn't touch your nose or any part of your face, you can keep it on. You can attach a nose covering that prevents the veil from touching your face," she said, gesturing to her nose.

That satisfied the ladies, and the teacher moved on. I used to wonder at the female guards at the Grand Mosque in Mecca who had these protruding devices on their noses with the veil draped over it.

After class, I stayed back to hang out with two of my Pakistani classmates whom I had befriended, hoping to get their reaction.

"If Prophet Muhammad established the rules of hajj and forbade women from veiling their faces, then why are we bending the rules?" one of the women who didn't veil asked the veiled woman. I leaned in to listen.

"No, no," the veiled woman responded. "That was a different time. *Zamana ab bara kharaab hai* (today we live in bad times). We have to protect ourselves against men of bad intent."

That was her belief, and no Saudi teacher was going to tell her otherwise. I kept my anti-veil opinion to myself. But I have to say that I was struck by their passionate defense of their belief, fighting for their right to conceal their faces, and prevailing. And these were young women—in their thirties. They didn't appear oppressed to me; they didn't seem voiceless to me. It was like: *No one's taking my veil away.*

Saudis are private, and one does not engage in probing questions about their beliefs and way of life; it feels intrusive and judgmental. So whatever impressions I gleaned were through observation or when the information was volunteered. So, if you ask me, "How does the younger generation feel about it?" or, "Do some women feel oppressed?" I have to say: I don't know.

On one occasion a woman volunteered to share her thoughts. She took the path of least resistance: wore it in situations where she was expected to be veiled and removed it when not. It was akin to adhering to a dress code and showing respect for the sensibilities of people. Consider western women who cover their hair when in audience with the pope. Pressure or respect? This reminds me of my mother in the 1950s, who would wear the burqa when she visited Multan where my grandparents lived. In that conservative city of Pakistan in those days, women were expected to wear a two-piece burqa in public (a cape covering the head and extending to the waist, and a buttoned-up gown from shoulder to the ankles). She would transition with ease from the fashionable woman in the military cantonment of Rawalpindi to the concealed woman in the bazaars of Multan. I was a little girl then, and my friends and I would put on the cape portion of our mother's burqas, veil our faces, and sneak out into the streets, feeling like grown-up ladies. A cousin of mine was so used to wearing the burqa that after marriage when her husband asked that she no longer wear one, she felt uncomfortable. She did remove it but at first had felt self-conscious and exposed.

Back to Saudi Arabia. One day, the veil got imposed on me. I had been taking Arabic classes when one evening, as I was leaving the school premises after class, I noticed the principal standing by the school gate.

"Sabeeha, you cannot go out like that."

"Like that" as in "unveiled."

A woman standing next to her beckoned me to follow her and took me into the office. She picked up a black veil from a pile, draped it over my face, and tied it around my head. *Consider it an adventure.* I stepped out. It was dark, the street was lined up with drivers waiting outside their cars to pick up the students. I saw my cab driver diagonally across the street and waved to him. He looked away. He didn't know it was me; he had brought me veil-less. I walked over to the car and called out, knowing that he would recognize my voice. He quickly jumped to open the car door, I took a seat, and even though he was practically our private cabbie, neither of us said anything about my new look.

Back home, I decided to surprise Khalid. Instead of letting myself in, I rang the doorbell. He found this veiled lady outside his door.

"Now you see me, now you don't," and I flipped off the veil. Khalid chuckled.

For as long as I was enrolled in these classes, I would put on the veil when stepping out of the car, off when indoors, back on when stepping out of the school, off in the car. Those were the rules of the school, and, like it or not, if I wanted to be a student there, I had to abide by the rules.

When I mentioned this to a Pakistani friend of mine who wore the veil, her response was:

"See! When you step out with the veil on, you feel protected."

I didn't feel protected. But I said nothing. If she felt protected, that's her conditioning. All I felt was: *How soon can I get this off my nose?* It felt stifling, it felt hot, and my driver cannot recognize me. Of course, in these COVID times, I had to get used to the mask. Yes, it's stifling, and it's hot, and yes, at times people don't recognize me despite my signature curly hair.

But I have a bigger issue with the veil, and that is one of principle. One evening I was hanging out in one of the compounds with my Pakistani friends, one of whom was veiled. At one point, she pointed to two men walking in the distance.

"That is Dr. Jamaal and Dr. Khan," she said.

That is when it struck me of the advantage she had over the men. She knew their identity, but they wouldn't know who *she* is. There was power in anonymity. And it wasn't fair. Concealed by the veil, she could observe without being noticed.

I respect the right of women to don clothing that conforms to their religious beliefs. But I draw the line at the veil. The face is your identity. To be accountable for your deeds, you must reveal yourself. Conceal your identity and you can get away with anything. And please give men more credit. Seeing a woman's face isn't going to make them go wild. Any restriction placed on women is—in my opinion—disrespectful to men. It's sending a message: men cannot be trusted, so cover your face. Really? I wonder if we need a masculinist movement, a men's lib of sorts, to level the playing field. How would women feel if men started veiling *their* faces, like bandits do? You'd never identify them in a line-up.

If I haven't convinced you of why the veil is problematic, how about this: One morning I heard that a man had entered the nurses' residence. Men are not allowed in the nurses' apartment building. That morning, the guard noticed that a person in a burqa leaving the nurses building was wearing men's shoes. He was apprehended, of course. Gave the hospital staff a lot to chatter about. And this is not the first time or the only place where this happens—the deception, that is. One of my colleagues told me that she went for *umrah* wearing the veil, riding in the front seat of the car with a male colleague driving. At the Mecca checkpoint her colleague said to the guard, "She is my wife." The guard wasn't going to ask her to reveal her face to compare it with her *iqama*. Women in Saudi Arabia date men—which they are not supposed to—under the cover of the veil, posing as a sister. In Pakistan, a terrorist tried to escape a police ambush by wearing a burqa. His shoes gave him away.

There is a reason why we have picture IDs.

There is a sad side to it too. This doesn't happen a lot, but when it does, it's heartbreaking.

In a meeting with a Saudi colleague, I noticed that he looked saddened.

"Is everything OK?" I knew him well enough to ask a personal question.

"My brother is sick. He is dying."

"I am sorry. Why don't you take a few days off and spend some time by his bedside."

"I have decided not to go."

"Why?"

"Out of consideration for my sister-in-law. You see," he paused. "I have never seen her face."

My eyes widened, and then I understood. He explained that his sister-in-law is spending every minute, day and night, by his brother's bedside. Being his wife, he felt that she had the first right to be with him, and his presence would mean that she would have to leave the room, and that would not be fair to her. So, it's best that he not impose on her time with her husband.

I came to my office and cried. Tears of compassion for my colleague, his sacrifice, and tears of frustration at the veil that separates brother from dying brother. Two days later, when I watched him sob at the death of his brother, I wept over the precious moments he gave up to respect the boundaries of the veil.

Two Faces of Women

One of my Arab American friends invited me to a party in her home—a woman's party. She wore the hijab. As the women started trickling in, I noticed that they were of Arab descent, all in the hijab. They emerged from their abayas wearing the most stylish clothing, some in miniskirts, and with their hair highlighted in streaks of brown and gold, styled to perfection. After a while I went looking for my host. I couldn't find her. Then I heard her voice coming from the dining room. I followed the voice and there she was, totally unrecognizable in her flowing blonde hair. I kept staring, trying to match the hijabi woman I knew with this utterly gorgeous blonde.

Women Power

I would often tell my friends in the US: "Mark my word. When change comes to Saudi Arabia, it will be women that make it happen." The women at the workplace were beyond excellent. Meet Farah: she headed the Appointments department, the most complex operation of the hospital. She knew how to manage a vast cadre of staff, keeping the patients and doctors happy, and was articulate, warm, friendly, good at heart, and a thorough professional. If that wasn't enough, she was also gorgeous, as in flowing hair (no hijab), big round brown eyes, tan complexion, chiseled features, and slim and tall. And she commanded respect. Meet Afroze, the head of Patient Relations. Now here was a woman who knew how to diffuse a patient's anxiety, comfort and reassure, and wore her mantle with pride. IT was loaded with Saudi women, energetic and driven. And it's not just the case with King Faisal Hospital; I noticed the same at the Arabic language school. The women ran a tight operation, were skilled at teaching, pleasant demeanor, and always working. I never saw them lounging around, socializing, or in downtime mode. Overall, in terms of diligence, women exceeded men. Sorry, guys!

It's All in the Name

Have you noticed that Saudis have long names? The first name is the personal name, the second is the father's name, and third is the name of the tribe. So you have Fahad Hussain Al-Saud. Some will add the grandfather's name: Fahad Hussain Kareem Al-Saud. Lineage is sacred; and in a tribal culture, your tribe denotes who you belong to and where you came from. Sometimes a conjunction word is added between two names as in Mohammad bin Salman, *bin* meaning "son of": Mohammad, son of Salman.

No Representation without Taxation

Saudis will not criticize the royal family. Not their extravagance, not their tight control over freedom of speech and assembly, not their double standards, not their flaunting of the law, not anything. Let me put it this way: they won't express it and definitely not with expats. So, any discussion with Saudis about policy is off the table. This remains one of my regrets: I could never have a heart-to-heart with a Saudi on politics, policy, and culture.

It was the cab drivers. They would impart information that we were not privy to in the sheltered environs of our compounds and the hospital campus. Mostly expats, as in Pakistani, Bangladeshi, Indian, they had their hand on the pulse. And they had their gripes, which we didn't because of how well we were treated. This is what we heard:

"They have been drugged in sweet opium."

"The royal family gives handouts, keeps them dependent and grateful, does not tax them, and in return, people accept their authority and keep quiet."

"They are not required to put in the hard work. Expats like us do all the work. Why would anyone complain if you get paid for no work?"

"They have given so much power to the *kafeel*. I do the work and my *kafeel* makes all the money. There are many people I know who don't get paid on time; the *kafeel* holds onto their wages, giving them a tighter grip on their employees, and there is nothing the employee can do about it. Anyone who holds so much power is bound to be content."

A *kafeel*: The *kafala* is a foreign worker sponsorship system. You cannot get a work visa unless someone sponsors you—a *kafeel*. The *kafeel* owns the worker who is tied to him. The *kafeel* controls their wages, their exit and re-entry visa, and alone can renew or terminate the worker's residency and work status; and without his approval, one cannot switch jobs between employers.

"The labor class is exploited here. We put in long hours, and our employers hold onto our pay. Every time we remind them, they say, *Bookrah In sha Allah* [tomorrow, God Willing]. If my family back home wasn't so poor, if job opportunities there weren't so dire, I wouldn't work here."

Tariq, one of the Haala Cab drivers, gave us a glimpse into his life. He was from Bangladesh. He lived in cramped housing and sent his earnings home to his family. Every few years, he saved enough money to buy back the taxi car, sell it, and then go home for a brief visit. He missed his family, but his earnings have gotten his children through school, and they own their house. That he says is the story of every expat cab driver.

"Every day I get into my cab, I pray that if I get into an accident, it is not with a Saudi. The police always takes the side of the Saudi; and you know what bad drivers they are. You are thrown in jail until your *kafeel* comes to get you out. Then he deducts the fine from your pay."

Speaking of bad driving: children were driving. Since mom cannot drive, if she desperately needed to get to some place, her twelve-year-old son would drive her. And that was OK. I am not making this up. I have seen boys driving who barely reached the height of a steering wheel. How did they even reach the brakes? Not to mention no driver's license.

This Is My Country

In all the years that we lived in Saudi Arabia, we never had an unpleasant encounter with a Saudi. But then, like anywhere else, there are exceptions, and of all places, in Medina, the place known to Muslim expats as the city of the nicest people.

We were visiting the Prophet's Mosque and stopped at McDonald's to grab a bite. As we sat down to eat our burger, the line at the order counter had gotten long. A Saudi boy in a white thobe, overweight—must have been around ten years old—stepped out of line and moved up to the front, elbowing aside a Pakistani/Indian man. The cashier—also a Pakistani/Indian man—told the boy that the man was ahead of him in line. The boy's father flew into a rage. He raised his voice and in Arabic, shouted at the cashier. How dare he tell his son to get in line; how dare he give a foreigner priority over his son. "This is *my* country," he yelled. The cashier was stunned. The manager, another Pakistani/Indian, came out from an office behind, apologized, served the father and son, did not charge them, and apologized again.

We wondered what became of the poor cashier. I wonder what kind of a man that ten-year-old turned out to be. I see him pushing his Saudi privilege, his sense of entitlement, his "*Saudi First*" credo.

And then I think about the resurgence of white supremacy in the US.

Hired for Life

A Saudi is never fired. At least that was my observation. When Khalid raised this over lunch with one of his Saudi colleagues, he said that incompetence and lack of performance are no grounds for letting someone go; employees have families to feed. In a tribal culture, protecting one's own was key to survival, and that instinct has endured and is embedded in the corporate culture. In the six years I worked there, if at any time a Saudi employee's performance became an issue, instead of firing him, he was reassigned. If it was a high-level executive, he would be given a new title, a comparable new office—if not better—a secretary, and of course, a salary. With no specific portfolio, he would come and go on his own time or not come to work at all. He was treated with courtesy, and life went on.

Disciplining the Saudi Way

Any of you who have worked in corporate America are familiar with the disciplinary process. An employee starts failing on the job, the supervisor counsels him or her, puts a note in the personnel file, a verbal warning. Employee continues to falter; supervisor issues a written warning. And finally, three strikes and you are out. Feel your jaw drop when I relate what a nursing supervisor told me: "If one of my staff is not doing their job, I don't issue them warnings. I call their parents."

He Showed His Cards

A circular driveway brought visitors to the hospital. While waiting for my cab at the entrance, I noticed that the cars were not moving. A huge SUV, double parked near the entrance, was blocking the traffic. I waited, like everyone else, for someone to get the car to move. It was getting late for my Arabic class. Looking around, I spotted the security guard, who was supposed to be directing the traffic. He just stood there doing nothing. I walked over to him. Young, good looking man in khaki shirt and pants, probably in his thirties.

"Can you please have this car moved. It's blocking traffic."

He looked at me apologetically and said, "It could be a prince."

Seeing the look on my face—I wish I had seen the look on my face— he gave me this helpless look, "We are a weak department."

I felt so bad for him. It took courage for him to admit that, and I wondered: What thoughts does he take home every night after work?

But then, don't some of our cops do the same on the streets of New York? Pull up wherever they please, leave their car standing diagonally taking up two lanes, and saunter off as if they own the streets. And they don't even carry a princely title.

Say, To You Your Religion, to Me Mine

That is straight out of the Qur'an, God telling humankind to be tolerant and avoid religious conflict. Ensuring religious freedom is one of the six objectives of shari'a; references provided upon request.

In Saudi, there are no churches, synagogues, or temples. There can be no religious gatherings in the homes either. Even Muslims cannot hold religious gatherings in their homes such as readings of the Qur'an, lest a different brand of Islam is propagated. One cannot bring in copies of the translation of the Qur'an unless they are by approved translators. In my stay there, I did not come across a Jewish person. Hindus, yes.

This is the land where the Prophet Muhammad laid the cornerstone for religious freedom, upholding shari'a. This is the land where God revealed the Qur'an to the Prophet Muhammad, calling Christians and Jews People of the Book (recipients of Torah and Gospel), commanding believers to embrace the Torah, Psalms, and Gospel as revealed to the Prophets Moses, David, and Jesus. This is the land where the Prophet Muhammad exemplified these teachings, marrying a Christian woman and a Jewish woman, and entering into a covenant to protect houses of worship.

Once or twice a year Khalid and I would go for *umrah* to Mecca and from there head on to Medina to visit the Prophet's Mosque. Driving on the highway, as you approach the environs of Mecca or Medina, a traffic sign appears saying Muslims Only, and the exit sign says, Non Muslims. I would cringe each time I read the You-Are-Not-Welcome signs.

One day I had to give a presentation on data collection for quality control. As I sat at my desk preparing my PowerPoint presentation, one of my American colleagues looked over my shoulder at my screen and said, "You can't do that."

"Can't do what?"

"That," he said, pointing at the graphic on my screen.

It was the final slide of my presentation, where I had placed an image of two roads intersecting, with the title: At the Crossroads.

"What's wrong with it?"

"It looks like a cross."

He then walked around to watch my jaw drop.

"It is a . . ." I had hardly finished my retort when it struck me. Crucifix.

He nodded as he watched me get it.

I gave him this "you're kidding" look.

He gave me the "I am not kidding" look.

"And don't even think about using the term 'crossroads.'"

By then two of my other American colleagues emerged, waving their finger at me.

I found a boring title for the slide—I can't remember what it was—and made it through the presentation. Actually, they liked my blueprint. Ah! Maybe I had titled it: Blueprint.

An Arabian Christmas

"It's Christmas Eve tonight," Samir said to me, speaking in a gentle, sentimental tone. "We should do something for the nurses on the floors."

I was surprised. Surprised because Christmas is kept under wraps.

I was moved. Moved because he was putting the sentiments of the staff above and beyond the cultural norms.

"Do you have any ideas?" I asked.

He adjusted his red-and-white-checkered headdress, draped one end over his white thobe, and was pensive.

"I going to ask Steve to join me in making rounds on the floors this evening and wishing them a Merry Christmas." Steve was one of the staff in our department, an American and a Christian.

Ahhh! I get it. Doing something for the nurses could not include gifts, cards, or anything visibly Christmasy.

Christmas celebrations were not permitted. And I don't mean no Christmas trees in the plazas, shopping malls, or even the front lawn. I mean no Christmas trees with sparkling lights visible from your window. No gathering of friends in your living room to sing Christmas carols, no Christmas cards in the stores or anything Christmasy for that matter. If expats want to celebrate Christmas, they were free to do so in the privacy of their homes, but even in their homes they could not have gatherings.

For that matter, no discussion on religion either. Or I would have pointed out God's revelation in the Qur'an on Jesus, Jesus speaking from the cradle, the miracles he performed, the chapter titled Mary, the annunciation, the miracle of his birth, and Mary as "the most exemplary woman of all times." A ban on Christmas?

Religious intolerance notwithstanding, expats of all faiths from Europe, North America, South Africa, Asia, and Australia flock to the kingdom. Every year at Christmas, some take time off to fly home and celebrate this joyous time with their loved ones.

On that Christmas Eve, Samir and Steve gave up their family time for the evening and made rounds on every floor of the hospital, extending their wishes and in a quiet way acknowledged their holiday. The next morning—Christmas Day—everyone went to work. A day like any other.

Gone Astray

"Guide us to the straight path. The path of those on whom You have bestowed Your Grace, not of those who have incurred Your wrath, nor of those who have gone astray" (Qur'an 1:7).

I was taking a test at the Arabic school, and the teacher asked me to recite the opening chapter of the Qur'an, verses one through seven. After I recited verse seven (above), the teacher corrected me. "You should have said: 'those who have gone astray, i.e., Jews and Christians.'"

Now, that is *not* what is written in the Qur'an. Yet, the Saudi printing of the translation of the Qur'an reads: "those who have gone astray [Jews and Christians]." Text within the brackets are "explanations or further elucidation." Incredulous? I have a version on my bookshelf.

One weekend we were entertaining my colleagues and their families at our home. Among them were European, American, and Arab families. While the children were playing in the garden, one of the little Arab girls came running to her father, telling on one of the girls, "She is playing with the *kuffar.*" *Kuffar* is a term often applied to "unbelievers," the Arabic version of infidel. She was referring to the European children, very white, very profileable as non-Muslims. She couldn't have been more than eight years old. Where was she getting that from? Not her parents, that I knew for sure. I wonder if it was the teachers at school.

A decade later, we would find ourselves on the other side of Trump's ideological wall, pushing against Islamophobia and antisemitism in the US.

Crime and Punishment

There is a plaza in downtown Riyadh that expats refer to as Chop-Chop Square. On Fridays, beheadings would take place in the square, in public. Capital punishment was carried out for murder, drug crimes, and some nonviolent crimes for both adults and juveniles. For theft, the punishment was amputation of the right hand. Flogging was carried out for acts like sodomy and adultery. There is no other way to describe it except to say that it is barbaric. We would hear that it serves as a deterrent to crime. No one I know ever witnessed it. It was a place to be avoided.

I recall that when Khalid and I first performed the hajj in 1986, there was no evidence of crime. When the *adhan* was called, store owners would put up a curtain in front of their stores instead of shutting and locking the doors and leave for prayers. No one ventured into the stores. A locked-door policy was nonexistent. For us New Yorkers, it was an astounding sight. During our initial years in Saudi, we always felt safe; safe from theft, safe from violence. By 2006, this was no longer the case. Car theft and break-ins into homes were on the rise, and at one point things got so bad that the CEO of the hospital had to call a special meeting of the hospital staff, urging them to keep their valuables under lock and key and "don't leave the key to your jewelry box on your dresser." Yet amputations were few and far between, while executions continued. If the victim's family accepts blood money from the murderer, the perpetrator will not be executed. By the way, drinking alcohol is punishable by up to five hundred lashes and can land you in jail.

Two-Door Policy

Let's shift gears to a less violent topic. Actually, not violent at all. If you ever get a chance to visit a Saudi home, you will notice two entrances to the house: one for men, one for women. Two living rooms, one for men, one for women. One dining room between the living rooms, with sliding doors connecting with the men's living room on one side and the women's living room on the other. And of course, the kitchen on the women's side. When it is time for a meal to be served, the sliding doors are shut on the women's side, opened on the men's side, men take their food, sliding doors shut, women's doors open, and women get their food. Got it! Isn't it interesting how the design and layout of a house is made to conform to the culture? When it's time to depart, one of the children is sent to the men's living room, telling Dad that it's time to go, or vice versa. Each departs from their respective exit doors and meets up outside. It works.

Walls

You know that in the US our front lawns are visible for the whole world to see. So is the front of our homes. In Saudi Arabia, homes are enclosed by walls, high enough to block the view to the top floor. If you build a three-level house next door, the walls of surrounding homes go higher. Privacy is premium. When my cousin from the Emirates visited us in New York, he wondered at the exposed houses: no walls, no curtains drawn, lights on. "How do people protect their privacy?" he asked me.

Saudi Hospitality

When our son Asim visited us, the hospital treated him like royalty. I had been sharing with the office staff the emails he was sending from Brazil where he was building houses with Habitat for Humanity. Samir was so moved by Asim's writing that when I told him my son would be visiting us in a few weeks, he called the Public Relations office and told them to make his visit a memorable one. Well, did they indulge him! While we were at work, they took him on tours and showed him the Riyadh that we never got to see, like academic and governmental institutions.

Children First

Go anywhere in Saudi Arabia and notice that facilities are family-oriented and outfitted with amenities for families and children. Hotels have playgrounds with all the swing sets, walking down the hallways one keeps running into Goofy and Pluto shaking hands with the children, malls have play areas, shopping centers have plazas for children to roller skate and bicycle, fast-food places have playrooms, supermarkets have play areas, museums have miniparks for children with man-made streams to swim in, etc. And Saudis like to have large families. Four or more children is the norm. When someone asked me, "How many children do you have?" I was almost embarrassed to say, "Two."

Making It Work

Every Saudi family we knew had a driver and a maid. A driver to drive the lady of the house around and take the children to and from school, and a maid to cook, clean, and nanny the children. Most of the domestic female help is Filipino or Sri Lankan; drivers mostly from Bangladesh, Pakistan, and India. Our villa had a maid's room with an attached bath, which remained vacant. We expats depended on part-time houseboys, and that was enough. You won't find a Saudi cleaning man or a Saudi maid, not in the homes and not in public places. They consider this as menial work and beneath them. So dependent are some of the families on domestic help that they are unable to clean up after themselves. Always when disembarking from a Saudi Airlines plane and walking past business class, we would find the seats littered with food wrappers and food crumbs.

My Morning Coffee

I didn't have a driver or a maid, but I did get room service; or rather, office service. Remember the tea boy in the office kitchen? Later, I had moved into a new office (more about that in Chapter 12) that was served by a large kitchen manned by Mohammad, a Sudanese man. In his fifties, short, plump, with a balding round head, he was always smiling.

Now, I am not used to being served, and until I moved into the executive suite, I actively resisted "ringing for tea." Being served by the wait staff in a restaurant is a treat. But having coffee brought to my office made me uncomfortable. So, I would walk into the kitchen first thing in the morning, greet the smiling Mohammad with a smile, and help myself. One morning I walked into a group of three young Sudanese men chatting with Mohammad, kind of like the water-cooler morning chat. As they shifted to make room for me, I felt like an intruder. Later, Mohammad came to my office.

"Madam Sabeeha, you don't have to come to the kitchen to get coffee. Just call me and I will bring you your coffee," and he put a slip of paper on my desk with the kitchen phone number scribbled on it.

The kitchen was his domain, serving coffee was etched in his job description, and I had been stepping on his turf. For the next four years, every morning at 8:00 a.m., I would dial the kitchen—actually, punch the kitchen number. Mohammad would arrive, putting on his warm smile, and with oh-so-much pride, place the coffee on my desk. Not a mug: a teacup, mini napkin between cup and saucer to catch the drips, and a tiny teaspoon. He would stand back and beam at his production, then leave with his head bobbing sideways. His adorable manner would continue to chip away at my discomfort at being "served."

Open-Door Policy

One day, I had a meeting with a new employee, a gentleman of Pakistani origin. As he walked in, he shut the office door. I jumped out of my seat and opened the door. Now I had to explain myself.

"It is an unwritten policy here that if a man and a woman are alone in an office, the door has to kept open."

I *had* to tell him that. There was just no other way. He turned red. A devout Muslim—as in very devout, someone who would never cross the line—he felt so embarrassed, he could barely look me in the eye. I had to quickly get down to business to overcome the awkward moment.

#MeToo

There was never a #MeToo moment, encounter, or scandal. The hospital was loaded with young western women, who were perceived as being socially liberal. Easy target? It never happened. Or let me put it this way: I never heard of any sexual harassment in the workplace. Now, granted that I was not much of a grapeviner, but I was practically the informal, unofficial HR person in the division, and nothing of the kind ever hit my airwaves. Now, in the #MeToo era when I reflect on it, I can't help but appreciate the ethics of the culture at King Faisal Hospital.

The Marvel of Arabic

Even though we never learned to speak much Arabic despite the five years of lessons, here is what we did learn from Fahed, our Syrian tutor. Whereas colloquial Arabic—the spoken Arabic of a particular region—is different from *fusha*, the Classical Arabic. If you speak *fusha*, you will be understood no matter what region you are in. But if you speak one region's colloquial Arabic in another region, no one will understand you. *Fusha* is universal. Yet *fusha* is only spoken by four categories of people in the Arab world: the royal family, teachers, news broadcasters, and the ulema (religious scholars). When you turn on the news on TV, they are speaking the *fusha* Arabic. Fahad told us that the vocabulary of Arabic has remained constant for fourteen hundred years since the Qur'an was first revealed. Not a single word has been added to the Arabic dictionary.

Do you want me to repeat that?

"How is that possible?" Khalid and I asked in unison. "New words are always added to a language. There is growth in medicine, technology, other discoveries. How could you get by or communicate if your language did not grow with the times?"

Fahad smiled. "We improvise."

"As in?"

"Take a look at the signage in your hospital. Radiology is written as *soora*, meaning picture; computer is written as *hisaab*, meaning calculation; surgery as *jarrah*, meaning cutting."

"What about words for which there are no matches?"

"Those words are Romanized, such as *telafoon* for telephone, or *telfazyoon* for television," said Samir, giving a few more examples.

He explained that the only reason why *fusha* Arabic has been preserved is because it is the language of the Qur'an. This is the language of poetry, of literature, and works of scholarship. Years later, we were surprised to learn that Fahad was a Christian.

I Never Want to Drive

We had gone on an overnight camping trip in the desert, organized by the hospital's Social Club. In our group was a Canadian couple, a Canadian woman, an Irish woman, a Saudi woman, and ourselves, and then of course our escort, Ahmed, a Sudanese. The Saudi woman, Noora, worked as a ward clerk at the hospital. Her presence was unusual. Saudis did not join trips that catered to expats—it was a touristy thing. Anyhow, we were met at our destination by Kareem, a young Saudi man, good looking, cheerful, and upbeat. Seeing Noora, he welcomed her with a "good to have you back again" greeting. *Now* her presence made sense to my sixth sense. A Saudi, twice on the same expat-y trip? *Hmmm! That's sweet.*

Let me dispense with the details of the campout other than to tell you that they installed a bathroom with running water, private tents for couples equipped with carpets, beds, and chairs; had a living room tent, and full-service hot meals in the dining room tent. It's the fireside conversation I want to get to. After dinner, which was served spread on the flooring, Kareem lit up a fire in the middle of the tent, and we gathered around it, reclining on cushions. His charm and informal style put us at ease. Our Saudi driver, Baba, a sweet old man, sat behind in the shadows, listening, and smiling. We talked about life in Sudan, Saudi Arabia, wet Ireland, icy Canada, our families, and it was wonderful being among people from different parts of the globe so easily sharing their personal points of view around the fire. Then we got into the real stuff.

"How do you feel about women driving?" an Irish woman asked him.

"Personally, I don't have a problem with women driving. But we have this mentality that a woman who puts herself in harm's way is asking for trouble. Let's say her car has a flat tire and she is standing by the roadside looking for help. To me, she is fresh meat."

Gasp!

He continued: "I say: Why did she put herself in this situation? So you see, our mindset has to change before we can have women driving."

Noora shook her head emphatically. "I would *never* drive."

A liberated Saudi woman who does not want to drive. Hmmm!

Now everyone turned toward her. She had on a brown hijab and wore a long skirt. By the way, all Saudi women by and large wear long skirts. Pants are considered immodest, as they reveal one's body contours.

"You are not veiled. Is that unusual for a Saudi woman? You are single, right?" a Canadian woman asked Noora.

"I am single. I don't wear the veil at work either. It is my brothers and uncles who insist that I wear the veil, not my father or my mother. When I am out with my brothers or uncles, I put on the veil. They believe that no man should see my face."

I just knew what was coming next. And it did.

"Do most Saudis have multiple wives?"

Kareem had the floor, and he didn't disappoint. I don't recall his precise words as it was a long discourse, but he was prepared. In a nutshell: polygamy is legal. It is prevalent in the royal family and in the Bedouin culture, not so in the middle class. In the royal family, the marriages are political, to forge relationships with tribes; and in the Bedouin culture, it is to ensure that a woman is never without a husband. In that culture, a woman needs a man's protection, so whether single, widowed, or divorced, she must always be married. It's a matter of survival. Desert life is harsh, and in a family of multiple wives, women work out an arrangement of division of labor tapping into one another's skills, who will cook, who will babysit.

We talked about the imminent war in Iraq and how each of us felt about it.

"If America does invade Iraq, what will happen to us? Will our lives be in danger?" a Canadian woman asked.

All eyes turned toward Kareem.

"You are our guests. It is our responsibility to protect our guests."

That night we saw the stars, walked the desert at sunrise. They took us dune-ing the next morning, riding up and down the sand dunes in four-wheelers, and on a safari on a land cruiser. And we got to see gazelles running off in the distance in a single-file formation, Arabian horses, and many animals. But it was the fireside chat that was most memorable.

Epilogue: A few years later, Khalid was attending to a patient when Noora walked in. "He is my uncle," she said, referring to the patient. "My husband and I would like to talk to you about his discharge plan." Her husband walked in right behind her.

Kareem.

My sixth sense hadn't been wrong.

Marriages

For the most part, they are arranged, like what it was like when I was growing up in Pakistan. The elders in the family—parents, grandparents, uncles, aunts, or elder siblings—decided on a match based on family status, family background, compatibility of the couple-to-be, and in the case of a daughter, the professional qualifications of the young man. Elders in the family command a respected status, particularly the parents, and their young sons and daughters defer to their judgment. Speaking from personal experience, I can vouch for that.

Flying with the Saudis

Here is the best part about boarding a plane in Saudi Arabia: they always board women first. If a man wants to board early, get attached to a woman, as in wife, daughter, or sister. She is your passport to early boarding.

The second-best part: before take-off, Saudi Airlines will broadcast a prayer over the PA system, a Qur'anic verse praying for a safe journey. It just puts you at ease, me at least.

Third: watching the Saudis transform. On international flights, when the plane starts approaching New York, Saudi women shrug off the abaya and scarf, emerging in tee shirts and jeans, with their nearly blonde hairdos in highlights. Saudi men line up at the toilets, enter wearing their white thobe and headscarf, exit in jeans and tee shirts, revealing their haircuts. I try to match the after look with the before look, and it's totally unrecognizable. When landing in Riyadh, the change in outfits goes in reverse. Do in Riyadh as the Riyadhians do. I think I just coined a new term.

Fourth: there is no fourth. From there on, it's the luck of the draw.

The unsettling experience of flying Saudi Airlines is that you can get bumped by the royals. We were at JFK airport checking in for our flight to Riyadh when we were informed that our flight had been canceled and we were being put up in a hotel to await the next flight. We learned later that some royals had made a last-minute decision to fly out that day and had commandeered our plane. The next day we were taken to the airport, and as we were handed our boarding cards, we noticed that we had been upgraded to first class. In fact, every business class passenger had been upgraded. Can you guess why? First, let me explain the layout of the plane. First-class seats are in the main cockpit area adjoining coach class. Business-class seats are on the upper deck and have the entire upper deck to themselves. The royal family preferred the privacy of the upper deck and had given up their first-class seats in exchange for the less comfortable business class. Privacy over comfort. I'll take comfort along with the royal treatment it offers.

Here is a story I related in an email, but devoid of the royal touch.

◆◆◆

Home-bound from Riyadh to New York

Saturday, July 10, 2004

Dear All,

I am home. Here is what happened en route.

"Mummy, could you please get me an Aborigine dot painting from Australia?" Asim had asked when we went on vacation to Australia.

"Sure, honey."

We had the carefully selected painting framed in Riyadh to avoid the high cost of framing in New York, and while we were at it, I also had a Vikings tapestry framed for my neighbor.

"How are we going to carry it?" I had asked Khalid.

"No problem. We will just hand carry it and put it away in the storage closet in the cabin."

"But will they let us do that?"

"Sure."

We were flying business class (don't get excited: it's an employer benefit), which meant that in addition to fully reclining seats and movies at your seat-side,* you have access to a small storage closet, big

---

* A luxury in 2004.

enough to accommodate paintings. Khalid, who has perfected the art of packing and packaging, wrapped the two paintings together in brown paper only and tied a string around them.

"Aren't you going to put some cardboard around it?"

"No. I want to be able to easily open it at security. And it's hand-carry, so no need to worry about the packaging."

Then the drama began.

Khalid checked in, and, as we proceeded toward Immigration, we heard one of the guards call out. "Are you taking that in the plane?"

He was pointing at the artwork.

Khalid walked over, showed them the artwork, and explained that it would be stored in the closet. No problem. Right?

Wrong! It was a big *Mushkila* (problem).

"You have to check it in."

"But it will break if I check it in. This is fragile."

"You have to check it in."

Another security official came running.

"I know him. He is a doctor at King Faisal Hospital. He is a cancer specialist. He is treating my mother." He was beaming and obviously very pleased to see Khalid.

"You have to check it in."

"Can I speak to the manager?" Khalid asked.

The patient's son went running to get the manager.

"Since this has glass in the frame, it is considered a weapon," said the manager. "You absolutely cannot take it inside. If you were going anywhere but the USA, we would have allowed it. I assure you, I will personally carry this package into the hold and place it myself in a secure position. We will label it, and don't worry. It will get to New York without any damage."

Standing on the other side of the security barrier, all I could see was all these officials shaking their heads politely, and Khalid speaking in earnest. When I saw them pick up the paintings and walk toward check in, I made a dash to stop them. I had to shove my carry-ons through the security scanner and make my way over to the other side.

"Khalid, let's call our driver and have him come and take these back. We should not check them in. They are bound to break."

Khalid and I had a back-and-forth discussion. Khalid prevailed, and the paintings were checked in, all framed, and wrapped in brown paper, the finest, most delicate of brown paper. I could picture it, the baggage handlers in New York, picking it up and throwing it on the conveyor belt, the noise of shattering glass, passengers shaking their heads, feeling sorry for the owner and wondering why they had wrapped it in brown paper only.

Whatever Will Be, Will Be. Worse things can happen. I have my health, I have my life, I have my children, I have my grandchildren. . . . So what's a few broken frames and some damaged expensive paintings. It's only paintings!

Think of it this way. It's been a long day, I am tired, and I can look forward to stretching out in those nice reclining seats in business class and watching my favorite movies in my seat. Right?

Read on.

The flight attendant on Saudi Airlines, an Arab woman probably from the Emirates, in a dark blue pant suit, with a scarf draped over her head and held in place by a cap, was showing us to our seats in the cabin. I gratefully sank into my seat, pressed the "recline" button and waited for the footrest to rise. There was a cranking noise as the footrest struggled to free itself from under the seat. I pressed the button again. Then again. This couldn't be happening to me!

"Khalid, this footrest is broken," I cried desperately, my world falling apart.

Khalid, who is not a certified footrest mechanic, leaped to work out the buttons. No luck.

I beckoned the flight attendant and announced that I was changing seats. Just then I saw a mechanic-looking person walk down the aisle.

"Excuse me, sir," I called. "This seat has a broken footrest."

"A broken footrest!" He was shocked. He immediately got working on it.

Khalid and I then proceeded to move to the next row. One seat worked, the other was broken.

No problem, there are ten empty rows. We will just move down the row.

Check it out first. One seat works, the other is broken.

Next row. One seat works, the other is broken.

Next row . . . until we exhausted all rows. Perfect pattern. One works, one is broken.

This is too perfect to be true. Maybe we missed a good seat. Let's start all over again. After all, we had the whole place to ourselves. This time the flight attendant got into the act and found a seat that was partially broken. Or partially fixed, whichever way you want to look at it. So, we relocated to the row with the working seat and the partially fixed/broken seat. We wanted to sit together, no matter what.

A few minutes later the mechanic ran past us down the aisle, calling out to us, "I can't fix it. I am going to log it in as inoperable. Meanwhile, please feel free to select any other seat." He never gave us a chance to tell him that every row had a broken seat. He also failed to notice that we had already relocated.

Then in walks someone with authority and tells us that we can stay in this seat until Jeddah, but from Jeddah onward, all seats are fully booked and we will have to go back to row #16.

"But it is broken."

"We will try to fix it in Jeddah, but if we cannot, you have to go back to it because this seat is allocated."

"Every other seat is broken."

"Every other seat is broken? Please write and complain." He then shook his head and walked away.

"Next time, why don't we just fly Economy. Why incur all this cost. Besides, Economy is all empty and you can use four seats and sleep, while here, you are locked into one seat because of the immovable audio system between seats." Khalid was being sensible, as always.

It didn't end here.

The plane pulled out of the gate, got to the runway, and was ready to take off when it changed its mind, got off the runway, and parked itself.

"This is your captain speaking. There has been a delay."

It's all for our good and safety. What's a little delay.

They served dinner.

By now I was getting very tired, and we still hadn't taken off. It was 11:30 at night, and Khalid had fallen asleep. I leaned over and whispered to him.

"I am going downstairs to Economy." It was a double-decker.

He smiled.

I picked up my pillow and blanket, walked down the stairs, and found the Economy section practically empty. A few passengers were seated on the window seats, dinner was being served, and the entire middle rows were empty. I stretched out purring like a cat, the ultimate in luxury, and dropped off to sleep.

The last thought that drifted through my mind as I fell into sweet slumber was, "Khalid is right."

I was suddenly awoken from my sleep by a blaring over the PA system.

"Please disembark the plane. Please take all your personal belongings with you." I bolted up. Khalid was standing beside me, bag and baggage in hand.

"We have to change planes."

My inner voiced called out to me. "It is all for our good and safety."

Back to the Riyadh waiting lounge.

We stood by the gate, all of us, not knowing whether to settle down or wait there, in case we had to board. An official came running: "New York, this way." We all chased after him, thinking he was leading us to the new gate for boarding; and then we watched as he parked himself by another gate, opened up cartons, and set up a snack counter for the passengers. Then another official came and announced, "New York, Gate 21." You guessed it. We all proceeded to Gate 21. Then we heard over the PA system, "New York, Gate 27." Back to Gate 27.

An hour later, we boarded a new plane.

Everything happens for a reason. In this plane, my seat won't be broken.

It was partially broken.

From Jeddah, the flight was full—business class, that is—so I settled into my partially broken seat, grateful for its width and the leg room.

How about a movie! Too wired to sleep and too tired to read this intellectually challenging Nobel Prize–winning novel. I just need to chill out with something soft and mushy. Just flip on the buttons, the screen lights up; just plug in the headset, right?

Wrong. No volume.

No problem, just raise the volume.

No volume.

My teacher always told me, "When solving a problem, look for the simple solution." I know, I must have plugged it in the wrong way. Let's unplug and flip it over. That should do it.

No volume.

Look for the simple things. Maybe the main system is not turned on. I looked around and noticed that all the children were sitting, headsets on, oblivious to the world around them, glued to the monitor.

So much for that.

"Khalid, I have no volume," as if Khalid were a certified volume mechanic.

I beckoned the flight attendant. "I have no volume."

"I will check the main system."

I pointed to all the children who were not having a main-system problem.

Maybe it was my headset. Let's try Khalid's headset.

No volume.

Khalid tried his system. It worked. My system was broken, and there was nothing that could be done.

Worse things can happen. I have my life, I have my health. . . .

For the rest of the journey, we took turns. When Khalid slept, I watched TV on his system; and vice versa.

A survey!

Flipping through the channels, I noticed the customer satisfaction survey. OK. Here is my chance.

Was the staff courteous? Is there enough leg room? . . . Where is the footrest question, where is the volume question?

"Was a complaint form provided to you?"

Aha!

"May I please have a complaint form?" I asked the flight attendant.

"Oh yes, of course."

She came back with two forms.

I gratefully pulled out my pen, spread out the form, and began. No. This wasn't a complaint form, this was a Customs declaration form.

"May I please have a *complaint form*?"

"Oh, I'm sorry."

She came back, "I'm sorry, we don't have any. Here is a postcard you can use instead."

Postcard it is, as long as I have an address to send it back to.

"Welcome to New York where the temperature is 26 degrees."

The paintings!

I had actually managed not to think about it the entire flight. How could I have, with all these distractions of luxury appointments gone awry?

The paintings emerged on the conveyor belt looking rather intact. We took the package down, shook it.

No sound of broken glass. We checked the edges. No signs of abrasion.

We came home and removed the fine brown paper.

Not a scratch!

All the best,
Sabeeha

* * *

Around the World in Six Years

All these broken seats and footrests didn't get in the way of exploring new lands, inside and outside Arabia. Mada'in Salih was the highlight in Saudi Arabia. If you have visited Petra, well, same idea but at a much grander scale. Performing *umrah* during Ramadan year after year was a blessing. Sometimes we would perform *umrah* in a day trip. And then there was a world beyond. Saudi Arabia lies at the center of the earth. You can fly anywhere in eight to ten hours. And if you are flying north or south, to Russia or to South Africa, no jetlag either. With all the vacation time we had, we got smart at maximizing it by taking five weekdays off, combining that with two weekends, and making a seven-day trip to places as far off as Thailand. Khalid and I traveled to Australia in the southeast; China and Japan in the Far East; Sri Lanka and the Maldives in the southeast; Morocco, Egypt, and South Africa in Africa; Lebanon and Oman in the Middle East; and most of Europe; along with many trips to visit family in Pakistan, only a three-hour flight away. My family and friends would wait for my long travelogues. It is all we expats talked about: Where are you coming from and where are you going? We would exchange Fodors travel books and maps, hand over leftover currency, and always have a slideshow on our return. It's what we lived for. It's how we survived being away from family.

CHAPTER 10

Ramadan in Mecca and Medina

We feel blessed to have performed *umrah* during Ramadan at the Grand Mosque in Mecca and *ziyarah* (visit) to the Prophet's Mosque in Medina. It became an annual ritual that we looked forward to, an experience steeped in spirituality, charity, festivity, and community. And it came with a price tag. Hotel rates in Mecca triple during the first week of Ramadan and increase another 50 percent during the last two weeks of Ramadan when the crowds peak, seeking the night of *Laylat al-Qadr*, the Night of Power.

When it is time to break the fast in the Grand Mosque of Mecca, it feels like the whole world is out there to take care of you. Small storefronts put up a sign and start giving away iftar packages to anyone and everyone who presents at the counter—free. And you don't see crowds jamming the counter. The package contains a few dates, a drink, a fruit, and either Laban (creamy yogurt) or bread. Three hours before sunset, trucks start pulling up to the curbside outside the mosque and unloading cartons and cartons of prepackaged food. These are from private anonymous donors. Two hours before sunset, donors start spreading out floor mats in the plaza outside the mosque, laying out rows of plastic sheeting for food service. As people walk by, they reach out and invite them to come join them for iftar, each donor group competing to be the most charitable. As people take their places on the floor mats, the organizers start walking between the rows, placing a package for iftar

226

in front of every pilgrim seated. Every food item is prepackaged, and copious. Take a step back and all you see in the plaza are rows and rows of people sitting on mats, chatting, and waiting for the *Maghrib adhan*, when they can break their fast.

Some people choose to break their fast in one of the many surrounding hotels. The five-star hotels go way out in their lavish and colorful display of buffets for iftar. Most people, though, go inside the mosque for iftar and take their own food with them. And there, too, people walk down the rows, handing out dates and Arabian bread. You don't say no, and accept it graciously even if one is loaded with food. Women dig into their food packs and hand out olives, more bread, cheese, a cup of Zamzam water, and anything else to women around them, the lady next to her, in the row in front, in the row behind, and you accept it with a smile. You are among your sisters-in-Islam, and you share bread; and as soon as the melodious sound of the *adhan* is heard, you break your fast together. None of us speak the same language, but we all know how to smile, extend a hand, and offer a nod of acknowledgment. In a few minutes the *iqama* is called: all rise, and we stand in prayer together, grateful.

There we stay until *Isha* prayer and through *Taraweeh* prayers, which lasts an hour and a half. Midway during *Taraweeh*, an older and senior imam, Shaikh Sudais, takes over. Khalid loves his voice. His voice resonates through the mosque, and the poetic composition of the Qur'an recited in his melodious voice is soothing. In the last unit of prayer, he raises his hands, and the entire congregation raises its hands in supplication, and he prays to God for His mercy, for His forgiveness, for a virtuous life in this world and in the Hereafter. After each supplication, the whole congregation of a million plus says "*Ameen*" aloud, and you are surrounded by the sound of his voice supplicating and the sound of all of us saying "*Ameen*," and people start crying with emotion. It ends on that note, every night for thirty nights.

Stores around the Grand Mosque display a popular black-and-white poster of the Kaaba. Many years ago, it had rained heavily, the Kaaba was flooded, and pilgrims performed the *tawaaf* by swimming.

After spending two days in Mecca, we would go on to Medina for *ziyarah* to the Prophet's Mosque where the Prophet Muhammad (Peace Be Upon Him) is buried and experience much of the same, except that Medina is festive and the Prophet's Mosque has a different feel to it. In Mecca you feel the presence of God; in Medina you feel connected to your history.

They have fixed times for ladies to visit the Prophet's *Rawdah,* the sacred chamber under the green dome of the mosque, where the Prophet is buried. The grave is not visible, as it is cordoned off by a gold mesh wall, and only one side of the wall faces the ladies' visitation area. It is so crowded that often I could not get close to the *Rawdah* and would stay back and say my *nafl* prayers in the open courtyard next to the *Rawdah.* The courtyard has many pillars that hold folding upside-down umbrellas. As soon as the sun moves directly overhead and the *Zuhr adhan* is heard, the umbrellas open up like tulips; and they close when the *Maghrib adhan* is called as the sun sets. I was there each time they opened and closed, and what a sight to watch as they gradually spread to form a blue-and-white roof. One doesn't have to get close to *Rawdah* to feel the presence of the Prophet. Just knowing you are standing in *his* mosque, the mosque he built, the place he called home, the place where he led the prayers, the place where he now rests, is deeply moving. It is tangible evidence of our history. And you are standing there, in his footsteps. It sends shivers to your core.

The Prophet's Mosque is so vast that you cannot see from one end to the other, as you look down the rows and rows of white arches and pillars with gold encasings. And at night, the shimmering minarets against the dark sky make one want to just keep looking.

During one of the prayers, I took my place for *Isha* prayers when a young woman in a long dress sitting next to me—must be in her twenties—struck up a conversation.

"Where are you from?" she asked in Arabic.

When I tried to respond in my broken Arabic, she asked in English, "Do you speak English?"

We hit it off. She was a friendly woman and kept smiling.

"I am a Palestinian, and I live in Jordan."

Wow! I had never met a Palestinian woman.

"I have never been to Palestine, just seen it on TV," she said.

Her mother sat next to me, with the saddest eyes, as I told them that I had been to Palestine. When I started talking about all the places I had visited, her mother's face grew sadder as she made gestures and sounds of anguish. Those are the faces I still carry with me.

The bazaars in Medina come alive after *Maghrib* prayers as people flock to get a quick bite of dinner before *Isha*. After *Isha*, the bazaars are thronged with pilgrims, and the vendors and storeowners stand calling out, "One riyal only, ten riyals only." Imam Sudais's voice reciting the Qur'an resonates through the streets from the tape cassettes played by shop owners.

If you happen to be outdoors when the *adhan* is called, you can hear its echo as the sound bounces off the surrounding mountains. It stirs the soul, particularly at night. As soon as the night prayers are over, the plaza is invaded by massive cleaning machines.

The bathroom facilities are a novelty. In the plaza they have escalators going down to the bathrooms. Below are hundreds of bathrooms, each equipped with a toilet, a shower, and an open closet with hooks. Then there are the *wudu* areas for ablution. Another row of escalators takes you farther down to hundreds more bathrooms—all in all, three underground levels. The ceilings are high, so there is no humidity or closed-in feeling. Some women were doing their laundry there. The area is clean! Female workers are constantly cleaning the place.

On one of our flights back from Jeddah airport, we literally had to chase the iftar time. That day, iftar was to be at 5:45 p.m. in Jeddah but at 5:15 p.m. in Riyadh. So we thought we would get to break our fast sooner. In the plane they handed out boxed iftar, and we were to break our fast as soon as the pilot announced it. What we realized later was that at the flying altitude, the sun sets a lot later. So, even though it was past iftar on the ground, because the sun was visible to us as we flew over the clouds, we had to wait, and we sat in our seats with our boxed iftar in our laps. As soon we descended below the clouds, the captain announced, "You can now break your fast." Then the flight attendant had to scramble to collect the empty boxes as the plane descended.

In all the years that we lived there, we always looked forward to coming back the following year to experience Ramadan in Mecca and Medina.

CHAPTER 11

Winds of War

I didn't believe we would invade Iraq. When I said this to Fahad, our Arabic teacher, he said, "All signs are that the US is going to war." Yes, the signs were there, but it is bound to be averted. Denial? For sure. But I believed that, at the end of the day, calm heads and good sense would prevail. It wasn't the first time I would be wrong.

In March 2003, we were home in New York on vacation when the US started bombing Iraq: shock and awe.

When we returned to Riyadh after our vacation, that is all expats talked about. Saudis were quiet, as usual. Pakistani expats were furious, and what I heard over and over again was: Syria is next. Western expats started leaving. Their families back home were pressuring them. Nurses left, and the hospital started closing beds. The director of Nursing, an American woman, went into high recruitment mode, reaching out to the Czech Republic. As more nurses left, the domino effect rolled in. Then Western doctors started leaving.

When the chairman of a clinical department called to tell me that he had accepted a job in the UAE, I asked why. "Sabeeha, we have no social life left here." The vibrant social life of Riyadh is what sustained us. The Pakistanis were not leaving, so my social life, dented and diluted, was still intact. But I missed my Canadian and American friends. As people left, school enrollment dropped, and the American and international schools closed. Then more expats left.

What was unsettling was the anti-American sentiment. We didn't sense this at the workplace. If the Saudis harbored these sentiments about our foreign policies, it did not spill over in their attitude toward us as individuals. We were still loved and respected. And appreciated. If anything, those of us who stayed were super appreciated.

Khalid and I would watch BBC TV in the mornings over breakfast and Al-Jazeera in the evenings. It didn't look good. It seemed like it was a matter of time before Saudi Arabia would be targeted by terrorists in their campaign against westerners. The US State Department was issuing travel warnings.

One of my colleagues—let's call him Greg—stopped by my office one afternoon. "Sabeeha, the Saudis are in denial."

"What do you mean?"

"I have been talking to them about possible terrorists strikes, and they say it will never happen here. They say terrorism is against Islam, and Muslims would never attack their own."

Iran-Iraq war? Iraq's invasion of Kuwait?

On May 12 we were awakened by the phone ringing at 2 a.m. It was Saqib calling from New York.

"Are you OK?" we asked in panic.

"Are *you* OK?" he said.

"Yes. Why?"

"There have been bombings in the western compounds in Riyadh." OMG!

It was daytime in NY, and he heard the news before we did. Three compounds had been attacked by suicide bombers during the night; thirty-nine people were killed, including nine Americans, and one hundred and sixty wounded. Twelve terrorists were killed; others escaped by climbing over the compound wall.

That morning, the hospital staff was in shock. Greg stopped by my office. "The Saudis who said it would never happen here are walking in a daze. I am calling a meeting to update our Disaster Plan. Are you available?"

The Disaster Plan was put in place with a roster of rotating on-call administrators. I was to keep a pager on me when it was my turn to be on call to activate the plan. As the on-call administrator, my duty was to initiate the call tree, a listing of heads of department and department chairmen to call and advise to execute their departmental disaster plan. For the Emergency Room, it meant that services would be limited to trauma only; for Security, it meant raising the security level to its highest notch; for Nursing, it meant increasing the staffing levels in surgery and intensive care, etc.

A crackdown followed and within weeks, six hundred terrorist suspects were arrested. I was told that in a tribal society, it is very easy to trace people.

So, what are they going to do with them? I asked a senior Saudi executive.

"They are being indoctrinated. It is being impressed on them that killing innocent civilians is not the Islamic way. It is hoped that by raising awareness, it will prevent terrorism."

A cab driver had a different take. "They took these people on a plane and dropped them into the Empty Quarter." The Empty Quarter is a vast desert covering the south-central portion of the Arabian Peninsula.

More expats left the Kingdom.

In November, another suicide bombing took place outside a compound in broad daylight. Seventeen people were killed, 122 wounded, including children. Those killed were mainly expat Arab workers. I was at the office when I got word that casualties were being brought into our Emergency Room. I rushed down to the ER. Stretchers were being brought in carrying Arab men in security guard uniform, bleeding. It seemed like the entire administrative staff had descended in the ER, and the staff were pleading with them to just leave and let them do their job. I left, but in the few minutes that I was there, I took note of the ER director's management of the situation. A Saudi, he was calm, in control, expediting triage and getting the casualties immediate medical attention. We were all shaken up. In all my years working in a hospital, I had never encountered bombing victims.

The next day I called the ER director and commended him on his handling of the situation. That same day, the US State Department issued a warning of further attacks.

More expats left.

We started getting pressure from our family to leave Saudi Arabia. Saqib wrote, putting us on notice. He had not been happy over our going to Saudi in the first place, but now in his own words, "I object." My uncle in Pakistan wrote: "I am really worried about you living in Saudi. Isn't it time you return to New York?" My mother wrote: "You have stayed in Saudi long enough. You have traveled and seen more of the world than most people. Now go back home." She was concerned that time and distance would impact my relationship with my sons.

It would be another three years.

You might be wondering why we stayed. Well, we didn't *feel* unsafe. We didn't *feel* insecure. One could rationalize the argument for leaving: with bombings taking place and expats being targeted, wouldn't it make sense to remove oneself from harm's way? Makes sense, at a logical level, that is. But it came down to how we felt. And we didn't feel the urge or the need to pack up and flee. Neither of us ever brought it up; in fact, the thought didn't even occur to us. When our family started pressuring us, we gently pushed back, trying to calm their fears and explain to them that violence occurs everywhere, in Pakistan and in the US, and when it happens, the news cycle creates a perception that a particular place is unsafe, but Saudi Arabia overall is a very safe place.

Not to minimize the circumstance, but during the 1980s, when I would meet people at out-of-town conferences, they would say to me: "I would never visit New York City. All that crime! Don't you feel unsafe living there?" Comparing apples and dates? How about this: In the years after our return to NYC, there were terrorist bombings in Chelsea, Times Square, and Battery Park, and many attacks were averted. I did not leave New York City. When COVID ravaged my city, apartment buildings emptied out as residents sought refuge in the suburbs; our family urged us to move into Saqib's home in New Jersey. We stayed. At the end of the day, it was our level of comfort, or discomfort, that drove the decision: to leave or not to leave.

May I loop back to Saudi Arabia? I am not done.

CHAPTER 12

Ripples in the Sand

When I was working in the Quality Resource Management department, each time I walked into the executive suite—the administrative offices of clinical operations—I would have this sense of longing. *This is where I belong.* Throughout my career in the US, I had been stationed in the administrative offices; it was the professional environment I had been groomed for and where I thrived. And now I was in a job well below the level of my qualifications and physically far removed from the nerve center.

Within a year, I had an office in the executive suite.

Things had moved fast, and it was the committee assignments that gave me the exposure I needed to find my place. Samir had assigned me to the Utilization Management committee, chaired by a senior administrator, a Lebanese doctor. I will call him Dr. El-Aziz. He knew how to run a meeting: have a clear agenda, set expectations, and get results. Our task was to ensure that hospital services were appropriately utilized: no unnecessary lab or radiology tests, no patients overstaying. We set targets based on clinical input, set up data-gathering systems to monitor our progress, and took corrective action. The committee was staffed by clinicians, the director of Nursing, and department heads of administrative services. I was most impressed by Jehan, the head of Admissions—a Saudi woman. What struck me even more was that she had Saudi men reporting to her. A firecracker, she knew how to move and shake things.

After our first meeting, during which—taking Samir's advice—I kept speaking up, Dr. El-Aziz asked me into his office.

"Sabeeha, you and I should meet weekly to keep this program moving."

I couldn't have been happier. We met every week for the next six years. As institutional priorities shifted, so did our agenda. We went from utilization management to electronic medical records, to adverse occurrence reporting system, to sentinel events, and on and on. He was methodical and organized, I was tenacious and organized; he was wise and steady, I was not-so-wise and too rushed; he was measured, I was pushy; we made a perfect team. Often, I wondered how he put up with me.

A few months into my job, I got a call from Eric, a Canadian administrator.

"Sabeeha, I am putting together a Policy & Procedure Committee . . . and would like you on it."

Of course, I jumped at the opportunity. It was beyond my job description, but seeing my excitement, Samir approved it. Not a wave, just a ripple.

Another call from Eric, "We need to have a system to process applications for adding staff. I am forming a Position Control Committee. It will meet weekly. I would like you to be on it."

Yes!

Samir cautioned me: "It's good to be involved in all these committees, but don't lose sight of your primary function."

Noted.

Now I practically hung out in the executive suite and felt totally at home.

Then came the call that clinched it. The executive director of clinical operations, a Saudi doctor, asked to see me. Seated behind a large desk wearing a white lab coat, he said, "I would like you to work for clinical operations." "In what capacity?" I asked. He explained, we talked, and I went flying to Samir to get his approval. The deal was that I would remain on the staff of my current department but would be assigned to clinical operations. Just my cup of tea. Well, Samir was not OK with it, and for justifiable reasons.

"If senior leadership recognizes talent in their departments, they should allow them to stay in place to help strengthen the department rather than take them away for themselves."

He had a point.

"But it's your decision. Think about it and let me know," he said.

I was in a contract and, without his release, I couldn't switch roles. I went to see him the next day.

"What's your decision?" he asked.

"I would like to accept the offer."

"OK. I will get the paperwork ready."

He rode the waves. I remain grateful to Samir for his generosity. He could have said no, but he didn't hold me back. For the rest of my tenure there, long after I had moved on and on, he remained my shepherd, stood by me, counseled me, and once even reprimanded me—in private—when I disappointed him.

The executive director promised me an office in the executive suite, "as soon as one is available," he said. The problem was that there was no office available. I kept an eye on the comings and goings of executive staff and as soon as I learned of staff relocation from one of the offices, I put in a request. Granted. I could move in as soon as it was vacated. One morning, Eric called me: "Sabeeha, the office was just vacated. You need to move in NOW before someone else grabs it." *Really! Someone else could grab it even though it was assigned to me.* I dropped what I was doing, picked up a folder and my desk name plate, and parked myself. I had come home.

By May 2003, I had a new title: Head, Decision Support. When one of Khalid's colleagues, a doctor, asked me what "decision support" means, I said, "It means: I make the decisions, and you support them." I wish!

Between the new office and the new title, things had moved swiftly. A Saudi doctor, Dr. Al-Jabbar, had returned from the US after getting his MBA. Samir took notice of this dynamic, bright, and energetic physician, and began engaging him in departmental programs, knowing that he would soon retire and needed someone to take his place.

Dr. Al-Jabbar, a thorough gentleman with a great sense of humor and a computer geek, soon became my new boss while Samir stayed on in a staff role. He must have been in his forties, a key consideration, since for the first time in my career, I was reporting to someone younger than me. He seldom wore the traditional attire, dressed impeccably, was polished and sophisticated, a straight shooter with a gentle touch and a penchant for American pop music. It was he who crafted the new job description for me, and at the time I couldn't tell whether I was more excited or he. As Head, Decision Support, my charge was to develop scorecards to monitor each department's performance. That meant working with every department to establish departmental plans, define indicators to measure achievement, have a data collection mechanism, and submit quarterly reports. I would analyze the reports for senior management and meet with chairmen of clinical and administrative departments to develop corrective action plans if they were unable to achieve their objectives. It was strategic and operational planning on steroids. I was in my element.

Senior leadership loved the program; heads of departments not so much. It was work, and they didn't see the added benefit, but they came onboard, and the program set sail. It got the CEO's attention, and he asked that we replicate it across the entire hospital. Now I was working with Finance, Buildings, Logistics, the whole gamut, most of them Saudi. And despite the extra work this program leveled on them, they welcomed me at the table and put up with me as I went through item by item with a, "So what are you going to do about this?" I valued their professional demeanor, their wit, and their resilience whenever I pushed a little harder. We forged relationships that endured long after my job changed once again.

Another two years, and I grew restless. I made a case to Dr. Al-Jabbar about upgrading my position. The work I was doing was far beyond my grade. He agreed. By now I was on the Sentinel Events committee, Ambulatory Care committee, Bylaws committee, and more, and my job was having an impact on the corporate culture. I believed that I deserved a promotion. What I didn't know, which I should have known by now, was that it is extremely difficult to upgrade a position. Dr. Al-Jabbar tried, went as far up the ladder as he could. I was crestfallen when he told me that he couldn't get the approval. A woman in her mid-fifties, I had still not learned to deal with disappointment.

I was going through menopause, and I was a wreck. I had mood swings I wouldn't wish on anybody. Sitting in a meeting, I would be ready to burst into tears over nothing. At one point I called Khalid.

"I have to go into a meeting, and all I want to do is cry."

"Close your office door, turn off the lights, stretch out on your sofa, and close your eyes."

My heightened sensitivities were off the chart—everything bothered me—and somehow, Dr. Al-Jabbar, God bless him, put up with it. He knew what my problem was because I told him. We were in a meeting and, realizing that I was overreacting, I said to him, "You are a physician so I can say this to you. I am going through menopause. I am not making excuses but just want you to know that this is not my usual self." The consummate professional, he kept a straight face.

Getting back to my promotion, or the denial of it. I was devastated to the degree that I decided to quit. Now when I look back, I am embarrassed. I was making too much of a deal out of what was *not* a big deal. Nevertheless, my plan—which I discussed with Khalid—was that I would retire, we would spend another year in Saudi Arabia by which time Khalid would turn sixty—the cut-off age for employment—and then we'd return home to the US. During this one year, I'd keep myself occupied by enrolling in Arabic classes.

I met with Dr. Al-Jabbar and informed him of my plan. Always a good listener, he heard me out. He didn't dissuade me but advised me to think outside the box. Now I had a bruised ego to deal with.

I sent an email to my parents and told them of my decision to quit and retire. Daddy's response was swift. *Don't even think about it,* he essentially said. "Don't be hasty. You are too young to retire. Have another talk with Dr. Al-Jabbar and explore options. You won't be able to handle retirement. Don't do it."

Daddy's urgent tone gave me pause. This was the first time in thirty years—my married life—when Daddy was telling me what to do or what not to do. A parental order.

I listened.

I turned to my ultimate guide; I prayed.

I did *Istikhara.*

Let me explain. *Istikhara* is a prayer asking for God's blessing and guidance in making a decision. I had done it once before when I was in a dilemma—job related, and He had guided me. It had given me the confidence to take a major step knowing that He would pave my way and He had my back. It's a matter of faith. I believe in the power of *Istikhara,* so I said a prayer, opened the Qur'an, and started reading. And God spoke to me. In the verses of the Qur'an, it said: "Wait."

Wait. Patience.

God was urging me to be patient; not to be hasty; wait.

That is what I read into it. And that is what I did.

I waited. And went about my business at work.

And then it happened.

There was a major change in leadership in clinical operations. A new executive director was appointed, a chairman of a medical department, someone I had worked with closely. Among all the chairmen, Dr. Ahmed was the one I admired the most. He had a remarkable career as a clinician, was a devoted physician, had published hundreds of papers, and as a chairman exhibited clarity of vision and purpose. He was principled and affable. It must have been his first day on the job, or maybe second, when I went in to see him and told him that I was considering leaving.

"Why?" he asked in a concerned and inquiring manner.

I told him.

His response was swift and resolute.

"Sabeeha, you are *not* going *anywhere*. I will do everything in my power to see that you get what you want."

Just the balm I needed. I felt myself relax. In that moment, that vote of confidence mattered. He advised me to look for job opportunities in other departments of the hospital and keep him informed. Other opportunities did open, and I did pursue them and kept Dr. Ahmed, Dr. Al-Jabbar, and Samir in the loop. They supported me, guided me, told me which job was a *"don't even think about it,"* which was a *"maybe."* And I was grateful.

Eric, the Canadian administrator, stopped by one morning, sat in the chair across my desk, and told me that he had accepted a job in one of the Gulf states. Eric held a senior-level, high-grade job, reporting directly to Dr. Ahmed. This job was tailor-made for me. The day Eric handed in his resignation, I went to see Dr. Ahmed and threw my scarf in the ring.

"Will you consider me for Eric's position?"

The day after Eric departed, I took over Eric's job. My title was administrator. It took some doing as I wasn't the only one vying for the position. No sooner had word of Eric's resignation gotten out than Saudi male staff lined up for the job. A high-grade position, it put you next to the seat of power. Dr. Ahmed handled the situation both the official and the Saudi way. While the applications made their way through the official HR process, he conferred with and consulted the leadership of the hospital and key department heads and sought their opinion about me assuming this position. I learned of this only after the vetting was done and he called me in his office to give me the news. Eric would later tell me that one of the Saudi employees, on learning that I would be taking Eric's job, said: "She is clean." I have no idea what that meant, but I will take it.

And thus began the most rewarding two years of my entire career. Isn't it ironic that one of my objections to coming to Saudi Arabia was that I believed I wouldn't be able to work there?

On my first day on the new job, I proposed to Dr. Ahmed that we meet every morning, one-on-one, for half an hour. "I need to get to know your work style and likewise. Once we are on track, we can reduce the frequency." It was one of the few times he readily agreed to my suggestion. Most of the time, he challenged me, so that I learned to be armed with reason and evidence before making a pitch. I didn't always succeed. But it kept me on my toes.

Every morning at 8:30 a.m., wearing his white lab coat, he stopped by Starbucks in the lobby, bypassing the teaboy in the kitchen (the hospital had three Starbucks on premises), bought two cups of coffee, walked in his office where I waited with piles of files, and handed me my cup. We sat at his glass round table, and I went through file after file, organized into the "updates" pile and "need-a-decision" pile. By 9:00 a.m. I walked out with a mile-long to-do list and an empty cup. The arrangement worked so well that for the next two years, until just a few months before I left in 2007, this was our modus operandi.

Will you be bored if I gave you a glimpse into a "day in the life"? Perhaps just a peek. I was responsible for the operating and capital equipment budget, which entailed developing a system to assess staffing needs, manage approvals for equipment, coordinate the risk management process, develop operational plans for ER and OR utilization, restructure Ambulatory Care, establish clinical quality indicators, and monitor the strategic and operational plan. What kept me on schedule was having a full-time secretary. A young Filipino woman, she organized my day, prepared all my meeting materials, took minutes, and handled all my correspondence. She was cheerful, spunky, sweet, and diligent to the umpteenth degree. I loved her. My ten-hour workday was consumed in meetings, so I ended up bringing work home. That meant dropping out of evening Arabic classes. By then, I was ready to give up on Arabic: I wasn't getting anywhere, and when someone said, "At your age learning a new language is not easy," it struck me that perhaps that was my problem: my age. It gave me the excuse to drop out.

Dr. Ahmed held me to high standards. Each time I thought that I had done a terrific job, he would raise the bar. And I would struggle to reach higher. And then he'd raise the bar again. He seldom commended me for a job well done, and I got used to his exceedingly high level of expectations. It motivated me to sharpen my skills and cover all bases; and that was energizing. He showed his appreciation in subtle ways: having me at the table with the senior directors to discuss crucial issues, inviting my opinion, and trusting my discretion on sensitive and confidential matters. From him I learned to appreciate the value of consensus building—he never acted alone, or at least I don't think he did. He welcomed voice of dissent. What made my life easy was that he was a man of principle, which made him predictable, which gave me clarity about where he would stand on an issue, so that I knew when to say yes or no when a request hit my desk.

A year into my new job, I started feeling the crush of workload. So, I made a pitch for a staff person, and Dr. Ahmed agreed. One of the female Lebanese doctors whom I admired recommended a Lebanese woman for the position. Fatima was slim and petite, light brown shoulder-length hair, stylish, and she interviewed brilliantly. I hired her on the spot. She took her charge and charged with it, exceeding my expectations.

Dr. Ahmed and the senior executives, all doctors, were the cream of the crop. Three were Saudi, one Lebanese. They had all been trained in the US or Canada, were visionaries, their hearts were in the right place, and they were smart, creative, methodical in their approach, and professional in their demeanor. They upheld hospital policy and the rules; and above all, it was their honesty and sense of ethics that put me at ease. It engendered trust in my relationship with them.

It was during that period that the accreditation survey came due, and Dr. Ahmed put me in charge of coordinating the survey.

Hide the ID Badge

The accreditation survey was only a week away, and I was doing a mock survey. A team of the Joint Commission on International Accreditation (JCIA) was flying in from the US to inspect the hospital and hopefully, re-accredit us. JCI accreditation is considered the gold standard in healthcare accreditation and the most rigorous evaluator of international standards in quality and patient safety. I had taken it upon myself to walk the halls and make sure that every employee had their ID badge visibly displayed. Why would that even be an issue? I mean, isn't that the whole idea? Read on.

In making my rounds, I came across two Saudi female employees walking in my direction. By now, I could tell a Saudi from a Lebanese or Egyptian. Both wore white lab coats and hijab. No veil. I walked into their pathway and intercepted them. Their ID badges had been flipped backward, concealing their name and photo.

"Hi. I am Sabeeha Rehman, and I am on the JCIA survey team. May I ask that you reveal your ID? It's a JCIA requirement."

They both smiled. "Uh. We will show it when the surveyors come."

"Employees are supposed to show it at *all* times. It's hospital policy." More smiles. And then nothing.

"Let me ask you. What is your hesitation in displaying your name?"

"The patients bother us."

"How is that?"

"If they know our names, they ask for us."

"What job do you hold?"

"Ward clerk."

My brows furrowed.

"They tell their families our names, and then their families call the hospital and want to talk to us."

Before I could ask my next question, they walked off.

I tried to process this. Why would the patients or their families be asking for a Saudi ward clerk instead of a nurse? Is it because the nurses are Western or Filipino and there are communication issues? Or they are asking for information or favors and know that they can prevail on a Saudi woman more than on an expat? I don't know. But one thing was clear: there is protection in anonymity.

Don't reveal your face.

Don't reveal your name.

Don't allow yourself to be identified.

Maybe it's a female thing; protection against harassment.

Wrong!

I was in a meeting with a group of doctors. All men. All wore white lab coats, all had their ID badges clipped on, and all IDs were concealed.

"May I ask my esteemed colleagues to please reveal their ID badges? We have a survey coming up," I said after the meeting was over.

Nodding at me, they quickly flipped their badges.

Two things struck me. One, that the reluctance to reveal one's identity is gender neutral. Second, they listened. These Saudi men took instructions from a woman and did as she said. No one dismissed me, no one patronized me with a "don't worry your pretty little head about this." They saw me as a professional, and the fact that I was a woman was irrelevant.

Now that is a place all us women would like to be.

The Role of a Woman

Then there were exceptions. I was hanging out in the executive suite when a doctor spotted me and walked up.

"I would like to make an appointment to see Dr. Ahmed."

I gave him this look.

"Aren't you [*pause*] his secretary?"

In a gentle and firm tone, I asked, "Why would you think that *I* was his secretary?" Emphasis on "I."

His face flushed with embarrassment. He looked at my ID, looked back up, and his face went redder.

He stammered.

Now I felt bad for *him*.

"That's his office, and you will find his secretary at his desk." By now Dr. Ahmed had a male secretary.

It's OK. Things take time to change. Go easy on it.

Exceeding My Authority

Khalid and I were not supposed to talk shop, particularly since we worked in the same institution. But we did. Talk shop, that is.

"Today I was sitting in my office when an Arab woman walked in and took a seat," Khalid began his story. "I was startled at the ease with which she invited herself into my office, because she was not an employee."

"How did you know that she was not an employee?"

"She was wearing an abaya and had no ID. A good-looking woman, all smiles, and before I could get in a word, told me that she would like me to open an account in a bank she works for."

"Wait, wait, wait. Soliciting on hospital premises! How did she get past security?"

"I have no idea. But that is what I told her, stood up, and opened the door for her."

"You have to report this."

"I did. I sent an email to the head of security, with a copy to administration and the chairman."

Anyone who knows Khalid, knows that he is a letter-writer. Give him a cause and he will write a letter.

Case closed? Hardly. A few days later Khalid spotted the woman making the rounds.

"No one has taken action."

One day, after Khalid and I had met up for lunch and were headed back to our offices, he spotted her again.

"There she is," he pointed to a woman in an abaya to the hallway on our right, chatting with a woman in a lab coat.

"You go on ahead. I will handle this."

I walked up to the woman—the banker—and interrupted their chatter.

"May I help you?" I asked.

She *was* beautiful, and her smile even brighter.

"No, thank you," the lab coat lady answered.

"I am speaking to her," I pointed to the banker. "How may I help you?"

Big smile. "Uh!" Another smile. "No, thank you."

"Are you a visitor?"

"Yes, yes."

"Do you have a visitor pass?"

The lab coat lady jumped in and tried to answer. I gave her the "I didn't ask *you*" look.

"Uh! No."

"Then what is your business here?" I knew exactly what her business was.

"I am a banker. I help people open accounts."

"We do not allow salespeople on premises without prior authorization. Do you have permission?"

The lab coat lady started to protest, and I gave her the look.

"Yes, yes. I have a letter."

"May I see it?"

The lab coat lady looked horrified.

The banker smiled. "I don't have it with me."

"Well, if you don't have the letter, and you don't have a visitor pass, then I must ask you to leave the hospital premises, now."

The smile finally dropped. The lab coat lady looked outraged and went speechless.

"Would you like me to escort you, or can you make your way out?"

"I know the way." She nodded hard.

"Very well." And I turned around and walked away.

Crossing the long hallway, when I made a turn, I found Khalid standing there.

"I just saw that lady walk out of the hospital. What did you say to her?"

"What I said doesn't matter. What matters is that I had *no* authority to do what I just did."

My justification: if the powers that be won't do their job, well, guess what!

It Will Never Happen Here

When I first interviewed with Samir, I was telling him about some of my work at University Hospital in New Jersey. When I mentioned that I had created a train-the-trainer program on corporate compliance and trained senior hospital staff to train department heads, he shook his head and said, "It will never happen here."

It did happen.

Saudis write in long sentences. Some sentences take up an entire paragraph. Just reading a sentence can put you out of breath. This is how it is written in Arabic, and it just spilled over into English writing. Don't get me wrong. English is their second language, and given that, it's pretty good. Very good, in fact. Except for the long sentences. So I made the case to Dr. Ahmed that we train all senior staff in business writing. He agreed. I collaborated with the Training department, enlisted trainers from among the management staff, got an American instructor to fly in and train the trainers on Business Writing, and launched the program hospital-wide. (That was a long sentence.) All chairmen of medical departments, heads of medical specialties, nursing management, heads of departments, and executive directors were asked to (actually, required to) enroll. An auditorium was made available, and I relished conducting the workshops. It was loaded with exercises, and attendees got firsthand experience in honing their writing skills. Hundreds went through the program. I appreciated the administration's willingness to recognize the need and put their weight behind it.

Executive Consultant

One morning, I received an announcement that all job descriptions across the hospital were being standardized, and my position was being changed from administrator to administrative assistant.

I threw a fit.

It had come from the Organization office that does just that: standardizes stuff. I went straight to Dr. Ahmed.

This was not acceptable.

In the US, administrative assistant is equivalent to being a secretary. I would never get a comparable job when I returned.

I ranted. I raved.

Dr. Ahmed saw my point. The senior directors saw my point. It was out of their realm. The Organization department controlled job descriptions, and approaching them would not get me anywhere. Everyone agreed that my only recourse was to go straight to the CEO. So I did. The senior directors coached me. The CEO, a Saudi, heard me out, picked up the phone, called Organization, told them to take care of it, hung up, looked across at me, and told me to go meet with the Head of Organization. I was struck: decisive and swift. None of the "I will look into it" or "Let me see what I can do" brush-off.

I went to see the Head of Organization. He said to me that once their department makes a decision, it stands. But since the CEO had instructed him to accommodate me, he was making an exception. He had done his homework, proposed two job titles, and showed me the job descriptions and qualifications. I went over the two and selected executive consultant.

Later people later said to me: what just happened never happens.

CHAPTER 13

The Passing of a King

August 3, 2005

Dear All,

This week one of our patients died after a long illness. He had been in our hospital for over two months, and early in his stay, it was apparent that his chances of leaving the hospital were slim. Every evening when I left the hospital, I kept my pager and my cell phone close to me, just in case. If this patient passed away, we might have to activate the contingency plan, for this was not just any patient. This was King Fahad of Saudi Arabia.

On May 28, Khalid and I returned to work after a two-week stay at home in the United States. As our shuttle bus pulled into the hospital, we found the gates closed and traffic diverted to the Tank Farm Gate. The gate was teeming with security guards, and every vehicle was being stopped. "What's going on?" I asked my fellow passengers in our mini bus.

"The king is in the hospital. He was brought in last night."

In the past, the king's presence in the hospital was a top-secret affair, and there would be no visible heightened security. This was a change.

King Faisal Specialist Hospital is the VIP hospital of Saudi Arabia, and this is where the royal family comes for treatment. We also provide medical personnel on a rotating basis to off-site locations: the Royal Clinic, the palace in Riyadh, the palace in Jeddah, and the king's vacations abroad. In the hospital is a department called Protocol, which is devoted to the medical treatment of VIPs and royals. It has an entire administrative infrastructure to manage this process, their security, privacy, and everything else that goes with it. And they manage it very well. The "regular" administration of the hospital, of which I am a part, has little direct involvement, other than to support the Protocol office.

The king's health had been failing for many years. I'd call up a friend to invite her over, and she'd tell me that her husband, a doctor too, was "at the palace" this weekend or out of the country "with the king." I found that exciting. They would assure me that it wasn't.

As I walked into the executive suite, I ran into a colleague—a Saudi doctor, who looked troubled.

"I heard the king is here," I said.

We are supposed to respect patient-doctor confidentiality, but as an administrator, I felt that I could venture at least that far with a very senior colleague.

He nodded, looking stunned.

"How is he?" I asked.

He just looked at me. It meant "not good." I nodded and said nothing.

Then I ran into another very senior Saudi colleague. He looked at me, dazed, with panic all over his face. I felt sobered as I realized what a burden they were carrying. Their king is in their hospital, they are responsible for him, his health, his security, his family's concerns, protocol, royal visitors, high-ranking government official visitors, foreign dignitaries' visitors, and it was obvious to me that medically, things were not looking good.

I came to my office, sat down, and took it all in. Only a five-minute walk away lay the king of this country. The king! And he was very sick.

For the next two months, security was like nothing you have ever seen. One day, it took so long to get into the hospital that Khalid and I had to get off the bus and walk. After a few bumpy starts, things settled down into such a routine that I am amazed at how smooth and seamless it was. Almost immediately, a contingency plan went into effect and lasted until the day the king died. It was so meticulously planned that even I, a career planner, was impressed. They must have this plan always ready in the hospital, always updated to account for new buildings and new traffic patterns (and new buildings come up like rabbits making rabbits). Traffic was re-routed, entrances were sealed off, and the fancy dining room was closed to redirect food services to the Royal Suite. Every car entering the hospital was searched by security officers and sniffing dogs. Beyond that, it was business as usual. We had a job to do, which continued, business as usual. Some days we actually forgot that the king was here.

Security personnel were stationed outside the king's suite just off the elevator. One day I accidentally ventured into the area and ran right into one of the guards.

"Yes?" he asked very politely.

"Wrong number," I said, and made a U-turn.

Doctors were flown in from all over the world, and every evening they would convene in the designated conference room to discuss the case. One day Khalid got a call from a friend who lives in New York.

"I am here in Riyadh."

"What brings you here?"

"I was flown in to see the king."

"Where are you staying?"

"At the Palace."

Wow!

And all this time, no one spoke of the king's medical condition. If they did, I didn't hear it. Here was a high-profile case, right in our hospital, and no one said anything. His privacy was respected, as was patient-doctor confidentiality. After a while we got so used to the security that we couldn't quite remember what it was like when the king wasn't here. Whenever we referred to the king, it was: "Our patient in D-2." D-2 is the king's suite.

What will happen when the king dies? I would wonder. Will there be a power struggle? An uprising? Instability?

For the contingency plan, I am first-in-line of call to activate the notification process. One weekend, I was going to a party in a restaurant where men and women are segregated into two different dining rooms. I thought of this scenario: I put my pager and my cell phone in my pretty little party purse, and as I go to get some food or socialize, I leave my purse on my table, the king dies, my pager beeps (to notify me of the king's death), but in the noise of the party, I don't hear the pager beeping. And my job is to trigger the contingency plan's call system. So, I gave Khalid my pager since he can wear it on his belt and hear it easily. If my pager beeped, he was to call me ASAP.

Some days after the king had died, I related this event to Dr. Al-Jabbar.

"My God! You women are so impractical. You don't have pockets, you don't have belts . . ."

The king's hospitalization had been reported in the Saudi news, CNN, the BBC, and all the networks. As the summer months rolled in, contrary to tradition, the top brass of the nation did not take their summer vacation, did not leave the country, and sheltered in Saudi Arabia. And it was going to be a long summer. Normally, Riyadh becomes a ghost-town as the residents flee to Europe, Beirut, and the Emirates. The streets were full at night, stores and restaurants were doing brisk business, and it trickled all the way down to the hospital level.

"The king is very, very sick," Greg told me on Saturday. He looked grave. I had wanted to see the CEO that day, but Greg suggested that I hold off. "He is going to be very occupied today."

"How is our patient in D-2?" I asked him on Sunday.

"The same," he said solemnly.

I nodded and asked no more.

On Monday, I was in my standing morning meeting with Dr. Ahmed when there was a knock on the door and Dr. Al-Jabbar and Edith, the nursing director for D-2 (the king's unit), walked in. Dr. Ahmed sensed what was coming and rose from his chair. Dr. Al-Jabbar said something to him in Arabic, then turned to me and said, "The king has died."

Edith stood by silent and gave me an inquiring look, which I understood only later.

I don't think that I will ever be able to describe how I felt at that very moment. Death is sad, death of a king is a historic moment, but this wasn't my king, so how am I supposed to feel? But he was the king of this country where I have been a guest for over four years, yet I still don't know how I am supposed to feel.

"*To God we belong and to him we shall return.*" I recited the Qur'anic verse under my breath and then just stared at my Saudi colleagues, not knowing what to say. I remained sitting at the table wondering what the protocol is. They were all standing in silence.

Should I offer my condolences? I decided to stay silent.

Dr. Ahmed picked up his pager and started to leave to go to the king's bedside.

"Before you leave . . . ," I said, stopping him. "Who is going to make the announcement?" I asked. And just as quickly, I answered my question. "I suppose it won't be the hospital giving a press release. It will be the Palace. If anyone asks us anything, what are we to say, officially, that is?"

"The announcement has to be made through official channels." Translated: wait for the official announcement.

As Dr. Ahmed left, the phone at his desk rang, and Dr. Al-Jabbar answered it.

Edith came and sat next to me. She is Canadian.

"Sabeeha, what am I supposed to say? Like, do I say, I am sorry? Like, what does one say to a Saudi when a Saudi passes away or when a king dies? Do you offer condolences?"

"I don't know!"

The king had been here for two months, and I had not prepared myself for this moment.

"Like, should I say, 'I am sorry about the king's death?'"

I didn't have an answer.

Meanwhile Dr. Al-Jabbar was on the phone taking a call from another colleague. "He had to go to D-2 on a very urgent matter. A very, very urgent matter." He was conveying what had happened without saying it and in doing so, letting the caller know that the news was not official.

He hung up and walked over to us. Neither one of us had the nerve to ask, "What does one say?" But I did ask a lot of other questions.

"Should the employees be concerned about any political unrest? Is there a reason for them to feel insecure? Should we go on high alert?"

"No," he said. "This was expected. The crown prince has been running the affairs of the country for many years; the transition has been taking place all along. This was a long sickness, and it is going to be a smooth transition."

It was the smoothest transition that I have witnessed.

"Will there be a state funeral?" I asked.

"I don't know. The last time the king died was thirty years ago."

We were still talking when Dr. Ahmed returned. Edith left, and the three of us sat down and started our next meeting. This was business as usual. I found that a little hard. The king had died, and we were working as usual. But then, should the hospital's work stop because the king had died? I struggled with that.

A knock on the door. A doctor walked in.

"I have a strategic question. We were planning to move _____ to _____and _____ to _____. Are we to go ahead or wait?" He was saying, "I know what has happened, I know we can't talk about it yet, but is it business as usual?"

"The move goes as scheduled."

"*Tayeb*." Fine.

This was a totally new experience for me.

I came back to my office, sat down, and took it all in. The king, now dead, was only a five-minute walk away from where I sat. This is history! Yet I couldn't pick up the phone and call Khalid.

An hour later, the phone rang. It was my colleague Sarah.

"Did you hear the news?" Sarah asked.

"I can't talk about it."

"OK, OK."

At noon, Khalid called.

"So, the king passed away," he said.

"I cannot talk about it."

"I think you can talk about it now. It's on CNN."

I walked into Dr. Al-Jabbar's office.

"When was the news made official?" I asked.

"Oh immediately! It was announced, the people gave their allegiance to the crown prince, and Abdullah is now king. The burial is tomorrow, and the day after tomorrow the public will go to the palace to pledge their allegiance to the new king. The new crown prince has been appointed—Prince Sultan."

I walked down the hallway to meet Khalid for lunch. The morgue is located off the main hallway. Standing outside the morgue was an armed guard and a security official. I knew then that behind those doors lay the king's body. Each time I walked by the morgue, I looked at these two guards with fascination. They are guarding the king's body. This is history.

Sarah called again.

"How come you didn't tell me that the king had died?"

"Because I am not supposed to."

"Do you know that the whole hospital was talking about it within an hour of his passing?"

This is precisely what happened a year or two earlier when the king had been admitted to the hospital (i.e., my lips were supposed to be sealed while the whole world was talking about it).

That day, Greg walked into my office. "Mum is the word. The king is here."

"The king!" I exclaimed.

"Mum is the word. He is having cataract surgery. Mum is the word."

So I said nothing.

The next morning, Khalid and I were on the bus going to work. A few nurses got on the bus at the next stop and were chattering excitedly, "the king . . . the king . . ." Khalid swung around to me, "Did you hear that?"

"Hear what?"

"The king is in the hospital."

An awkward silence.

Khalid realized immediately that I knew.

"Why is he in the hospital?" he asked.

"I can't say."

"Yes, yes." Khalid understood.

That evening, Fahad came to our house for our weekly lesson. He sat down at the table and said, "So, the king is in your hospital for cataract surgery."

Khalid looked at me and smiled.

King Fahad was buried the next day. The burial was to take place after *Asr* prayers in the late afternoon. The news reported that Prince Charles, President Chirac of France, et al., were coming. That morning, out of curiosity, I walked down the hallway to the morgue entrance. The armed guard was still there. So how was this going to work out—the state funeral, that is—if there was going to be one? And what is the protocol for the visiting dignitaries? Prince Charles would not be participating in the *salat-al-janazah* (funeral prayer), so how would that be handled?

At 2 p.m., I walked past the morgue again. Now a third man stood by. He was not in uniform but had a walkie-talkie. It signaled to me that the body was about to be moved. The king had lain there since his death, and it appeared that his body would be taken directly to the mosque for the funeral prayer and then to the burial ground. There would be no lying in state. This was to be a simple, very simple, affair.

At 3 p.m. I went to see Dr. Ahmed. He was not in his office.

"He went down. They are taking the king's body for burial. The new King Abdullah is there, the king's wife, the crown prince, the princes, the princesses, they are all downstairs," his secretary said.

I flew out. This was history, and I wanted to witness it. The royal family downstairs, the king's body being taken away, the funeral procession . . .

As I came down to the hospital entrance, I saw a gathering of Saudi employees outside on the front lawn, all in their white thobes and white lab coats, standing quietly. That is when sadness overcame me. This was their king and they had assembled outside to pay their respects. I was their guest, and I was going to join them in paying my respect to the departed. I tried not to walk hurriedly, out of respect, and slowly made my way to the crowd that had assembled outside the Flower Shop. People stood quietly. I walked up to the front, found a shady spot under the canopy, and waited. Security cars were stationed there and other than that, people were just waiting. It was very hot.

"Is there a hearse?" I whispered to one of my Canadian colleagues standing next to me. As soon as I asked, I realized that there was going to be no hearse. A funeral in Islam is a simple affair, and more so in the Wahhabi tradition of Saudi Arabia. After about fifteen minutes, there was a flurry of activity by the entrance, and I knew that they were bringing the body out. Security cars pulled up—just two of them—and then an ambulance rolled by, with two security cars behind. The king's body had been taken away in an ambulance. Simple as that! Then all the cars of the dignitaries rolled behind. I tried to catch sight of the familiar faces, King Abdullah, Prince Sultan, but they all wear the same garb, and it is hard to distinguish one from the other in a moving vehicle. I saw Dr. Ahmed walk hurriedly after the last car had pulled out, just to make sure that all had gone well. And that was it! Simple as that! The whole top brass of Saudi Arabia pulling out of the front of the hospital grounds, all in one place, with no ceremony. The simplicity of it all struck me. It felt sad, and appropriate.

His body was taken to the mosque. All dignitaries from Muslim countries joined in the funeral prayer. There was no hearse, no casket. His body was carried out of the mosque on a wooden cot-like structure with a thin mattress; his body was wrapped in a white shroud and was draped with a brown sheet, and the family members served as pallbearers, carrying the cot on their shoulders.

The body was then taken to the family burial plot, and he was laid to rest in an austere, unmarked grave. Only small stones marked the sites of the graves in this simple-looking graveyard. And all day, the Saudi TV channels recited the Holy Qur'an.

Prince Charles, Jacques Chirac, and Dick Cheney arrived later that evening. The next day, the public went to the palace to pledge their allegiance to King Abdullah. An email flicked on my screen saying that the hospital bus would be taking employees—Saudi males—to the palace and anyone who wanted to go could go.

I marveled at the smooth transition. The king died in the morning, and by afternoon the hospital's contingency plan had been lifted. When we left for home, the security guards were no longer at the gate. The next morning, the bus brought us in through the regular route, no security. It was as if a switch had been flicked off. The entire nation transitioned smoothly. There are some things this country manages very well. One is hajj, and the other is the logistics of the royal family.

Within hours of the king's death, a warden message hit my email from the US embassy, advising US citizens to be cautious. A few e-mails came from department heads, acknowledging the passing of their king, and the next morning, the home page of the hospital's website had a small photo of King Fahad with a one-line tribute to him. That day I attended a meeting and before starting the meeting, the chairman—a young Saudi physician—put up a few slides for "reflection." Two were photographs of King Fahad, one in official robes and one in a moment of relaxation, followed by quotations, one of them from the Qur'an, the other from the Bible, tastefully presented. It didn't make you sad, it made you reflect. And that is at the heart of the Saudi tradition in dealing with death.

That same day, I was in a morning meeting when one of my colleagues showed a second colleague an email he had sent out to his staff on the passing of the king. Nicely done. The second colleague read it and asked, "Are we in mourning?" The nation that is.

"I don't know," the first colleague answered.

"Oh yes, the mourning is for three days," I was quick to answer.

"Where did you hear that?" they both jumped at me, incredulous.

"On television," I said with confidence.

"Are you sure?" They were so sure that I was wrong that I had to rethink.

"I take that back," I said. "The news reports said that Arab nations were going to have a three-day mourning." I had assumed that Arab states included Saudi Arabia. In the Wahhabi tradition, death is not mourned.

Pakistan had seven days of mourning.

Arab states had three days of mourning.

There was no day of mourning in Saudi Arabia.

Be well,
Sabeeha

CHAPTER 14

Farewell

We returned home for good in the spring of 2007. Our grandson Omar had been diagnosed with autism, and we were shaken to the core. He had been growing up like any typical child: chatting, laughing, hugging, smiling, and then like the flip of a switch, one morning he stopped talking, stopped making eye contact, and retreated into his own world. This was a new experience for us, we didn't know how to handle it, how to manage it; all we knew was that we had to go back and be there for our children and for Omar. By now Omar had a little sister, Laila, and each time we went home for a visit, our grandchildren had to get to know us all over again, and by the time we bonded, it was time to return to Riyadh. We wanted to see them grow, to hold and to cuddle, to be there when they had their first of many firsts. Khalid and I started talking about an exit date. Our younger son, Asim, and his fiancée, Brinda, set a wedding date for May, and that nailed it. It also coincided with Khalid's contract expiration date. He went ahead and accepted a job as attending physician at Our Lady of Mercy Hospital in the Bronx.

We informed our family, who welcomed the news with relief. Khalid informed his chairman, and now came the hard part: I had to tell Dr. Ahmed. He asked me why. "I miss my family. . . . I need to be closer to my children . . . my grandchildren." He reasoned that even when families live in the same city, parents seldom see their children; children are busy with their lives. But he could tell that my mind was made up. Later he stopped by my office and raised it again. I walked over to the credenza, picked up Omar's framed photo, and sat on the chair next to him. "This is Omar, our grandson. He has been diagnosed with autism."

He closed his eyes in pain. We talked about Omar, the intervention he was receiving, how he was responding. He didn't press further. A few days later, he came to my office.

"*Ya*, Sabeeha," he always addressed me that way, as in *O Sabeeha*, or hey. "Can you delay your departure till September?" He explained his reasons, which I understood. Asim and Brinda's engagement photo sat framed on my desk. As I showed it to him, I explained that I needed to be at home to welcome our new daughter-in-law, help her get settled into the family, and make her feel at home. He looked at the photo for a while, then placed it back on the desk and gave me his blessings.

Fatima, my Lebanese administrative assistant, took it the hardest. She broke into sobs just as Dr. Ahmed walked into my office.

"What's the matter?" He got very concerned.

"I just told her about my plans," I said.

Sobbing through tears, Fatima said, "You know, sometimes I make mistakes. She never made me feel bad, she always. . . ."

That is all I remember because by then my tears were rolling. I called off our meeting and took her for a walk in the park where we sat and had lunch and talked.

A few days later, one of the senior Saudi executives met with me and asked me to reconsider my decision. "Your sons belong to their wives. After a few months, you will be telling them, 'Maybe you should replace this rug.' You will just get in the way. You will be gossiping with your friends about your daughters-in-law."

"Oh no! I am very protective about my daughters-in-law, current and future. People know that no one can say anything against them. They are the love of my sons, and I love them to death."

He smiled. "Really?"

"Really."

I was sad. Sad about leaving. My colleagues had become family, and I was going to miss them. One afternoon I was in a meeting in Dr. El-Aziz's office with Dr. Ahmed and the executives, when Dr. Ahmed said to me, "Sabeeha, you are looking so sad."

"Of course, Sabeeha is sad," said Dr. El-Aziz. "She is leaving us."

That is all it took for my tears to roll. I wasn't embarrassed.

"Get Sabeeha some water," Dr. El-Aziz called out to his secretary.

Someone put a box of tissues in front of me, and I let the tears flow. The agenda was scrapped, and it became all about sad Sabeeha. And I got sadder.

A Parting Gift from the Queen

One of Khalid's patients was the widow of a former king. Khalid had made arrangements for another doctor to take over her care after he left. Then he told the queen that her next visit would be his last visit with her; he was going back home.

My office phone rang. It was Khalid.

"Today was my last visit with the queen, and after the visit was over, she asked her assistant to give me a gift. He handed me an envelope. Ten thousand riyals. I don't know what to do with it. I can't accept it."

"Turn it in to your department." That was the compliance officer in me.

Khalid went to see his boss and handed him the envelope.

"What is this?"

"It's a gift from the queen."

"Why are you giving it to *me*?"

"I can't accept it."

"Yes, you can. And why give it to me?"

"The department can use the funds."

He explained that one does not turn down a gift from the queen, or king for that matter. Besides, the accounting department wouldn't know how to account for it. It's not as if there is a line item on the financials for "royal gifts returned."

"Keep it and have a good vacation."

A Farewell to Remember

Dr. El-Aziz took it upon himself to organize a farewell reception for Khalid and me. Everyone we had worked with came, including the CEO. We were moved by the presence of so many well-wishers. There were speeches and gifts, food and good wishes, and we both felt enveloped in warmth. Khalid gave a heartwarming speech. I enjoyed making everyone laugh as I picked on each of the senior staff. But Dr. Ahmed was teary-eyed.

We left feeling that every moment of our life there had been a gift: the friends we made, the sense of fulfillment in our work, how welcome we felt, and the warmth of the people who touched us.

EPILOGUE

I left my career as a hospital administrator to form the New York Metro chapter of the National Autism Association. For many years, autism was front and center in my life. Witnessing the aftermath of 9/11, I also immersed myself in interfaith dialogue. In 2014, I switched careers again and began writing.

Khalid retired from medical practice after being diagnosed with multiple myeloma. With the Grace of God, he is doing well and stays engaged in anything and everything. *Alhamdulillah.*

We have been back to Saudi Arabia just once, in 2008, when I presented a paper on autism at a conference in Medina. We went to Mecca for *umrah* and made a quick trip to Riyadh to meet up with friends and colleagues. Dr. Al-Jabbar took us out for lunch. Our wonderful Pakistani friends organized a dinner party at LaSahni restaurant, and it was a joy to see all those friendly faces again.

Over the decade, some friendships endured, some faded away; some colleagues I stayed in touch with, some I was not able to. Khalid would run into his former colleagues at medical conferences in the US, but once he retired, those encounters ended. Sangeeta and Dr. Pai moved to the US, and whenever they are in New York, we meet up and it's delightful to see them. A few Pakistani doctors repatriated to the US, none to New York, and we stay in touch; some moved to the Gulf, the rest have stayed. Every year, I send a year-end email to all my Pakistani and expat friends. In the beginning, they would all respond, but over the years, the replies have become fewer and fewer. Every year, I send Dr. Ahmed a birthday greeting; he writes back, always generous, always gracious. Eric and I occasionally exchange a note on LinkedIn. Samir retired, and we lost touch. Dr. Al-Jabbar's children live in North America, and whenever he is in town, we meet up; in between, Facebook keeps us Liked and Commented. The ones I am in constant touch with are my Lebanese female friends; and whenever we talk, we talk until there is nothing left to talk about: new babies, a new job, sickness and death, heartaches and breakups, joys and grief. The stuff that friends talk about.

My friends in Saudi Arabia keep me updated on changes in the culture and the workplace.

The ubiquitous woman driver on the streets of Riyadh has been the most visible and welcome change. I asked one of my Saudi colleagues if *men* are the ones celebrating their freedom, now that they don't have to drive their wives everywhere. When my Saudi friend Jamal accompanied his wife to obtain her driver's license, he thought the male staff would shame him for allowing his wife to drive. He was pleasantly surprised when the man told Jamal that as an Eid gift, he should get his wife her own car.

Mobility has opened doors for women in the workforce in public arenas. They man the checkout counters in stores (beyond just the Kingdom Mall)—or "woman" them; work as saleswomen, waitresses, driving school instructors; are in military uniform; and a woman sits on the Cabinet.

Whereas wearing the abaya is no longer a requirement, most women observe the family tradition, albeit in color and with a touch of style. In shopping malls, abayas dominate, though you see a few with the veil, some with only the hijab, and a few in tight jeans and clingy shirts.

Decades-old societal norms are not easy to wipe out. The law of the land has removed many restrictions, but in practice, the will of the father and the husband prevails. It is countercultural to go against one's father's wishes, puts a woman at risk of hurting her reputation, and hurts her marriage prospects.

Jamal tells me that his mother and sister always wore the veil. His mother still does, but his sisters do not. When he asked his sister why she had decided to give up the veil, her answer: "None of the women at work are veiled, so I stand out." His mother says she no longer recognizes the place she called home: veilless women, that is. Some women are not happy with the veil being lifted, concerned that now their husbands can see the faces of other women; some are insecure about their looks, others prefer the anonymity of the veil. Jamal tells me that in high-end selective restaurants, they post a sign with a cross across a picture of the *niqab* with a sign saying, "Respect our dress code."

The *mutawwa* are around in small numbers, but their power has been drastically reduced and they are banned from pursuing, questioning, asking for identification, arresting, or detaining anyone.

Male guardianship rules have been relaxed for women, but a woman still needs her father's permission to marry. Most marriages are still arranged, as the country bends toward culture and tradition. Women over twenty-one years of age are now allowed to work, live alone, and travel abroad without a male guardian's permission. Yet traditions endure, and this freedom is being exercised only with the nod from the parents or husband. Jamal told me that women are now checking into a hotel with a man without showing proof of marriage.

In the weeks before the hajj in 2021, the Hajj Ministry officially allowed women of all ages to make the pilgrimage without a male relative, on the condition that they go in a women's group. What hasn't changed are the risks and challenges pilgrims encounter before and during hajj. Saqib and Asim were blessed to perform the hajj in 2012 and 2016, respectively. Saqib had planned to perform hajj in 2011, but the travel agent took off with his money and declared bankruptcy. Saqib did perform the hajj the following year, but was put to the test when he got pickpocketed during the *tawaaf*. In 2015, thousands were killed in a stampede in Mina. Whereas transportation has been modernized, particularly the monorail connecting the holy sites, chaos at the stations forced Asim and his friends to walk from Mecca to Mina. At one point, they had to form a human shield around people who had fainted on the street. These people, who were severely dehydrated and depleted of energy, had opted not to drink fluids or eat so they wouldn't have to deal with bathrooms. Asim's patience was tested when he had to wait in the bathroom line for forty-five minutes in Muzdalifa.

But what also hasn't changed is the soulful experience of hajj—of absorbing the positive energy of the devout, embracing the camaraderie of the faithful, being in awe of the gathering of nations and tribes, and the joy of recharging one's spiritual connection with the Divine. Everyone comes back a changed person.*

The country remains an autocracy. It controlled the COVID outbreak by dictate.† Vaccines were mandated; one could not enter a public place without proof of vaccination through a government-issued app on their phone. It compelled the vaccine-hesitant to get their shots or risk getting locked out of supermarkets and restaurants.

Mass executions continue. In March 2022, Saudi Arabia put to death eighty-one people convicted of murder, rape, arms smuggling, links to terrorist groups, and other crimes, in the largest known mass execution in the history of the kingdom and the most in the country in a single day. The form of execution and its location were not disclosed.

The Saudi crown prince has a new plan to deradicalize militant extremists. Ha'ir state-security prison near Riyadh has a counterterrorism program aimed at religious reeducation and rehabilitation. One of

---

* Due to the pandemic in 2020, hajj was limited to 1,000 pilgrims with no international travelers; and in 2021 the number of pilgrims was limited to 60,000 (versus 2 million).

† As of April 2022, it ranked seventy-third worldwide, with approximately 750,000 COVID cases, compared to the US number-one ranking with approximately 81 million cases. The rate of infection in Saudi Arabia was approximately 21,000 cases per 1 million population, compared to the US rate of approximately 245,000, and the worldwide rate of approximately 63,000.

the programs involves corporate training, song and music, and poetry readings.*

At the workplace at King Faisal Hospital, my expat colleagues tell me that there is more and more Saudization. While gen-Xer expats sense that their generation of Saudis continues to value expatriate employees, such is not the case with the millennials. Seems like a global trend. The number of western expats has declined over the last few years. Most American and Canadian staff are nurses, with few doctors and executives. The number of Saudi nurses is increasing as the stigma fades away. Long-term care and chronic rehabilitation continues to be provided in acute care hospitals.

The dependence on government largesse has lessened. Crown Prince Mohammed bin Salman has imposed heavy taxes and has tried to neutralize the pain by giving Saudis social freedoms such as mixing of the sexes, concerts, and movie theaters. However, Saudi citizens continue to receive free healthcare.

How people living there feel about these changes depends on who you talk to. Like any nation, Saudis are a diverse people. Some applaud the freedom offered women; others oppose it, believing that it corrupts the society. Some welcome women driving; others fear that it puts women in harm's way. Some support the right for a woman to work; others believe that it impedes a woman's chances of finding a suitable match and the husband and children are neglected. Most people I am in touch with welcome the relaxed climate. Yet, a few feel that the pendulum has swung too quickly and too much to the extreme.

Time will tell how the intersection of tradition and modernization plays out. Meanwhile, keep an eye on the change-makers of Saudi Arabia: the women.

---

* See if you can get a copy of the April 2022 cover story in the *Atlantic* magazine, *Absolute Power: The Crown Prince, a Murder, and the Future of Saudi Arabia,* by Graeme Wood. The description of Ha'ir prison program is fascinating.

ACKNOWLEDGMENTS

If my friend Jyothi Pamidimukkala had not suggested that I send daily letters about my experiences in Saudi Arabia, this book may not have been written. And if I did write the book, it would have been devoid of the excitement of real-time reporting. It did more than that. I discovered that I enjoyed writing. Thank you, Jyothi.

When I returned from Saudi Arabia, I received an email from Dr. Faroque Khan. He urged me to write a book about my life in the kingdom. I certainly took my time in taking his advice, but here it is, finally. Thank you, Dr. Khan, for believing in me.

Last summer I decided to embark on this project and compile the letters—emails actually—into a book. I wasn't sure if that structure would work. My friend Madhu Mazumdar, who knew what I was struggling with, surprised me with a gift: a memoir constructed entirely of emails between the author and her recipients (*I Signed as the Doctor*). That nailed it. Thank you, Madhu, for giving me the confidence to allow emails to drive my story.

A big thank you to my sons, Saqib and Asim, for allowing me to share their emails, written to us when the towers fell in New York on 9/11.

Over the summer of 2022, I started sharing my writings with members of the Yorkville Writing Circle at the New York Public Library. Over several months of weekly meetings on Zoom, they offered their critique. Thank you Ron Trenkler-Thompson, Caryn

Schlesinger, Joan Penn, Nancy Benson, Nancy K, Madhu Mazumdar, Kirsten Simone, Michele Duffy, O'labumi Browne, Lou-Ellen Barkan, Renee Bray, Nadia Bongo, Andrea King, Maryann Giarratano, Jane Weart, Charles Schwartz, Eric Rosenbaum, Pat Weich, Elisabeth De Nitto, and my husband, Khalid Rehman.

Then there is my Writers Group that Michele Duffy and I started when we took a memoir-writing class at Hunter College in 2014. Eight years later, we still meet every month. Thank you all for offering your invaluable feedback: Michele Duffy, Alice Cody, Caryn Schlesinger, Ron Trenkler-Thompson, Walter Ruby, Jackie Schecter, Pat Weich, Lou-Ellen Barkan, and Andrea King.

You have heard the phrase "to be a good writer, you have to be a good reader." For that I am thankful to my bookclub friends who keep me on track with my reading, exposing me to books I never would have picked on my own, but more than that, providing me with insight on how readers respond to the written word, or audio word for that matter. Their incisive critique enabled me to anticipate a reader's reaction to my writing. If you are an author reading this, you know how valuable that insight is. Thank you, Ilene Singh, Jyothi Pamidimukkala, Maria Biancheri, Joan Mistrough, Loulou Saleem, Seshu Tyagarajan, Bobbie Keers-Flood, Kiera LoBreglio, Margaret Kazancioglu, Toni Siegel, Frank Tamburello, Laila Al-Askari, Caren Singer, Elizabeth Degear, Michele Duffy, Margaret Jaworski, Larry Roth, Khalid Rehman, and Kausar Zaman.

I am grateful to Dawn Raffel, for developmental editing of the draft manuscript. Her guidance in shaping the narrative, ensuring that it maintained a brisk pace, anticipating the question's in the reader's mind, and instructing me on areas that needed more emphasis, or less, was invaluable. The hardest part for any writer is what not to include, and cutting paragraphs and pages is painful. Dawn, in her gentle and firm manner, made that decision easy for me. Thank you, Dawn.

Do believe me when I tell you that picking the title for the book was harder than writing the book. I cast my help-me net far and wide to friends, family, colleagues, neighbors, passers-by. . . you name it.

My niece, Komal Kazim, took time during her lunch break to brainstorm over the title. Lou-Ellen Barkan, over a long phone call, multitasked between thinking through and combing titles on the internet and came up with some marvelous suggestions. Thank you to my granddaughter Laila Rehman, my sons Saqib and Asim, my husband Khalid, my morning-walk friends Caryn Schlesinger and Michele Duffy, my friend and co-author of *We Refuse to Be Enemies*, Walter Ruby, and my developmental editor Dawn Raffel for pondering over and recommending some terrific titles.

Next was the book cover. My family was totally into it with my eighteen-year-old granddaughter, Laila, an artist, leading the pack, and my sweet twelve-year-old granddaughter Sofia putting pen to paper drawing samples of the cover, with Asim not far behind. Of course, Arcade's artist was to design the cover, but anyone and everyone wanted to have a say in the theme. Thanksgiving chatter was all about the book cover. Ideas were flying off the table faster than the turkey and trimmings. I kept sharing these ideas with Arcade, and each time the artist sent me a few cover samples, Laila, Sofia, Asim, and Khalid weighed in. Thank you to all of you: Saqib, Asim, Laila, Sofia, Khalid, Farheen Mahmood, Mahmooda Raza, and Shafaq Asghar for your indulgence and your ideas.

Let me not leave out the person who brought all those ideas to life, Erin Seaward-Hiatt, Arcade's artist. I cannot thank her enough for her patience and her responsiveness in taking our suggestions seriously as we went back and forth on the book cover. She did a fabulous job, don't you think?

Laila wasn't done with me. Once my prologue was written, she went through it carefully—she is a podcaster (*GreenMe*)—and gave me the go-ahead to run with it. Authors, if you are reading this, trust your grandchildren to give you the best advice, i.e., if you are old enough and lucky enough to have one, or more.

Calvert Barksdale, executive editor, Arcade Publishing, who guided me to ensure that this book, which relates decades-old experiences, has relevance today in the shifting landscape of Saudi Arabia. That in fact was the most challenging facet of the book. Here, Cal's instructive review was instrumental in keeping the content up to date. It was Cal's prompt that nailed the title of the book, when he asked, if I was to write a daily blog on Saudi Arabia, what would the title be. This is my third book with Cal, and it's a partnership I respect. What makes working with Cal stress-free is his responsiveness. I have never had to wait more than a few hours to get a response to my email query and he always makes himself available for a quick phone call. That means something to an impatient person like me. Cal, I have said this before, and I am going to say this again: You are the best.

My heartfelt thanks to my colleagues at King Faisal Specialist Hospital and Research Center (KFSHRC), Riyadh, who welcomed me, offered me opportunities to achieve my potential, accorded me the respect every professional desires, and enhanced my understanding of Arab culture. Here I spent six memorable years of my life, made possible by my colleagues. I hope I have done justice in portraying their values and the corporate culture of KFSHRC.

Many thanks to my Saudi and expat Pakistani and Lebanese friends and colleagues in Riyadh, who keep me informed about life in Saudi Arabia, what has changed, and what remains unchanged. Thank you particularly to my Saudi friends in the US whom I relied on to share the Saudi perspective both from a personal and professional aspect. I couldn't have written this book without their help.

The greatest praise goes to my beloved husband, Khalid, who is my biggest supporter in any and every way. He has taken over almost all my responsibilities to allow me the time to pursue my passion of writing. In reviewing the manuscript, Khalid would remind me of anecdotes I had missed, he spent hours helping me with the graphics, and dug out the photos he had carefully archived, preparing them to be print-worthy. But, most of all, it is his companionship and moral support that I treasure. He is the source of my strength, both emotional and intellectual.

Above all, I offer my gratitude to God, who has given me the gift of life, and endowed me with the capacity to embrace His blessings in all its forms. From Him I seek the positive energy and patience to steer me through life. *Shukr Alhamdulillah.*

GLOSSARY

Words and phrases translated from Arabic

Alhamdulillah: Praise be to God

Allahu Akbar: God is the Greatest.

Ameen: Amen

Asr: One of the five mandatory daily prayers for Muslims. The third prayer of the day, its time begins approximately when the sun is halfway down from noon to sunset.

Dhul Hijjah: The last month of the Muslim Hijra calendar, and the month during which the hajj is performed.

Fajr: One of the five mandatory daily prayers for Muslims. The first prayer of the day, its time begins at dawn, ending just before sunrise.

Fatwa: A formal ruling or interpretation on a point of Islamic law given by a qualified legal scholar, known as a mufti.

Fusha: Literary or Classical Arabic (vs. colloquial).

Ghutra: A traditional Arab headdress fashioned from a square piece of usually cotton cloth.

Hadith: The collected traditions of the Prophet Muhammad, based on his sayings and actions.

Hafiz: Literal meaning is "guardian" or "memorizer." Depending on the context, it refers to one who has completely memorized the Qur'an, or protector. When saying goodbye or ending a conversation, many Muslims say, "Allah Hafiz," meaning, "May God protect you."

Hajar-al-Aswad: The Black Stone is a rock set into the eastern corner of the Kaaba (the ancient building in the center of the Grand Mosque in Mecca, Saudi Arabia). It is revered by Muslims as an Islamic relic that, according to Muslim tradition, dates back to the time of Adam and Eve.

Hajj: The Muslim pilgrimage to Mecca that takes place in the last month of the Muslim year and that all Muslims are expected to make at least once during their lifetime, if they can afford it.

Hajji: A pilgrim performing or having performed the hajj.

Haram: Sanctuary. The word is commonly used by Muslims to refer to the holy sites of Islam and the area surrounding them.

Hijab: Headscarf worn by Muslim women.

Hijabi: A woman wearing the hijab.

Hijra: Migration. It refers to the Prophet Muhammad's migration from Mecca to Medina in 622 CE to escape persecution. Hijra also refers to the Islamic calendar, which dates its beginning to 622 CE.

Iftar: Breaking of the fast with a meal at sunset during Ramadan.

Ihram: A sacred state into which a Muslim must enter in order to perform the hajj or *umrah*. Men must wear two pieces of unstitched white cloth.

In sha Allah: God willing; If God wills.

Iqama: (1) The second call to Islamic prayer, given immediately before the prayer begins. A call for all the congregants to rise and stand in prayer.
(2) Residency permit issued to expatriates who arrive in Saudi Arabia on an employment visa.

Isha: One of the five mandatory daily prayers for Muslims. The fifth and last prayer of the day, its time begins at nightfall. The end time varies; Sunnis end at beginning of dawn, Shias end at midnight.

Istikhara: A prayer of seeking counsel from God, performed by Muslims who are in need of guidance when facing a decision.

Jamaraat: The three stone pillars in the tent city of Mina. Stoning these pillars is a ritual of the hajj in commemoration of the Prophet Abraham's pelting Satan when Satan tried to dissuade him for carrying out God's command.

Jannah: Paradise or heaven in the life hereafter.

Jumma: The Muslim congregational prayer held on Fridays. Held in a mosque, it includes a sermon by the imam and is in lieu of the obligatory noon *Zuhr* prayer.

Kaaba: The cubic structure in the courtyard of the most sacred mosque, the Masjid al-Haram in Mecca, Saudi Arabia. Built by the Prophet Abraham and his son Ishmael, it is the most sacred site in Islam. It is considered to be the House of God and is the direction Muslims face when they perform the five daily prayers. When performing the pilgrimage of hajj, this is the first and the last site that pilgrims visit.

Kafeel: An in-country sponsor, usually the employer, who is responsible for an expat migrant worker's visa and legal status. The kafeel assumes responsibility for the worker and must grant explicit permission before the worker can enter the country, transfer employment, or leave the country.

Kiswah: The cloth that covers the Kaaba. It is replaced annually on the second day of hajj when the pilgrims leave for Arafat. Qur'anic verses in gold thread are embroidered across the black covering.

Labek Allahumma Labek: "Here I am O Allah, here I am," is chanted repeatedly by pilgrims as they begin the journey of hajj and get closer to the Kaaba.

Laylat al-Qadr: The Night of Power. It commemorates the night on which God first revealed the Qur'an to the Prophet Muhammad through the angel Gabriel. It is believed to have taken place on one of the final ten nights of Ramadan in 610 CE, though the exact night is unclear. Muslims stay up late into the night praying and seeking God's blessings.

Maghrib: One of the five mandatory daily prayers for Muslims. The fourth prayer of the day, it begins at sunset and ends at nightfall.

Mahram: A member of one's family with whom marriage would be considered *haram* (illegal in Islam); and with whom, if he is an adult male, she may be escorted during a journey.

Mashallah: A term used when something good has happened. It's literal meaning is "what God has willed" in the sense of "what God has willed has happened."

Mataf: The open white area immediately around the Kaaba where hajj and *umrah* pilgrims perform the "tawaf" or circumambulation.

Meeqaat: The principal boundary at which pilgrims enter into a state of *ihram* and make the intention for pilgrimage.

Mimbar: A short flight of steps used as a platform by a preacher in a mosque.

Muezzin: A man who calls Muslims to prayer, usually from the minaret of a mosque.

Mushkila: A problem.

Mutawwa: Religious police in Saudi Arabia whose duty is to ensure strict adherence to established codes of conduct.

Nafl Prayers: Optional Muslim prayers, believed to confer extra benefit on the person performing them.

Niqab: A veil for the face that leaves the areas around the eyes clear.

Qasr Prayer: The practice of shortening the prayer when travelling over long distances. It involves shortening Zuhr, Asr, and Isha prayers.

Qibla: The direction of the Kaaba toward which Muslims face in prayer.

Qirat: The various ways of reciting the Holy Qur'an. These are different lexical, phonetic, linguistic, morphological, and syntactical manners permitted with reciting the Qur'an.

Qiyam-al-Lail: It means "standing in the night" and pertains to when you spend some part of the night (even if only one hour) in prayer, recitation of the Qur'an, in remembrance of Allah, or any acts of worship between Isha and Fajr prayers.

Raka'ah: A single iteration of prescribed movements and supplications performed by Muslims as part of the prescribed obligatory prayer. Each of the five daily prayers observed by Muslims consists of a prescribed number of raka'at.

Raka'at: Plural of *raka'ah*.

Ramadan: Month of fasting during the ninth month of the Muslim Hijra calendar. Muslims fast every day from daybreak to sunset, abstaining from eating, drinking, and sexual relations.

Rami: Literally: to throw. During hajj, the act of throwing stones at the stone pillars (*Jamaraat*) is known as rami.

Rawdah: An area of the Al-Masjid an-Nabawi mosque in Medina, the Prophet Muhammad's mosque. Muslims are keen to visit the Rawdah, a place located between the Prophet and his wife Aisha's house and between the Prophet's Minbar (or pulpit).

Saee: One of the integral rites of hajj and *umrah*. The meaning of this word in Arabic is "to strive, walk, or pursue." During hajj and *umrah*, it refers to the ritual of walking back and forth seven times between two small hills of Safa and Marwa, which are located adjacent to the Kaaba in Masjid al-Haram. It is performed to commemorate and pay homage to Hagar, Abraham's wife, who ran back and forth seven times between the two hills looking for water for baby Ishmael.

Salaam Alaikum: Muslim greeting meaning "peace be upon you." The response is: *Wa Alaikum Assalam*, which means: "peace be also with you."

Salat-al-Janazah: Muslim funeral prayer.

Shari'a: The sum total of God's commandments in the Qur'an. From shari'a is derived the Islamic law. In Arabic, the word means "the path." In the desert of Arabia, it was referred to as "the path to the watering hole" (i.e., the path to sustenance).

Shukran: Thank you.

Suhur: Meal taken before dawn before starting the fast in Ramadan.

Sunna: The example established by the Prophet Muhammad (i.e., his actions).

Talbiah: Muslim prayer invoked by the pilgrims as a conviction that they intend to perform the hajj only for the glory of Allah. It is repeatedly chanted as pilgrims put on the *ihram* and begin the journey of hajj and as they approach the Masjid-al-Haram.

Taraweeh: Special prayers offered during Ramadan after the Isha night prayer. It involves reciting long passages from the Qur'an, with up to twenty units of prayer and lasts up to one hour.

Tawaaf: Circumambulating seven times around the Kaaba in Masjid-al-Haram in Mecca. It is an essential rite of hajj and *umrah*. Muslims perform this ritual when they visit the Kaaba, walking counterclockwise in a circular fashion to symbolize their belief in and worship of the One God.

Tawaaf-e-Ziarah: Tawaaf performed after returning from Muzdalifa. It can be performed between tenth and twelfth of Dhul Hijjah. It is an essential rite of the hajj.

Tayeb: That's good. Fine.

Thobe: Ankle-length robe with long sleeves worn by men in Saudi Arabia and other Arab countries. Thobes are usually white in summer and darker colors in the winter. (Also spelled "thawb.")

Ulema: A body of Muslim scholars recognized as having specialist knowledge of Islamic sacred law and theology.

Umrah: Islamic pilgrimage to Mecca that can be performed anytime during the year (unlike the hajj, which occurs over specific dates that coincide with the Islamic lunar calendar). It has two essential rites, the *tawaaf* and *saee*, and is considered the lesser pilgrimage.

Wa Alaikum Assalam: Response to *Salaam Alaikum*. It means: "And peace be also with you."

Wahhabi: Adherant of Wahhabism, a strictly orthodox Sunni Muslim sect founded by Muhammad ibn Abd al-Wahhab in the eighteenth century. It advocates a return to the early Islam of the Qur'an and the Prophet Muhammad's Sunna, rejecting later innovations. It is the predominant religious force in Saudi Arabia.

Wudu: A ritual of cleansing parts of the body and purification, or ablution, performed before entering a state of prayer. It involves washing the face and arms, cleaning the nasal cavities and ear canals, wiping the head, and washing the feet with water.

Ya: Means "O," a common prefix before personal names, e.g., "Ya Sabeeha."

Ziyarah: A form of pilgrimage. For a Muslim, to visit a place of historical significance in Muslim history, e.g., the burial place of the Prophet Muhammad or the plain of Karbala in Iraq where the Prophet's grandson, Imam Hussein, was martyred in battle.

Zuhr: One of the five mandatory daily prayers for Muslims. The second prayer of the day, it begins at noon when the sun is at its zenith and ends as the sun begins its descent.

ABOUT THE AUTHOR

Sabeeha Rehman is an author, blogger, and speaker on interfaith under-standing. Her memoir *Threading My Prayer Rug: One Woman's Journey from Pakistani Muslim to American Muslim* was a finalist for the William Saroyan International Prize for Writing, named one of *Booklist*'s Top Ten Religious and Spirituality Books and Top Ten Diverse Nonfiction Books, awarded honorable mention in the San Francisco Book Festi-val Awards, Spiritual Category, and was a United Methodist Women's Reading Program Selection. Sabeeha has given more than 250 talks in nearly a hundred cities at houses of worship, academic institutions, libraries, and community organizations, including the Chautauqua Institution. She is also the author, with Walter Ruby, of *We Refuse to Be Enemies: How Muslims and Jews Can Make Peace, One Friendship at a Time*, and has given more than eighty book talks nationwide and overseas. She is an op-ed contributor to the *Wall Street Journal, New York Daily News*, and *Baltimore Sun*. She lives with her husband in New York City.